John Greenwood.

Robert Stephens

Robert Stephens was born in Bristol in 1931. He trained as an actor in Bradford where he met his first wife Nora Ann Simmonds by whom he had a son, Michael. His second marriage to actress Tarn Bassett produced a daughter, Lucy. He formed a golden partnership with Maggie Smith at the National Theatre where they were acclaimed in George Farquhar's *The Recruiting Officer*, Zeffirelli's *Much Ado About Nothing* and Ingmar Bergman's *Hedda Gabler*. They had two actor sons – Christopher and Toby.

After periods of uncertainty and occasional glory, Robert Stephens' career came full circle in the 1990s when he joined the RSC to play Falstaff and King Lear. In 1995 he was knighted and received the 'Best Actor' Award from the Varity Club of Great Britain. He lived in north London with his fourth wife Patricia Quinn until his death on 13 November 1995.

SCEPTRE

Knight Errant

Memoirs of a Vagabond Actor

ROBERT STEPHENS

with

MICHAEL COVENEY

SCEPTRE

In fond memory of Ralph Richardson who told me to wait ten years and not to do this.
Well, dear Ralph, I waited ten years . . . and did it anyway.

Copyright © 1996 by Robert Stephens and Michael Coveney

First published in 1996 by Hodder and Stoughton
First published in paperback in 1996 by Hodder and Stoughton
A division of Hodder Headline PLC
A Sceptre Paperback

The right of Robert Stephens and Michael Coveney to be
identified as the Author of the Work has been asserted
by them in accordance with the Copyright, Designs and
Patents Act 1988.

10 9 8 7 6 5 4 3 2 1

British Library Cataloguing in Publication Data

Stephens, Robert
  Knight Errant: Memoirs of a Vagabond Actor
  I. Title
  792.028092

ISBN 0 340 65460 0

Typeset by Palimpsest Book Production Limited,
Polmont, Stirlingshire
Printed and bound in Great Britain by
Cox and Wyman Ltd, Reading, Berkshire

Hodder and Stoughton
A division of Hodder Headline PLC
338 Euston Road
London NW1 3BH

CONTENTS

INTRODUCTION

By Michael Coveney

Towards the end of March 1995, on a bright sunny afternoon, Sir Robert Stephens was lying in a bed in the tenth floor Hassall Ward of the Royal Free Hospital in Hampstead, London. He was smoking and talking and making calls on his mobile telephone, gossiping about what he had read in the paper that morning, planning a recording session with Prince Charles and telling me exactly what he thought about Chinese food, Tony Richardson, the films of Gérard Depardieu, the character of Iago and the life-giving properties of champagne.

He had undergone a routine biopsy operation that morning to see how his new liver was coming along. It was coming along just fine. How did he feel? Grand, wonderful, pluperfect, that's how. The nurses smiled in amused tolerance through the fug of the cigarette smoke. One doctor asks if he has been smoking. 'Smoking? Me? Not at all. Just one or two. Nothing to speak of.' Coffee in polystyrene cups is not Robert's idea of the good life. The cups had better double as ashtrays, stuffed with butts and pocked with burning holes.

I first met Robert Stephens in 1973 at an end-of-term platform discussion at the Royal Academy of Dramatic Art. As a young critic, I was invited by the principal, Hugh Cruttwell, to field questions on a panel also comprising Robert, Miriam Karlin and the senior critic J.W. Lambert. I always remembered Robert telling me how little Lambert thought of his work and how much he respected his opinion.

It was clear that I was dealing here with an unusual performer. No huffs or tantrums or standing on dignity with Robert. All would be well with a drink or three at the bar. Even for an actor, Robert is unusually tactile and bear-like, both of which characteristics I now know he inherited from his father, a huge shipyard labourer who was born in West Hartlepool but moved to Bristol to find work, raise a family and finish his working days as a quantity surveyor. Robert and his father would often listen to plays on the radio in floods of tears. Some Britons can, after all, wear their hearts on their sleeves.

Robert has delicate hands and small feet, a ready smile, a cheerful disposition. He is open, transparent and almost entirely devoid of malice. This is unusual in anyone, let alone a member of the acting profession. And it is partly because of these apparent qualities that I believe Robert has earned a special place in the affections of British theatregoers. His life has not been easy but you could not tell in 1973 that he was going through hell. His marriage to Maggie Smith was finished. He was drinking too much. He had been committed to a mental hospital. A few years earlier, with his big chance in films apparently evaporating on the difficult shooting of Billy Wilder's *The Private Life of Sherlock Holmes*, he had attempted suicide.

But he bounced back, rather erratically, to be sure, and regained the respect of his peers and the undying admiration of his audiences in his two titanic interpretations of Falstaff and King Lear at the Royal Shakespeare Company in the 1990s. Robert blames no one for his misfortunes and expects no favours. His phenomenal powers of physical endurance have seen him through illnesses that would have killed off lesser mortals at least ten years ago. In this, he is similar to his great friend and mentor, Laurence Olivier, who also had more than his fair share of physical afflictions. Their friendship, and falling out, is one of Robert's main themes.

Robert always takes you by surprise, with his laugh, with his energy, his appetites and his incorrigible cigarette smoking (always untipped Camels). He is just a few years older than his admired contemporaries Albert Finney and Alan Bates, so that his background encompasses Northern tours and weekly rep, the hard, formative slog of an unglamorous apprenticeship before he came to attention in the early days of the Royal Court.

At the Court, he was a notable young actor in a company of rising stars – Alan Bates, Kenneth Haigh, Joan Plowright, Keith Michell – who were cannily mingled by George Devine and Tony Richardson with some of the most respected names around: Peggy Ashcroft, Joan Greenwood, Nigel Davenport, Esmé Percy. And he scored a great personal success as John Osborne's George Dillon in the play that

Osborne wrote with Anthony Creighton before *Look Back In Anger* changed everything in 1956.

For playgoers of my generation, Robert is a symbol of the best new theatre at the Court and subsequently at the new National Theatre at the Old Vic. In both arenas, Laurence Olivier was a pivotal figure, appearing in Osborne's *The Entertainer* in 1957 and symbolically exchanging his personal life with a great Hollywood star, Vivien Leigh, for the down-to-earth contemporary affiliation with a brilliant new performer, Joan Plowright. In a curious way, Robert's emotional development was the opposite, or mirror image, of Olivier's domestic life at this time: he moved from a marriage with Tarn Bassett, born of his younger touring romance with the theatre, to a whirlwind liaison with a major box office star talent, Maggie Smith.

I used to queue for three-shilling slip seats in the Old Vic gallery during those early National seasons, where Robert transformed himself as Atahuallpa, the glistening Inca sun god in Peter Shaffer's *The Royal Hunt of the Sun*, strutted gloriously in Restoration comedy and Zeffirelli's *Much Ado*, then shrunk and surprised us still as the befuddled Loevborg in Ingmar Bergman's *Hedda Gabler* and the sweet-natured Tom Wrench in *Trelawny of the Wells*. He strikes to the heart of any audience and by dint of sheer hard work and years of experience, had developed a formidable voice and an immediately attractive physical presence.

He was always someone who *gave* himself on the stage. Although there have been fine film performances, Robert is an actor who really inhabits the flesh, exists on the boards. His worst film performances are always those which have cast him because of his theatrical nature: Stephen Poliakoff's *Century* is a good case in point, and the worst of all is probably as the oddly named Max Lopert (Max Loppert – double 'p' – in real life is a perfectly respectable, indeed distinguished, white South African music critic who reviews concerts and operas for the *Financial Times*) in Howard Davies's naff and technically abominable film version of David Hare's *The Secret Rapture*.

In this gormless travesty of a wonderful stage play, Robert's role – one day's work on the film – was that of a tacky, one-scene invention (who did not appear in the original play), a ridiculous publisher, unrecognisable in the real world. Everything about his wild and intemperate performance in this five-minute scene – some of it irrationally shot from beneath his desk by a camera looking up his crotch and up his nose – explained why.

It is sad to see such talent traduced. But Robert has always risen above shoddy circumstances. He's a real actor, a primeval spirit who touts his trade as an extension of the Life Force, not a sop to stupid vanity. Robert is vain but only on the most silly and likeable of levels. He is entirely bereft of any sense of self-importance.

He emerged in the early 1960s as both a star and a classic character actor, combining elements of fire and earth, the swagger of Olivier and the spiritual density of Wilfrid Lawson or Ralph Richardson. No one, with the possible exception of Michael Redgrave, has conveyed so movingly a sense of tragic waste or valedictory emotion. Three of his best performances have been as failed writers: George Dillon, Loevborg and Chekhov's Trigorin in *The Seagull*.

Robert was playing Trigorin when I first met him. In the subsequent years, he has sometimes disappeared from view, then re-emerged with a memorable performance on stage, film or television. He has remained a vagabond and a true spirit. I think of him in some ways as a naughty boy. And as such I have encountered him over the years.

I dislike actors who are too grave, too precious, too grand, too secretive, too coy. Robert's all up front. So I had no hesitation in accepting his invitation to help him write his life's story. Robert is very special to me. I admire him because he has lived his life as he has lived his work. He is the kind of character I thought the theatre was supposed to incarnate but only too rarely does.

He speaks my language. In this book, it may be possible that I have really made him speak as much of mine as of his. But that is only as a result of shaping his wonderful stories and confessions for the demands of the cold light of syntax, structure, chronology and readability. I hope I am right in saying that I don't think my interventions have distorted any of his meanings. He has been kind enough to say that they do not.

I have spent, and indeed enjoyed, many hours with Robert over the past twenty years. There is no such thing as a wasted moment in his company, for the simple reason that no moment in his company *is* wasted. He glints and reflects all the time, he spills gossip, he spills opinion, he is forever wonderfully alive, and fascinatingly committed, to the other world of other people. He's an actor, true bred. He's the kind of artist who makes it possible to contemplate our times. Because we love him.

When he bounced back in Stratford with the RSC as Falstaff in 1991, he became a focal point in the life of the company. He gave example to the younger actors and was befriended by many of them. In the Dirty Duck, the actors' pub, he became a loyal customer of the manageress, Pam Harris, and never had any qualms about mixing with her regular clientèle among the critical fraternity. One night after supper there, Jack Tinker of the *Daily Mail* invited myself, Pam, Robert and the mountainous new comic star, Desmond Barrit, to join him for a nightcap in his suite at the Welcombe Hotel.

We took with us some champagne from Pam's fridge and proceeded in a brace of taxis to the outer limits of the town, where the Welcombe nestles in the margins of the Warwickshire countryside. Jack was occupying the Lady Caroline Lamb suite, and we instantly formed a club of which we five were, and as far as I know, still are, sole members – the Lady Caroline Lamb club. The evening was one of riotous high spirits and unforgettable gaiety, although it would have been even more unforgettable if we hadn't all drunk so much.

The longer Robert lives, against the odds, behaving badly, overcoming each day the set-back of debilitating illness and physical misfortune with the most sumptuous disregard for his condition, and with a complete absence of self-pity, the more interesting he becomes, which is more than can be said of the rest of us. I had already written a biography of Robert's third wife, Maggie Smith, and was loath to traverse similar territory. But I soon discovered that this was a very different assignment. Robert's a one-off, and a special case.

We met to talk. We met to drink. We met to have lunch. Mostly, over a couple of weeks at the start of 1995, we met in Denville Hall, the actors' home of retirement and recuperation, in order to go out and get some real food. Robert required nursing, his feet bandaging, and his diet watching, and he had therefore been accommodated in Denville Hall for a few recuperative weeks. The burden of caring has fallen in the past, and would again fall in the very near future, on his fourth wife, and partner of twenty years, the actress Patricia Quinn, but she had lately completed an exhausting national tour in *The Rocky Horror Show* and in order to prepare for the weeks, months and (knowing Robert's survival instincts) almost certainly years ahead, she had wisely removed herself to Goa with a girlfriend for a much-needed three-week beach holiday.

Denville Hall is a pleasant nursing home with the atmosphere of a country hotel in the middle of golfing territory near Northwood in Middlesex, just about twenty miles from Central London. Visiting Robert there was an eerie experience, like wandering into a production of Noël Coward's *Waiting in the Wings*. Veteran artistes like Anne Dyson, looking wonderful, and beautifully turned out, would wander through the lounge *en route* to lunch, carrying their careers in their heads, their performing pride in their very aspect, their billing – large or small – in their brows.

The great Old Vic actor, Robert Harris, sadly deceased in May 1995, appeared in his grey slacks and carpet slippers one afternoon and gave the tea trolley an especially hard look: 'Is that what they call a *bar* nowadays?' he uttered loudly and to no one in particular. Doris Hare, a robust comic actress who was in the National Theatre company when Robert was in his pomp, was planning a return home after a brief stay and looking forward to her ninetieth birthday party. 'You deserve it, dear, have a bit of rest and put your feet up,' chimed in Fanny Carby, encouragingly. Fanny Carby, a stalwart of Joan Littlewood's Theatre Workshop days at the Theatre Royal, Stratford East, in the 1960s, had been staying for a few days while recovering from a sprained ankle. She also appeared at the Royal Court with Robert, and had lost no time, he remarked ruefully, in reminding him of times past.

One day before lunch at Denville Hall, an elegant old biddy in a wheelchair turned on me as I was waiting for Robert to come downstairs and asked me how long I had been resident. I said I was merely visiting. She then tried a different tack and accused me of being a writer. I said that I was, of sorts. She said that she had been married to a *real* writer.

No doubt, I huffed, asking disinterestedly who that might have been. 'Sean O'Casey,' she replied, and I recognised at last the beautiful Eileen of my Dublin acquaintance twenty years previously. She was a shadow of her former self – she died peacefully in the second week of April.

Robert was averse to such demands. As the residential inmates sat down to lunch in the dining room, he staggered on his pins and steel crutches, and urged escape. To Uxbridge. He knew of a restaurant there. In the heart of Roland Maule country. Maule was the importunate wannabe dramatist satirised by Coward in *Present Laughter*. It is very unlikely that he would have known about a place like Giovanni's, a wonderful Italian restaurant near the Denham film studios, which became our preferred stomping ground for several hours each day in the last week of January 1995.

The food is excellent and the tolerance of the staff even more so. One of Robert's great skills is his restaurant rap. He speaks cod-Italian, cod-French, cod-Spanish. He walks in to a place and charms the pants off everyone. He loves the theatre of food, and the staff anywhere immediately recognise a theatrical foodie. He will study the menu with vicious concentration and finally decide on the most obvious components: a simple pasta, osso buco, baked fish or sautéd veal. He relishes green vegetables, a good salad, an honest, unpretentious bottle or two of wine. He's perfect restaurant company. And he'll stay in one all day and all night if necessary or desirable.

Our Denham lunches are the basis of this book. But only the basis. Robert spills over into everyday life in a way that is both alarming and delightful. There is no template. I used to arrive during our few weeks of intimacy at the front door of Denville Hall to find him crouched in expectancy by the hall door. He couldn't wait to escape, rather like some unhappy detained boy in a remand home or a minor public school.

He was anxious not for my company, but for any company. And for lunch. What might the special be? What the wine? Occasionally, he was not waiting there. This only meant that he was trussed up with some medication or other, or having his feet bandaged, or giving a nurse a bad – which is always, by his lights, or anybody else's – a good, time. I could therefore study the playbills in the reception area, the signed photographs of Noël Coward, Laurence Olivier and Richard Attenborough which are left about the place to jolly up the declining residents.

When Robert had shaken off the shackles of besotted attention that clanked around his every step, we'd negotiate the car. His bandaged, slippered feet would be a problem to everyone except himself. He'd slide into the passenger seat with the flamboyance, and the physical tact, of major royalty. His stick would be scuppered on the door or roof of the car, but this would cause no problem to him. We rallied round. His feet would be tucked in, his stick accommodated.

We would speed to Denham. One day, we sped so fast that I had forgotten to close all the car doors, and we went around a corner at fifty miles an hour without knowing that half the car's chassis was heading in the opposite direction to Watford. Several fellow road-hogs kindly pointed out the error of our ways in a series of honks, hoots and jovial expletives that left us only more determined to enjoy our lunch.

We did so. Another day, as we joined the A40 to take the little bit of motorway we needed for Denham, I casually remarked to Robert that we might as easily, were we freer, stay on the motorway for Oxford.

How lovely to lunch in Oxford, I mused out loud. What a mistake! It was the worst day of the year so far, with driving rain, sheets of hail, ice-floes, almost nil visibility. 'Of course, darling, let's go immediately. I can't think of anything more exciting!'

As we pounded up the motorway through scenes of devastation and danger, Robert chortled away about this and that, old actors and new actors, good times and bad times, people we knew. He told jokes, performed impressions without really thinking about them – he's an absolute whizz at Burton, Hopkins, Richardson, Gielgud, Olivier and the whole damned lot – and chattered so brilliantly that I felt that if the worst came to the worst and I steered uncontrollably off the road, hit a treacherous patch of black ice or grey water, at least I would die happy in the company of a man whose life enriched the comparative poverty of my own.

And this man was someone who had no right, really, to be alive. But every justification for his claim. He was cramped, he was struggling to be comfortable. He had a metal walking stick. He had undergone the most dangerous of all transplant operations and he had at that time no serious prospects of employment. Yet here he was, merry as a grig, chortling and chirruping away like a rogue robin on a spring branch. Robert absolutely refuses to look on the dark side. He's been there; he prefers the light.

We arrived in Oxford after the most terrifying road journey of my life – to which Robert had been completely impervious – at just after 1.30 pm. I parked on a double yellow line outside the Randolph Hotel in Beaumont Street and rushed inside to announce our requirements. Hotel parking. A large table. Quiet. Good food and wine. Respect. This was *Sir* Robert Stephens and he was recovering from serious illness.

They didn't really know him from Adam, but they pretended they did. A posse of waiters saw Robert from the car to the table. We were served magnificently. We lunched superbly on pies and soup and quail and desserts. Robert had a few drinks. We talked. We drove home at teatime, messing up our motorway interconnections and dicing with even more death on the M25. Nothing is ever quite safe or settled with Robert. He always wants to fly, and take us with him, which is the hallmark of his acting, I think. He dares beyond the immediate circumstances.

In the hurly-burly of these recent months, Robert never allowed himself to slow down. By the end of March, growing stronger after the operations and recovering his weight, he started to behave almost manically, as a result of the steroid treatment and other drugs. He recorded the role of the poet John Dryden in his old friend John Osborne's last script, a film about Henry Purcell. Simon Callow played Purcell and recounted in a newspaper article his joy at encountering once more the generous, full-hearted Robert of old, the actor he admired and loved from a distance when he, Callow, was working in the box office at the Old Vic in the mid-1960s.

Mid-morning on the first Monday of April, I visit Robert with the first full draft of his own manuscript. The sun shines brightly over Primrose Hill and floods through the high windows of the living room in the apartment he has shared with Patricia Quinn since 1975. Pat has been out most of the previous night and early morning at a *Rocky Horror Show* convention – she originated the double role of Magenta, and of the usherette, in 1973, and is still with it – and at one point barges sensationally into view in her silk nightdress, sleeping mask and facial glitter.

Robert's hair is dyed blond and curled in preparation, he says, for the touring production he plans of an Eduardo de Filippo play, *The Local Authority*. This is first-time news to me. When is he doing this play? The minute he gets back from a month's holiday in San Antonio, Texas. Ah, yes. When is he going to Texas? This Saturday, with Pat. Fine. The play is a comic masterpiece, he says, and the source of Mario Puzo's idea for the film of *The Godfather*. He is playing the godfather.

Sitting in his blue dressing gown on a capacious sofa, his spindly legs haphazardly bandaged, his cigarettes on the go, his glass brimming with champagne, you feel this man could do anything. I have booked a table in the nearby restaurant, Odette's, for lunch. Robert asks me to go ahead and he will get dressed and join me. Having gone ahead, I have no idea how he manages to do this. It is as if he has spirited himself downstairs and across the road. He travels on pure willpower.

Over lunch, I ask him about food and drink. For years he had an account in La Cappanina in Romilly Street, where he first went with Franco Zeffirelli, who told him that the food there was the best Italian fare in London. He found that it was. He favours the chicken liver risotto in Rule's, and is indeed on this occasion lunching on a broad bean risotto (he loves broad beans) in Odette's. He reminisces about a tiny broad bean risotto made with Parmesan cheese that he enjoyed in Rome. In London, he eats often at the Caprice, the Ivy and Green's off Park Lane. Drink? Today, just a little wine, but when fully fighting fit, Robert is, or was, partial to anything. 'Old-fashioneds', bourbon and ginger beer, are a particular favourite. He loves Margaritas, any number of whisky cocktails, and is very keen on a lethal gin-based, Campari cocktail called a Negroni. At a nearby table, the retired ballet dancer David Wall and his colleague Jane Sanig – currently dancing Giselle with the London City Ballet – invite us to join them for liqueurs and coffee. They know Robert from way back, and the extraordinary performance of stories and quips is rejuvenated. I slink away towards teatime. David and Jane say they will see Robert home. If they don't, he will manage it anyhow.

In the event, the trip to Texas was postponed. Robert returned to the Royal Free in mid-April for more tests and a period of supervised recuperation. He was speeding too much on his medication and needed to be calmed down and readjusted to his new limits and capabilities. We continued working together, and no session, however brief, was devoid of a telling anecdote, a superb impression, a raft of memories.

In trying to deal with Robert's life, our endeavours have been greatly assisted by Pat Quinn, who has been a tower of strength to him in recent months; and, indeed, for the entire twenty years of their partnership. Pat has organised and rallied much important material, and many photographs. Robert's second wife, Tarn Bassett, provided the correspondence between her and Robert in the early years of their relationship, and generously filled in many biographical details. As did Jacqueline ('Jackey') Finch, Robert's younger sister; Jeremy Brett, the actor Robert first met in their days together in the Library Theatre company, Manchester; and Christopher Downes, Robert's dresser at the Old Vic and a close friend and confidant of both Robert and his third wife, Maggie Smith.

We are especially grateful to Helen Osborne, widow of John Osborne, for permission to reproduce in full her late husband's extraordinary letter to his old friend after he had been to see the RSC *King Lear*. Thanks are due, too, to our effervescent editor Rowena Webb, and her assistant Rachel Bond, at Hodder & Stoughton.

Robert has revealed both more and less of himself in this book than he knows. He has honestly, and sometimes painfully, compiled an extraordinary document of the life of a working actor, and a very great one, during a tumultuous era of British theatre. And he has done so during a period of intense personal anxiety and physical trauma. Robert has been ill for years, and seriously debilitated for months on end. Would you be able to tell that? Would you know a hawk from a handsaw?

Michael Coveney
Theatre critic, *The Observer*
London, June 1995

PROLOGUE

My life was saved, not for the first time, on Monday, 19th September, 1994. My new liver and kidney organs were flown into North London by helicopter on the Sunday night, and the operation was performed at the Royal Free Hospital the next morning. I had been given three months to live. Now I felt that I could start again.

Prince Charles sent me a bowl of fruit and John Gielgud a huge box of chocolates, apparently and touchingly unmindful of the fact that I am a diabetic, a slight physical failing that runs in the family; my mother was diabetic, too.

With the single exception of my first wife, whom I have not seen since the day we parted, very young, and very unsuited, my entire extended family has rallied around me: my second wife, Tarn Bassett, our daughter Lucy, my third wife, Dame Maggie Smith, and our two boys, Chris and Toby, and of course my darling Pat, the actress Patricia Quinn, whom I finally married after years of loving partnership and suspense on 11th January 1995.

The kidney, the doctors said, was so perfect a match, it could have come from my own daughter. The operation costs £25,000, which is the amount the Italian government pays for all the Italians who are in the same hospital having it done. Mine, thank Heavens, was performed on the good old National Health Service.

After the operation, I was kept in for another six weeks of recuperation. Looking at the same four walls for over three months was not much fun, nor was the hospital food. I am rather particular about my food. I like lots of it. And I prefer it to be extremely good.

On top of everything else, I fell over and broke my hip. It would make very good copy to say that I fell off my exercise bike, but it was all much more banal than that. I was putting a yoghurt pot into the waste-bin in the room, I turned round, slipped, fell, hit my shoulder on the sink and bumped my bottom on the floor. The X-ray, to my astonishment, showed that I'd fractured the hip. So, that added complication held me back even longer.

In addition, because of staying in bed for so long and pushing myself up into a sitting position, I developed some sores on my heel, and a cut on the sole of the other foot, and they had to be treated and bandaged every day. I had to be careful, because the last thing you want is any ulcerations.

From the Royal Free I moved for a few weeks into Denville Hall, that wonderful home for retired actors and convalescing thesps, such as myself. On New Year's Day 1995, my knighthood was announced for services to the theatre, and I felt prouder than if I had won an Oscar.

Pat and I were desperate to get married, but she got cold feet and cancelled a couple of times because she was not sure if I could get through the ceremony without collapsing in an embarrassing manner. In the event, in the middle of January 1995, I didn't collapse, but I did totter. The registrar asked us to stand, and as Pat did so, I sort of keeled over to my right. Luckily, Pat's son Quinn caught me, abetted by her brother. Much to everyone's relief, the registrar then said, rather urgently, 'You may remain seated!' In my case, there wasn't much option.

After our marriage at St Pancras Registry Office, and a tumultuous lunch in the Ivy restaurant, Pat took herself off for a well-deserved three-week holiday in Goa. She had just completed an exhausting tour of *The Rocky Horror Show*, in the same role she had been playing in the original production when we first met in 1975.

Pat returned in time to accompany me to the Variety Club Award ceremony in the Hilton Hotel on 7th February, 1995. I was to be named Best Actor of the Year for my performance as King Lear with the Royal Shakespeare Company. Shirley Bassey was Showbusiness Personality of the Year. And Maggie Smith was named Best Actress for her performance in Edward Albee's *Three Tall Women*. It was strange, and strangely moving, to be on the same stage with her again after all our years together.

Usually reticent to the point of anonymity, Maggie accepted her award with a speech of tremendous volubility, thanking her author, the author's step-mother on whom her role was based, her fellow actors, the welcoming theatre, the stage management, the stage doorman, everyone bar the usherettes. Luckily, she hadn't exhausted everybody's patience by the time I was called to the stage, and I was immensely moved and gratified by the warmth of the ovation. I had a bit of a struggle, as I am not too quick on my pins at the moment but, with Pat supporting me, I felt ten feet tall.

I thanked my doctors, the staff at Denville Hall and the lady beside me whose stoicism and determination had seen me through a tricky few months. I also thanked Adrian Noble, the artistic director of the RSC, who had directed me as both Falstaff and King Lear in the past few years. I really had come back from the dead. And looking in the direction of Shirley Bassey, one of her best known song titles came to mind, and to my lips: 'What now, my love?'

Finally, to complete a staggering few months of high points and low points, the highest of all: my date at Buckingham Palace in the first week of March 1995 to receive my knighthood from the Queen. I had already received a letter from Prince Charles congratulating me on becoming one of his knights of the realm. I felt like Falstaff receiving a reprieve from Prince Hal. But the Queen's charm and solicitousness were equal to her own son's decency towards me.

I left my hospital bed to keep the appointment. I could not sleep a wink the night before. Her Majesty looked charming in a powdered blue frock, and the band, which had struggled through the entirety of *Oliver!* and 'Feeling Groovy' suddenly, as my turn came, struck up a soupy arrangement of Topol's old hit from *Fiddler on the Roof*, 'If I were a rich man'. God knows why. If only I were! I suspect you have to be a jockey to have any sort of meaningful conversation with the Queen, but she rather surprisingly said, 'There's a lot of work to be done in your area, isn't there?' To which I could only reply, with a silly grin, 'Yes, ma'am.' And that was that. Of course I should have said, 'No, ma'am, I'm afraid there's not a lot of work in our area; most of us are out of work a lot of the time.'

The doctors have to keep an eye on my progress, pump me up with a few steroids and take the odd biopsy to see how the new liver's bearing up. But there was no way I was going to miss that entrance at the Palace, the proudest day of my life. And now I am guaranteed a good table in any restaurant I choose to eat in. Shall there be no more cakes and ale? I sincerely hope not.

1

Early Days in Bristol

One can always smile and smile, and be a villain, as Hamlet says, but it is impossible to fool an audience for even some of the time. I am, and always have been, an impetuous boy, and I make no apology for the fact. That is what an audience sees in the theatre, that I am a flawed and open creature who will share my fears and hopes with them for an hour or two. I am a person of impulse and spontaneity, and I have always had an alarming capacity to let myself go: in life, and on the stage.

If I am indeed a good actor, it is partly because I am not, I hope, a dull man. It is impossible for a dull man to be a good actor. I am easily bored, and I love to live in the moment as well as in the spotlight. But my background could not be more ordinary. The actor Jeremy Brett, with whom I have been close friends since our days in repertory in Manchester in the early 1950s, was kind enough to describe me once as 'a fairly nice old sweetheart from Bristol', and I dare say that sums it up.

My parents were married on 31st May 1930 in St James' Parish Church, Shirehampton, a mile or two from the port in Bristol. The marriage certificate records that Reuben Stephens was a labourer, and Gladys Millicent Deverell, a chocolate worker. He was born in West Hartlepool in 1905 and called Reuben merely because my grandmother plucked the names for all her children from the Bible; of course everyone thought he was Jewish. My father had come to Bristol with his family in search of work. My mother was a born (1906) and bred Bristolian, who met Dad through his sister, Auntie Lou, who also worked in the Fry's chocolate factory. My mother had very dry hands, and was always assigned to the packing of 'special occasion' boxes.

I was born on 14th July 1931. Bristol was a great port in those days, and all the petrol and oil came in there for Shell and British Petroleum, who kept their oil tanks down there. Not that any of this wealth came our way. We never owned the house we lived in and to this day, for one reason or another, I never have owned the house I live in. I'm a roving actor by temperament as much as by inclination.

I had a terrible childhood, with no money, no love and no prospects. I was the oldest of three children and always known as 'our Bob' – a big fat Bristol baby I was, weighing in at ten and a half pounds; at school I was known as 'Tubby' Stephens. My sister Jacqueline, 'our Jack', or Jackey, was born in June 1940, nine years younger than me; my brother John, born in March 1945, nearly fourteen years younger. I hardly knew them at all. Jackey and John remain close to this day, but I drifted away from them very early on.

I grew up, in effect, as an only child, in 34 Priory Road, Shirehampton. I have hardly kept in touch with my brother because I never really grew up with him. And there are few pictures of my early years for the simple reason that no one we knew had a camera. Reuben lived to a ripe old age, dying in the Evesham General Hospital in 1985; Mum had pre-deceased him, dying of diabetes-related gangrene ten years earlier.

My father's family in West Hartlepool all worked on the boiler-making side of the shipping trade. When the industry failed on their own doorstep between the wars, and they stopped making ships, they all moved down to Avonmouth near Bristol, thick North-Eastern accents and all. I couldn't understand a single word one of my uncles said.

They all soon discovered that there wasn't that much shipbuilding going on in Avonmouth, either, so they mostly all turned to the building trade. My mother's family, the Bristolian Deverells, were all in the building trade, either as painters or decorators. My father went into steel bending and fixing for a time, which was very hard labour. He was entirely self-taught, with no education, and he worked very hard. Money was unbelievably tight; my father would buy packets of just five cigarettes.

He was a huge man with a big nose and a kind smile and, like me, he was as strong as an ox. He worked very hard and eventually became a costing surveyor. He was admitted as an associate of the Building Surveyors' Institute in June 1954; so he made a great advance in his life. Dad was a very keen golfer and took part in a lot of amateur competitions. I have never had the slightest interest in sport and never took part in competitive games. I love swimming and being by the sea, or by the pool, but that is not quite the same thing!

To start with, we all lived with my father's parents from West Hartlepool. Proximity did not breed affection. My father, despite the gentle giant image, was rather frightening, a bit like myself, physically, but rather an exaggerated version. He was prone to fits of violence which explains my abhorrence of all unnecessary physical aggression. Some of this he worked out on the golf course. My mother, who was very small, had to put up with his everyday brutality, so she had no qualms about giving me a good clip round the ear and indeed rarely stopped there. She used to knock me about quite heavily.

Social workers today would undoubtedly say that I was an abused child, though the abuse was merely violent, not sexual. And my early experience of what I took to be normal, everyday violence, has undoubtedly made me both inwardly revolted by such activity and curiously immune to taunts and fits of bad temper. I hate violence in all its forms, and I have never in my life raised a finger in anger against anyone.

My mother used to whack me with the boiler stick she used to push the washing in the copper. One day when I was very little she whacked me across the back with it; the stick had been soaked in a lot of water so it wasn't like cracking your teeth, but nevertheless she could have broken my back. My grandmother said, 'Look, you've broken his back, you've killed him.' My sister Jackey plays down this maternal walloping, saying that we all got walloped, and it was nothing unusual.

My mother used to go and visit her mother almost every day and they used to like wandering around a Woolworths store in town. On one of these outings, I had been given a silver threepenny piece – I must have been aged three or four – and I managed to get it jammed into the roof of my mouth. All hell broke loose, and they went into a dreadful panic, my Mum and Grandma. But the minute the coin was released – probably with a firm smack round the head – they went on and on at me as if I'd committed the worst crime in the world.

Much later on, when I was about seventeen, my mother told me that she never wanted a baby, and certainly not when I came along. I always thought that was an odd thing to say to me. She suddenly came out with this extraordinary confession about how, when she was pregnant, she sat in a bath with a bottle of gin and took a crochet hook while sitting over a pail and tried to . . . well, of all the clichés. I said, 'Jesus Christ, why are you telling me this?' But she said she had to tell me, she had to get it off her chest. 'Thanks a lot,' I thought to myself. 'Nothing like being made to feel welcome!'

I didn't want to know about all this and she was just puzzled by that reaction. I think she didn't want me because she wasn't happily married to my father. I remember he once hit my mother and knocked her clean over the sofa, when I was about three. The two of us left home and went to live with my grandmother, her mother, until he calmed down and we went back. Life may have been frugal but it was never dull. I lived in permanent fear of physical attack. At the hands of my parents.

For this reason I have always cherished whatever happiness I have found in life. The only happy times of my childhood I associate with my maternal grandmother. I was sent to her house in Bristol, about five miles away, every Friday night and returned home on Sunday afternoon. There was Grandma, my grandfather, my Uncle George and my Auntie Wyn – she's still alive, aged about ninety-three – and my Auntie Lily, who was deaf and dumb; I spent every weekend of my childhood and most of my holidays with them. So I recall much more about their house and the way they lived than I do about my own home and my parents.

I used to go on my own on the bus and come back every Sunday night. I loved going there, not just to get away from Mother, but also because they spoilt me and looked after me. My deaf and dumb aunt took me to the cinema every Saturday night when they showed silent pictures: I saw Charlie Chaplin, Laurel and Hardy, Rudolf Valentino and John Barrymore, all with sub-titles.

When I was older I always felt I was much more loved by my grandparents on my mother's side than I was at home. They had Irish, and beyond that, Polish, antecedents; my mother's mother's family were called Huntley, originally O'Donnell.

There is some sort of artistic genetic strand: Jackey has always been a dab hand with the needle and thread, and has never stopped sewing, while John is an expert screenprinter. At one stage, John wanted to be a writer and indeed had a play of his produced at Bristol University which was taken to the Edinburgh Festival fringe, where it was awarded a prize of some sort. And I was an actor. Some say this is all down to the fact that a distant aunt on my mother's grandfather's side was reputedly – or disreputedly – a dancer with the Folies Bergères in Paris.

When I was eight or nine, I was playing Cowboys and Indians with some of the other boys in my street. The Indians tied me to a lamppost and disappeared home for their tea. I just stood there, waiting to be relieved by the Cowboys. But they never turned up. They'd gone for their tea, too. Luckily, Auntie Wyn came round to visit my parents before it got dark, and she asked me what I was doing. I'm told I replied: 'I'm a Cowboy and the Indians caught me and I'm waiting for the Cowboys to come back and rescue me.' I have always been generous with my trust, and always give people the benefit of the doubt. Much good did it do me on that occasion! Jackey says that this story demonstrates my placid nature. Mother on the other hand, was very quick-tempered.

I was very cowed by my mother. When we finally left my grandparents' house and went into a house of our own, a council house, she was much happier. I was an isolated child and I suppose I must have steeled myself against all the unhappiness.

As I grew up, I only saw my father very rarely. One odd thing I remember about him: he had an obsession with going to the lavatory. He always announced it in the most unsavoury manner: 'Well, I think I'll just go and have a shit'; or, 'Come on, give us the paper.' He also used to say, 'I think there must be something wrong with my guts, it must be that beer; one day I can paint the door with it, the next I can bolt the door with it.' And I think to this day I always feel as though I should ask to go to the lavatory.

During the war, my father used to travel all over the country, on his work of National Importance, anywhere there was a need for building or repairing. Twice we were all evacuated to Midsummer Norton in Somerset. Dad was building an Italian prisoner of war camp at Bridgewater, and we all stayed there with a farm labourer and his wife. It was the most ghastly experience of my childhood. There was nothing much to eat. All the vegetables they grew were sent off to market. The lighting was from oil lamps, we were only allowed to have the wireless on for the news, and this great big horrible labourer would stretch out in front of the fire warming his chilblains. Mum and I were dying for fish and chips, so we just left Dad to it and went back to Bristol.

Dad would also build great big storehouses for tinned food, just in case of invasion and emergency. Naturally, a bomb hit one in Bristol, and we suddenly came by all this tinned food: tinned ham, tinned jam, tinned lobster, tinned beans, tinned corned beef. He just filled the back of a lorry with the stuff from the burnt-out warehouse and every cupboard in the house was filled to bursting point.

The trouble was, all the labels were burned off, so you never knew what you were opening next. We had some very peculiar meals; we used to shake the tins and try to guess what was inside before we opened them. If it was dense and solid, you couldn't tell what it was going to be. He once came home with a week's supply of butter. This was the ultimate, and for a short while we had landed in the lap of luxury.

During the war, I had a friend called David Rendle. When we were about ten or eleven, we began to produce our own Punch and Judy shows. My father carved for me all the puppets heads out of applewood and made me the framework of the theatre. I researched assiduously in the local library, and found out everything I could about the Italian characters, Pulcinella, Pretty Polly, the courtier who talks to Mr Punch as his neck grows longer and longer, the crocodile, the Devil and Jack Ketch. It is terrifying, compulsive stuff, and I have never lost my addiction to those stories or the powerful theatrical instincts they represent.

We used to perform wonderful little shows for the Aid to Russia fund, charging a penny a head for entrance – and indeed we were given a medal by the Lady Mayoress of Bristol for so doing. The operation expanded into the air-raid shelter in the garden, where we put together a Haunted House exhibition with bits and pieces of hardware and crude special effects, and we charged a penny admission to that, too. We continued with the puppets for a few years, doing lots of charity shows. I also started to keep some money back for myself.

I did all the voices for the puppets and crocodiles and things. I didn't have a ventriloquist's squeaker! As a consequence of all that vocal strain, my voice broke very early, and I could no longer sing in the church choir as I had done for a couple of years, so I had to sit by the organ in church and pump the bellows. I hated doing that, and if I'm honest I probably sat there, pumping away, thinking about ways of resuming a performing career. The bug had bitten. When the war was over, our puppet shows switched their charitable loyalties and contributed towards the Aid to China fund. If I'd been in America, I would certainly have been imprisoned for being a Communist.

Because of the age gap with my brother and sister, and because my father was away a lot for his work during the war, I became, as it were, the man of the house. It was a very hard, tough life. My mother went out to work every day as a cleaning daily, my father came home once a month at the weekend, and I had to look after my sister.

She was a miserable child and grew up almost exclusively in an air-raid shelter, though I am glad to say she has grown up into a reasonably jolly woman. So it is just as well really that I saved her life, which she claims I did. I had taken her out shopping during the war and as we came back over the hill, the sirens went off. The German bombers had come up the River Severn to bomb Bristol and now they were going back to the Channel over Avonmouth and dropping on the way back whatever they had not already dropped. It was very frightening. I grabbed Jackey out of the pram and dived into a privet hedge with her and stayed there until the all-clear went.

At home, whenever the alert was on, we all slept on the floor of the Andersen shelter and Jackey slept over our heads in a cradle my father had made for her. I used to get in such a state when the sirens went off. One day, the panic was farcical: rushing to get down to the shelter, I pulled on my short trousers, putting both legs down one hole! Talk about going for cheap laughs. When I left home at seventeen, Jackey was still very young and my brother John only about three. I never saw much of him at all.

In later years, when I went on holiday to Ibiza (my favoured holiday haunt in the late 1950s and early 1960s), John came out with his then girlfriend, now his wife, Betty, to run a bar for a friend of mine. He, too, finally wanted to get out of Bristol, whereas Jackey was always quite happy to stay in the neighbourhood. John bought an old car and took it down to Ibiza in the late 1950s, and my mother and father finally went out to stay with him. They were so entranced by Spain that my father taught himself Spanish and read *Don Quixote* in the original at the age of about seventy.

We were never a close family, and grew no closer down the years. Jacqueline lives in Upton-on-Severn, Worcestershire, now and is married to a very clever man in electronics. They have a son, Stephen, who is a statistician. John teaches silk screenprinting in London and has written two books on the subject. He has two daughters. Jacqueline and John are a bit like me, they both have the same sunny nature! (Though my sister can still be a bit of a misery.)

John sometimes comes and sees me on stage, but Jacqueline rarely does. What really impresses them all is when one is on television. My father was forever saying, 'You want to get on the television, boy; Atahuallpa in *The Royal Hunt of the Sun* was very good, and that's all very well, that National Theatre stuff, but it wasn't on the box, so it wasn't *that* good, was it?'

I never remember my dreams, so I have no idea what the sensation is like. But my waking dream as a child was that I might find something better than the life we had. I wanted to get out of it somehow. Our poverty ensured that we had very little pleasure in life. I had no idea where the pleasure might lie, or how I would find it. I was very taken with the films when I went to see them, because I could see that they were acting – that man up there, John Wayne, he's acting being a cowboy, I'd tell myself, he's not really like that, nor is James Cagney really like that gangster he's playing. And I did think I'd like to be that, not a cowboy or a gangster, but someone other than myself. I'd like to be acting.

2

Bradford and Weekly Rep

I was not a show-off as a boy, quite the opposite in fact. I was terribly shy and placid. My mother cowed me, which I think affected me in later life. I always found it hard to speak out for myself, because I wasn't allowed to when I was little. But, of course, you can't go on being shy; you've got to break through that. And I suppose that was what attracted me to the theatre. It gives you a chance to speak out, but as somebody else. When you play a part all your energies go into that, and it's not you.

I went to Portway Boys School, not a grammar school, just an ordinary secondary school in Bristol, where I was a dunce. That role required no acting at all from me. But I was always very good at verse-speaking. I won several prizes for it, including one which allowed me to go to a local elocution teacher called Hedley Goodall, who was also very big in amateur theatricals in Bristol. I was fairly well-behaved and I never got into scraps or fights. I did have a Bristol accent which I was encouraged, quite rightly, to lose later on at drama school in Bradford, and I made an effort to speak properly.

When, a few years after me, Albert Finney, Peter O'Toole and Billie Whitelaw arrived on the scene, drama schools encouraged people to keep their regional accents, which I think was disastrous. So when, years later, Albert played his Hamlet, I didn't believe a word he said, because Hamlet would not talk in that flat, boring, dull way which leaves you no freedom to go up and down the scale. The words don't sound right. Whatever so-called experts like John Barton might say about Shakespeare sounding more like Cornish or mid-Western when it was first spoken, that's how everybody else spoke as well; they don't now, so it simply won't work.

It was the same when I finally joined the RSC to play Falstaff in 1991.

This young actor came on to the stage at Stratford-upon-Avon sounding like a navvy, declaring that he was the Earl of Westmorland; nobody believed him. I certainly didn't. There are all these people teaching voice – Cecily Berry and her assistants – at Stratford who should never have allowed all this slack-jawed, regional, lazy nonsense to happen.

I remember reading Wordsworth and not understanding a word of it, though I understood the rhythms – the music, if you like – but I used to speak quite well, thanks to Hedley Goodall. I did drama at the National Association of Boys Clubs which the Duke of Edinburgh encouraged after the war, as a way of keeping young people off the street, and giving them something to do, even if it was only a game of ping pong.

There was a training centre for youth club leaders in Cranborne in Kent, and you'd learn how to form a drama group or a football team. On the drama courses they had to have twelve or more boys so that club leaders could learn how to direct plays. Boys like me could go there on a two-week drama course and be used as training fodder for them. Then they had tours that went out, with the boys from the boys' club; we took one-act plays and bits of mime and revue around youth clubs to show them what could be done with a minimum of scenery and costumes. I went on one of these tours when I was about fifteen or sixteen, and then I went on another one a year later.

One play we did, *The Hewers of Coal*, won a prize at a youth club festival. I played a miner in a cap and necktie which I managed to convince myself constituted a real theatrical costume. A fellow cast member was Mavis Williams, my first true girlfriend, with whom I was deeply in love for a very short time. Her parents were not at all keen on the idea of me hanging around, so I made my excuses and left her, but not before we had sampled those physical delights which hasten the departure of the virginal condition. I had discovered the lethal cocktail of theatre and sex, and it seemed like a very good idea indeed.

I must have made some sort of thespian impression on the powers that be as the advisor on drama, a very nice, encouraging man called Tony Thomas, asked me if I would like to pursue this as a career. I said I would. He said that the two best drama schools were the Old Vic School in London run by George Devine and Michel Saint Denis, and Bradford Civic Theatre School run by Esmé Church in Yorkshire. I won a place at the latter and a free scholarship from the local authorities in Bristol.

Esmé was an extraordinary woman, very large, very refined and rather intimidating. You never saw her without her cigarette holder. I loved her very much; she was like a mother to me. She had previously been at the Old Vic with Tony Guthrie as his assistant before the war, when Larry and Ralph and Alec Guinness and all those other great people were there; she'd opened the school in Bradford because she believed in decentralising the drama schools, challenging the hegemony of London. And she also felt that there was an enormous amount of talent in the North that remained undiscovered, partly for financial reasons, partly for lack of encouragement.

She opened the school at a time when people leaving the armed forces could easily get a grant, and it ran very successfully for about seven years. I was there between 1949 and 1951. She was a truly wonderful teacher of acting, if indeed you can teach such a thing. She also had a man called Rudolf Laban who taught in a big studio in Manchester, and he used to come over every Thursday to give movement classes; Christopher Fettes and Yat Malmgren, who later ran the Drama Centre, source of many fine young actors, especially at the Royal Court, were totally influenced by Laban. He ran the Ballet Joos, and was the first man to notate modern dance steps. He used to be master of movement at the Berlin State Opera House during the Hitler years before the war, but he got out.

Esmé Church's school was associated with the Bradford Civic Playhouse, an amateur theatre. With them, she formed a children's theatre which produced plays for children in the Civic on Saturday mornings. These shows would then tour to Leeds and around the West Riding.

I was a tall, dark and not very handsome young man by that time; I always thought I was rather plain, in fact. If anyone else thought I was good-looking they never said anything about it. I played character parts mostly, old men and rascals, never juveniles; parts like Noah! The person I really thought was handsome when I met him in Manchester was Jeremy Brett. *That* was a young handsome leading man, a Gentleman Jim type. I was never one of those.

It was a two-year course at Bradford, and that's plenty; students do three years now and I think that last year is a complete waste of time. The Moscow Art Theatre used to give their students five years of the Stanislavsky method: I once met two old Russian actors at the National when they were touring during the World Theatre season at the Aldwych and I took them out to dinner. I asked them about the Method, because I'd seen American actors in New York using their version of it and it was so awful, amateur and inept and stupid. And they said to me, if you have a copy of Stanislavsky's *My Life in Art* or *An Actor Prepares* just take it out and throw it into the river. If it was bilge to them, it was certainly no use to me.

I saw Esmé Church act twice for Guthrie, once in his production of *The Matchmaker* and once in a play of his own called *The Top of the Ladder*, and she directed Edith Evans in the famous *As You Like It* with Michael Redgrave. She used to say that if you get one successful student out of a two-year course you've done your bit. The only other person I know about from my time there was Bernard Hepton, and you could see that he was brilliant. It was a crying shame that the school closed. But there you are; all the rough Northern lads like Albert Finney (who's about five years younger than me) were trying to get into RADA! You couldn't get away with talking with any kind of rural accent with Esmé.

I hadn't seen that much theatre at that point – John Gielgud's *Hamlet* and the Lunts – but they certainly spoke just plain, well articulated English. When I was training, I knew that I wouldn't get on unless I did something about my voice. If I was going to talk like a country bumpkin, then that's all I could expect to be playing. And I didn't want that. Mind you, when my voice changed and I went back to Bristol, they were all mortified; especially my grandmother who said, 'What do you want to do that for, you don't want to do that; actors are all spivs!' Lovely word, 'spivs', but not quite right for actors. Rogues and vagabonds, maybe.

I don't think anyone in my family really understood what it was all about. If they came and saw me in anything, all they would ever say was, 'It was very nice, very nice,' as if that was any bloody kind of useful criterion or assessment. No one ever said it was brilliant, or wanted to know how I had managed to do it; it was just 'very nice'.

Being away so much I really grew away from home. My father was always very encouraging about going on the stage, but not my mother, or my grandmother. Not many working class kids went to drama school when I went; the change hadn't come yet, and most of the students at Bradford were middle-class. Most of the girls were there treating it like a finishing school, using up two years before they got married.

That's where I met Nora Ann Simmonds, my first wife. Her father was an estate agent in Londonderry. She was very pretty and I fancied her like mad, but she came from another class of people. We had an affair and it quickly became serious, although we were both far too young to be signing our lives away. The trouble was, Nora Ann became pregnant as I came to the end of my second year, so we had to get married as I left the school in 1951. It was the classic shotgun wedding. The minute Nora Ann gave birth to our little boy, Michael Christopher, she went back to Londonderry. We had hardly been together at all. I was nineteen.

Nora Ann's parents made it very clear to her that I was an unsuitable partner, and no doubt I was. As soon as we were married and our child thus ratified, she went home to live with her parents. I was on the road in my first theatrical job – which meant everything to me – with the Caryl Jenner Mobile Theatre Company, which I had joined the minute I left Bradford. It was a logical extension of all the children's shows I'd been involved with, but I could hardly be of any material use to Nora Ann and the baby with an income of just eight pounds a week. My prospects did not seem glittering, and rushing around the country on one-night stands with an obscure fit-up company was not the way to impress her family. Nor did I want to, particularly. We were married for just about a year.

We were hardly together at all. I was not considered to be from the correct social stratum, and of course I wasn't. I was not what was required. It was exactly like the situation between Jimmy Porter and Alison in John Osborne's *Look Back In Anger*, only five or six years earlier! I was very hurt at the time that our separation should be presented as a *fait accompli*. Obviously it didn't take her long to wake up to the fact that she had probably made a very bad mistake. I had, too, but I just bumbled along in my usual, amiable manner. I had no plans to be a good husband, or a good father.

I did, however, want to be a good actor. All Nora Ann's friends were marrying lawyers and so on. I was in no position to put up any sort of fight because Nora Ann very soon agreed with her family on the subject of my unsuitability. But primarily the marriage couldn't work because I wasn't there and I wasn't earning anything. Things were no better when I quickly progressed into rep. That paid twelve pounds a week, and you ended up even poorer because you had to find all your own clothes: dinner jacket and three suits, sports jacket and flannels, which I bought on Hire Purchase. I was simply unprepared for, and unwilling and unable to engage in, domestic life at that stage.

We had some terribly upsetting scenes. I went over to Londonderry to see the baby, little Michael, for the first time since his birth, and picked him up. Nora Ann came into the room, pulled him out of my arms and forbade me to hold him. I walked out of the house, and out of the town, and never returned. Nora Ann's brother adopted Michael and brought him up. I had no idea what happened thereafter or how he matured, until I met him years later. Nora Ann went back into the theatre, but she never really made any impression.

With Caryl Jenner, I did a play about Queen Victoria and a whole lot of children's sketches and plays. It was donkey work, but quite fun. I didn't learn very much, but it was a job. It was a start. In the summer, we played in weekly rep in Seaford, in stalwart repertory pieces like *The Hollow* and excellent popular farces like *Rookery Nook*. That appealed to me much more. After Caryl Jenner, I moved on to weekly rep in Morecambe. They had a rather ambitious programme, mixing genuine crowd-pleasers with a regular input of more serious and challenging stuff, such as Sartre's *Crime Passionel* or tricky, demanding Shakespeare, such as *Julius Caesar*.

I had no objection to doing my National Service. While still at Bradford I had been passed A–1 on the medical test. But when I returned to Bristol after completing the course, I had to undergo another test. They accused me of having flat feet, a condition which I could not in all honesty deny. I was therefore excused service, and continued my apprenticeship in repertory theatre.

I was at Morecambe in 1950/51 for about fifteen months, acting in a different play each week. The great thing about it was not so much the technical practice, or the learning of anything new, as the discipline of going on however miscast or unhappy you were. You learned a sense of reponsibility, which in my case was something to which I did not very easily take. I was cast as the husband of the actress Mabel Constandouros, who was about seventy, while I was only twenty. I even had one scene in bed with her, which was the only time in my life I can remember being in bed with a woman and remaining chaste in thought and deed with absolutely no difficulty whatsoever!

Ralph Lynn, the great farceur, came up to Morecambe, too; such great stars would come and do 'special', or 'guest', weeks. Ralph Lynn used to direct the other actors on the stage while the play was going on, so you were both acting in a play and appearing in a Ralph Lynn master-class. He'd say a funny line, get a huge laugh, and then say under his breath, 'Don't say anything yet.' Then he'd say, 'Now say it;' you'd say it, and get another big laugh so he'd say, 'There you are, you see.' And then he'd say, 'Face the front, face the front,' and push you round to face the front. He once told me: 'In drama, you can act with your back to the audience, in straight plays you can act in profile, but in farce they've got to see the whole play on the face; so when I'm talking, look at me, and when you have to answer, look out front.'

He was about seventy-two then, but twice as quick as anyone else on the stage. I went to see him in a play called *Wild Horses* in the West End with Robertson Hare in 1952. Apart from his brilliant technical craft, he operated on sheer personality. In the first scene, the doorbell rang and Robertson Hare went offstage. You heard this voice say, 'Thank you, thank you, thank you . . .' and without him even appearing on the stage, there was a huge laugh and round of applause. When he came on, there was another huge round of applause. He walked straight to the front of the stage, stood there, looked around, walked back and began the scene. Amazing. A farceur par excellence. He told me that when Ben Travers wrote the Aldwych farces, the acting team – Ralph, Tom Walls, Mary Broughton, and so on – had all taught him how to write them. Robertson Hare could hardly act at all, but the others taught him, too.

Another big star in Morecambe was Thora Hird, who had been born next door to the Theatre Royal, so she came back every year to make a guest appearance in a special week. The play, invariably, was *Ma's Bit of Brass*, which was very funny, though I can't remember a single thing about it. People were hanging from the rafters, you couldn't get a seat. Thora is an extremely adroit and skilful actress – John Osborne's favourite actress, for what that's worth – with an extraordinary ability, rather like Maggie Smith, to twist on a sixpence from being terribly funny to terribly touching. She's a bit mawkish, sometimes, but a brilliant comedienne. The tops.

A die was cast for me in a different direction in Morecambe when the director Tony Richardson turned up and saw me in *The Little Foxes*. He said that he and George Devine were planning to start a new company somewhere in London and would I be interested in joining them. This was way before they started the English Stage Company with John Osborne and Co at the Royal Court. I think they were hoping to get the Saville; and they were hoping to produce brand new plays. I said, of course, I would like to join, but I heard no more about it for the time being. I still had time to serve in the reps, and some important relationships were looming.

3

Falling in Love with Tarn . . .
and Jeremy

After Morecambe, I joined a touring production of a salacious little farce, *Not a Clue*, by David Cross. I was cast as the villain of the piece, replacing some hopeless actor who had played the role as an Italian; it was re-written as an Arab called 'Ali Chumna' which was probably no improvement at all. I had to wear black make-up and a white turban. It was all totally ridiculous. We toured this wretched play for about six months. It never came into London, though it was supposed to.

The stars were Claude Hulbert, brother of the more famous Jack, his wife Delia Trevor, and another fine comedian called Sonny Hale, who had been married to Evelyn Laye, a great musical comedy star, but had ditched her and later married another, Jessie Matthews. It always fascinated me that when Sonny had abandoned 'Boo' Laye in 1929, she was appearing at Drury Lane in a Sigmund Romberg musical called *The New Moon* and she had to sing 'Lover, come back to me', every night and could not get through it without bursting into tears. More a case of 'Boo-hoo' Laye. I felt keenly for her in retrospect, even though Sonny was a gross, unfunny person offstage and someone, on the whole, to avoid.

In the *Not a Clue* company, sometime in 1953, I met the actress Tarn Bassett, who was to become my second wife. I had no real girlfriends at the time, and I fell head over heels in love. The play involved a game of strip poker in which Hulbert and Hale unfunnily cheated on each other while Tarn innocently disrobed until she was naked inside a large white towel.

She was instantly irresistible. Tarn, who was and is the sweetest, loveliest person in the world, was even more of an Alison Porter to my Jimmy in that she was extremely middle-class; her father was a retired military gent who had served with the British army in India. Tarn was born in Bangalore. She was less dark than Nora Ann, more mousey and lighter complexioned, but she was also very beautiful.

People say I eventually grew out of the relationship. But I'm not sure about that. Ours was not a relationship. It was an extended love affair. Tarn, lovely devoted Tarn, stood by me for eleven years and sacrificed her own career to making a success of mine. I was never ambitious in the material sense, but I did hunger for recognition and the bright lights. You did your time in rep but all young actors of any talent knew that was only the apprenticeship. In those days, the thing was to get noticed by H. M. Tennent's, the big West End producing company run by Binkie Beaumont.

At first, I did not tell Tarn about Nora Ann, or about my child. The whole unhappy episode was deleted from my consciousness. But I was determined to settle down with Tarn. After *Not a Clue*, we were separated by our work and we wrote to each other all the time. Our correspondence shows how stuck on each other we were. We used to write almost every day. It's difficult these days to imagine such a correspondence, but in the early 1950s we had no money for telephone calls and little more for train journeys. We made love to each other via the Post Office. And courtesy of a piece of paper, an envelope and a twopenny-halfpenny stamp.

Tarn was the youngest of three children, and her mother was Irish, which explains the sense of fun and the spirit she always exuded. Her father's family had emigrated to New Zealand, where her father was born. He was a wonderful old character, and never stopped kissing people of either sex, which was an unusual and very remarkable trait in an army officer.

Tarn's background was totally conventional. She had attended the Old Vic Drama School as a middle-class girl in need of 'finishing.' In fact, she got a darned sight more than she, or her family, bargained for: a life-long friendship with her fellow student Joan Plowright (Tarn is Joan's daughter Tamsin's godmother), lectures from Laurence Olivier and Edith Evans – who used to teach people how to use fans – make-up classes from Alec Guinness and concentrated tuition from George Devine, Glen Byam Shaw and Michel Saint Denis.

There you have her connections in a nutshell. Tarn was plugged into the new British theatre even before it happened. But we didn't even give it a second thought. We were completely in love and trying to make a go of being actors in rep. I was bound on a wheel of fire, which took me from Morecambe to Preston and into some very peculiar lodgings!

Tarn had graduated from the Old Vic School and joined the touring Young Vic Company. I have always written letters to my loved ones. But only Tarn's are preserved. In later years, I think Maggie Smith burnt everything I wrote to her, and Pat Quinn has lost all my missives. But my letters to Tarn are an extraordinary reminder of what life was like in the last days of regional weekly and three-weekly reps. My days in Preston and Manchester formed my career.

After *Not a Clue* I joined the rep at the Hippodrome in Preston, which was run by Reggie Salberg of the famous theatre producing dynasty. Reggie ran reps all over the country: Hull, Salisbury, Birmingham. I was in Preston for a few months, then they shut the place down. Nothing to do with my performances, I hope. It was doing all right, but they turned it into a shopping mall or something. I became great friends at that time with an actor called Peter Wyatt, and I wrote to Tarn about the passion harboured for him by the local theatre critic. The silly old fool kept leaving *billets doux* for Peter at the stage door, which amused us mightily and led to absolutely nothing.

On pieces of paper headed 'The Hippo' in my own scrawl, I asked Tarn such questions as, did she think *The Little Hut* was too risqué for Preston? And I recounted my adventures in finding digs: 'I'm sharing a room with two other blokes, one of whom sleeps in his shirt and socks! I don't see the point in someone getting up in the morning to put on a tie over a creased shirt they've just slept in. But I'm moving downstairs to a room presently occupied by one of the 'Soldiers in Skirts'! I've not seen him, but I can smell him; Chanel Number 5 has nothing on that one!'

My landlady in Preston kept me well fed, and I started to put on weight. And I developed a compensatory stoop on stage which became a bit of a trademark, right up to the Royal Court performance as George Dillon in *Epitaph for George Dillon* by John Osborne and Anthony Creighton in 1958. I have a big frame, but small, dainty hands, and small size eight shoes. I started to hunch myself together and I was also prone to fits of inaudibility. All of these things I worked on assiduously over the next few years. In addition, I had terrible acne all over my back, another consequence of poor food in digs, but nothing ever seemed to weigh me down too much. I had boundless energy and plenty of enthusiasm.

While I was appearing in Preston in Rattigan's *The Sleeping Prince* the man running the Library in Manchester, Peter Lambert, came over to see it and offered me Iago, Biff in *Death of a Salesman*, and Cassius in *Julius Caesar*. He was a good director, but he never fitted in to the West End way of things when he went there to do a play. He was a bit like Kenneth Williams, which may not have helped him all that much – highly strung, with an odd mixture of sudden extrovert campiness and brooding, withdrawn bouts of obsessive secrecy.

Lambert left after my first season and was succeeded by David Scase, who was an even better director, and a much nicer man. Scase had worked with Joan Littlewood's Theatre Workshop around Manchester after the war. During his time at the Library, where he stayed for many years, he became an important and influential figure in his own right. He was my first real mentor in the theatre, and someone whom I have always held in deep affection and high regard. Later I was always trying to persuade Tony Richardson to talk George Devine into taking on David Scase as an assistant at the Royal Court, but they never listened to me.

All the work I did at the Manchester Library was very good. We had a month to rehearse, rather than a week. You learned more. I played the advocate Voltore in *Volpone*. I loved it, having done nothing like that before. I played Biff in *Death of a Salesman*, a part I enjoyed very much, Iago in a not very good Edwardian production of *Othello*, and Horner in *The Country Wife*. I started to go swimming a lot and generally taking much more care of myself. I was blossoming physically, and I had learned to stand a lot straighter.

Tarn had gone off to work in London, and was living at the address which was soon to become our home, her parents' house at 38 Glebe Place, London SW3. In early 1955 I played Dunois in a fine production by David Scase of Bernard Shaw's *Saint Joan*, in which Jessie Evans was superb in the title role – she was the Welsh response to Siobhan McKenna's more fashionable, but no better, Irish version in London at the time – and my letters touched a peak of bubbling, romantic euphoria:

> 'Everything I do and shall do is for you. For us and for you, as Joan says, "I shall dare and dare and dare until I die', truly, baby, with all my heart, all of me ... Tarnie, I love you ... to stop loving you would be to stop living ... People keep asking me if I am writing a book as I'm always here [in the Green Room] writing, during the Trial Scene, or they say, "Is she worth it?" and I say "*Oh, yes!*" – I love you.'

The experience of *Saint Joan* – which convinced me that the best company of actors is the happiest company of actors, bound in a common purpose with democratic, shared objectives – made me so happy that I thought, on the last night, during the epilogue, that my heart was going to burst. Jessie Evans was never sentimental in the role. The other two great Joans I have seen – Siobhan McKenna and Joan Plowright – both became somewhat mawkish in the cathedral scene. But Jessie never did. One really felt one was in the presence of greatness, and yet she remained a peasant girl, too.

She always was an underrated actress, and because of her ordinary, unaffected appearance, was usually cast as maids in Restoration comedy. When she was given the chance to go further, she invariably soared. At Manchester, she also played Margery Pinchwife in *The Country Wife*, and was absolutely brilliant – better, I would say, than either Maggie Smith or Joan Plowright, both of whom laid very effective claim to that role later on. But for me, Saint Joan was Jessie's biggest triumph. She was very kind to everyone, and took me a little under her wing. She treated us all to champagne and we even thought at one point that the production might be transferring to London, as a 'compare and contrast' with Siobhan McKenna's. But it wasn't to be.

I had only been reviewed by the local papers up to this point, but in Manchester we attracted a lot of attention in the *Daily Telegraph*. My Dunois, according to the *Telegraph*, had a 'gentle charm'. And there was the unfortunate headline in the same newspaper referring to 'The Have-a-cigarette *Othello*'. On the first night, Cassio, played by Jeremy Brett, offered me (Iago) a cigarette, a piece of stage business that had slipped my mind altogether. I was looking the other way when I heard Jeremy utter the un-Shakespearean invitation to 'have a cigarette'. I'm not sure if I replied, 'Thanks very much, don't mind if I do', but it was a moment fraught with dangerous anachronism, even though we'd set the play in Edwardian dress anyway.

The Othello was a Welsh actor called Brendan Barry who was a little out of his depth in the role. He became so upset by the performance on the first night that he left the stage in floods of tears. When he fell into Othello's epileptic fit, Cassio forgot to make his entrance, so after my evil imprecations, I just left old Brendan lying there on the stage and went off to the dressing room to find Jeremy. No wonder he had a good cry later on and remained on edge throughout the run. At one particularly noisy schools' matinée he simply stopped the show and told all these chattering kids to shut the hell up. Which they did for about five seconds.

Jeremy Brett was the juvenile lead and he quickly became my best friend. We have looked out for each other ever since those days. Jeremy was gorgeous, simply irresistible. Being a country bumpkin, I had never before met anyone so elegant, so charming, so 'Etonian'. He had, of course, been to Eton. And, like Tarn, Jeremy's family background was both impeccable and military. I was entranced.

Jeremy, although I scarcely appreciated it at the time, was having trouble. He was far too young for his leading lady and was about to be sacked. He always says that he was moved and touched when I appeared, because I had this vulnerable, slightly stooped, appearance, and I was both benign and gentle, which is true. I was also overweight, because the landlady at Preston had fed us all very well.

Jeremy snuggled up to me, and to Tarn. We became inseparable best friends. He was terribly good-looking and always suffered for it. At school, he was known as 'the tart of Eton' because he sang like Elizabeth Schwarzkopf, but was giving out all the wrong signals to unsuitable men who kept trying to pick him up. And I was the gentleman's relish who sat between him and the rather heavy old queers in the company. I winkled him out and we bonded – as platonic friends, never sexual partners. We balanced up the classes between us.

I moved in with Jeremy Brett over the Astoria Ballroom. The lettering used to light up at night. A character actor called John Saunders, who was very sweet on Jeremy, had a room over the first 'A' which he shared with two cats, and Jeremy had two rooms over the last 'A'. We used to follow Johnny into the bathroom, which he always left smelling nice and meticulously tidied up after the cats had been in there.

The rooms used to change colour in the summer. They'd be dark blue with damp and general fug in the winter, and light blue in the summer when they dried out. Mrs Park was our cleaning lady, but she spent most of her time on her knees downstairs, trying to clean all the chewing gum off the ballroom floor. When she went round our flat, she sometimes overdid it. Once, she chucked out a pot of stock we were saving for soup, which infuriated us for a couple of weeks.

There were fights downstairs in the ballroom every weekend. Not between me and Jeremy, who was and remains my dearest friend. Neither of us would go down when these terrible fights were going on, in case we were trampled to death. It wasn't a very glamorous life, but we were always screaming with laughter. We went regularly to the pub of course, and every Friday night we'd treat ourselves to a strong, hot curry. Often we'd have a chicken or a prawn vindaloo and then the walk back to the ballroom would gradually turn into a race for the lavatory. Those vindaloos went straight through you like a dose of salts.

In June 1955, Jeremy went off to make the King Vidor film of *War and Peace* in Rome, with Audrey Hepburn and Henry Fonda. I found a letter of farewell from the book, and gave it to him to read on the plane. He told me how touched he was and very kindly said to Tarn and I that, if we could find our fares in the next three-week break, he would pay all our expenses. So we went to Rome, a city which I have adored unreservedly from that day to this, and we were billeted in a flat with Robert Graves's daughter, Diana. Jeremy, bless his heart, gave us pocket money from his own salary.

By now, Tarn and I were committed to marriage and I had set the wheels in motion for my divorce from Nora Ann. I had tried to do the right thing by Nora Ann and let her divorce me. But as she had left me right at the start, I was advised that she could not secure a divorce on that basis. So eventually it all had to be done on the grounds of her desertion.

A new phase in my life was opening up. Our time in Manchester was coming to an end: when Jeremy came back from Rome, he went to London to join the Old Vic, and around the same time I finally came to London to join the English Stage Company. George Devine and Tony Richardson had at last managed to find a theatre to launch their new writing plans: the English Stage Company was to open at the Royal Court in Sloane Square in the spring of 1956.

Tarn, who was working in television and acting with the Artillery Theatre in Woolwich, had remained friends with Devine since her days of studying with him at the Old Vic School, and she had told him about the exciting work we were doing in Manchester – she quite shamelessly recommended me, as well as Jeremy and a fine character actor called Bunny Warwick. She was always going on to him about us because she genuinely admired the work we had been doing. Coincidentally, I suddenly heard again from Tony Richardson.

Richardson rang up the theatre and asked me to go and audition for George Devine on the coming Sunday. I went down to the Royal Court and waited in the wings. There was a young man sitting on the top of a stool who took my script and offered to prompt me. I did a bit of Cassius and a bit of Biff. The man in the prompt corner was John Osborne, who was employed to read scripts and help out at the auditions. My audition obviously must have gone well, because I was soon invited to join the original English Stage Company.

Tarn and I were married, it felt like inevitably, in April 1956, at Saint Columba's Church in Pond Street, Chelsea. We had enjoyed the most wonderful affair for three or four years and now we were at last living together in London. Jeremy was my best man, and Tarn's parents, who lived in a manor house in Winchester, rented to us their small town house in Glebe Place, just off the King's Road, ten minutes' walk from Royal Court. I was almost twenty-five, I was happily married at last, I had served my professional apprenticeship. Things seemed to be on the move.

4

At the Court of John Osborne

Although I joined the English Stage Company, which was founded by George Devine and Tony Richardson, in what proved in retrospect to be a momentous season in the history of twentieth-century British theatre, the year of *Look Back in Anger*, it did not feel like an awfully big adventure at the time. That, for me, had been the period at the Library Theatre in Manchester. But it was work, and I felt that something might come along for me which would allow me to build on the experience I had accumulated.

Tarn and I were living happily enough in Glebe Place. I would trudge up and down the King's Road to the theatre in Sloane Square with a packet of sandwiches and my cigarettes while the course of British theatre was busy being changed. Our house was in the eye of the storm and became a meeting place for all the leading participants in the company. People would drop by after rehearsals and have a drink or a cup of coffee. Tarn was an excellent hostess and made everyone feel welcome.

The first production of the ESC, opening on 2nd April 1956, was Angus Wilson's *The Mulberry Bush*; George Devine's big idea was that great new plays were going to be provided by contemporary British novelists. He was entirely wrong, of course, and *The Mulberry Bush* was dreadful. That play's company was expanded for the second production, *The Crucible* by Arthur Miller, which ran in repertory with *The Mulberry Bush* for a month. It opened one week later, on 9th April, and I played Judge Haythorne. Others in the cast were Mary Ure, Joan Plowright, Rachel Kempson, Alan Bates, Kenneth Haigh and John Welsh, as well as George Devine, who also directed – very badly.

The third production, opening 8th May, was indeed *Look Back in*

Anger, in which I understudied the father played by John Welsh — I never went on — and one month later I was in Nigel Dennis's *Cards of Identity*, another dreadful play, in which John Osborne and I played two commentators and stole some wonderful notices. I was pretty miserable most of the time. I read *Look Back* before it was cast; I was mortified by it. It was shocking. I didn't think it was a bad play, but I thought it was monstrously offensive, and I think word got back to George Devine and the rest of them that this is what I thought.

I failed to recognise the humour of Jimmy Porter in *Look Back*, and Kenneth Haigh, who played it, certainly failed to recognise it, too. But there was no argument with the impression it made, once Kenneth Tynan's review and the impact of a television excerpt had filtered through. In 1989, when Kenneth Branagh wanted to produce and appear in the play, and televise it, he asked me how should he go about getting the rights. I said, 'Just write to John,' which he did, and so he got the rights.

I also advised him not to make the same mistake that Kenneth Haigh made, which was to just bellow the role. Jimmy Porter is an effective role if played wittily and lightly. Kenneth Haigh was really responsible for the angry young man soubriquet; he was so unpleasant and noisy and offensive, and I thought, 'I wouldn't sit in the same room with you for five minutes.'

I knew that Jimmy Porter was really John Osborne, although John would never be offensive in public; but in his writing, yes. I became really very close to him. He was the most marvellous company and we enjoyed many nights of shouting, laughing and drinking together over the next few years. He was really the sweetest, most sensitive man, generous to a fault. I never once saw him bawl out anyone in public. He could, of course, be quietly and devastatingly sarcastic.

But he was too cowardly to be Jimmy Porter, really. And he was heterosexually insatiable. The recent attempt to brand him a homosexual hypocrite really is a shocking misrepresentation to fit some journalistic agenda. At that time, John was married to Mary Ure, he had a mistress round the corner and another courtesan at the Savoy Hotel; I don't know how he managed it all. I wouldn't say I behaved perfectly, but he was astonishing.

When success hits you it changes your life completely, and I noticed this with John particularly. When I first knew him he used to wear red socks and sandals, whatever the weather. It was a freezing cold February and I remember asking him in Sloane Square why he was only wearing socks and sandals. He replied simply that he didn't have any shoes. When *Look Back in Anger* opened, he didn't change *personally*, but everything else did, slowly. He began to have his hair cut properly and more stylishly, and gradually his jackets, trousers and shoes all improved. Then he had all his teeth capped. He really did transform himself into a Regency-style dandy.

John had an opinion on everything in the world and wrote articles in any newspaper that asked him to. At the same time, however, he'd sue anybody who wrote disparagingly about him.

He once sued for defamation of character and got £20,000, which was a lot of money in those days.

His success, overnight, was extraordinary. I remember him saying to me, 'I've got to spend £60 a week on lunches or cigars; got to get rid of it, otherwise the taxman gets it.' So he was endlessly taking me out to lunch, or buying shirts and ties. He loved to laugh and have fun. As he says in *Epitaph for George Dillon*, the play which made my name in 1958, 'Laughter is the only thing that saves us from sainthood'.

One day he came rushing up to me and said, 'You must come and see my new motor car.' It was the latest thing. You pressed a button and the windows went up and down. There was every conceivable mod con in it, including a cocktail cabinet in the back. And he whizzed me off in it down to the river for a drive along the Embankment. It was like a bloody great hearse. It was enormous and incredibly ostentatious. He dropped me off home and about twenty minutes later he called on the phone and said, 'The most terrible thing has happened; just after I left you a great big lorry drove into me and the car's a write-off.' There was a great big irreparable dent in the side and he took it straight back to the garage and turned it in.

We look back now and say what a glorious new era of British theatre that was, and so on, but only the Osborne play was that. The rest of it was pretty dreadful and not exciting at all. I dare say I felt this mainly because I wasn't playing anything worth playing. But the whole attitude to everything was flaccid. And it was all personified in the crass and bogus opportunism of Tony Richardson, the director of the Osborne play and George Devine's right-hand man. He wasn't a good director, but he was a good operator and wheeler dealer.

He manipulated people to suit himself. Nor was George Devine a great director by any means, and he certainly wasn't a very good actor. So the whole first year was crummy, I thought. We only had two successes in the opening season: *Look Back in Anger* and *The Country Wife*, a classical Restoration play with a really beautiful performance by Joan Plowright as Margery Pinchwife. Joan was going to be their girl; she'd been in the Old Vic School with Devine.

There was a certain amount of ideological, uninformed, left-wing nonsense talked at the Court about Brecht, but it never cut very deep. *The Good Woman of Setzuan* in that first season was a particularly dreadful production by George Devine. You always got a great long lecture before rehearsals about alienation and Brecht, but once you started you never heard another word about it. You just went on and did it in the same way as you did everything else. We had all this ghastly Chinesey music.

Peggy Ashcroft as Shen-Te had a song to sing about the need for a great blanket to cover the people of the city. She was wearing a half mask and a moustache, and old Teo Otto, who had done the music for the Berliner Ensemble, bellowed from the back of the stalls: 'No, no, no, no; this is Ashcroft, not Shen-Te.' She was terribly upset because she didn't know – none of us did – how to do alienation acting. There is, of course, no such thing.

But Peggy made the mistake, which she couldn't really help, of identifying too closely with the character, so that her acting became sentimental. Nobody could or would help her find another way of doing it. I've never seen a Brecht producton that worked, not even one by William Gaskill, who is a great Brecht director; somehow, any cast will always contain some actors who are not 'tuned' to it. I've come to the conclusion that it must be a very German way of acting.

As an actor you certainly didn't feel you were part of the changing face of British theatre, though it certainly did change with *Look Back in Anger*. We were a mixed bag of actors, not a company really: Alan Bates, Nigel Davenport and Joan Plowright were the only prominent ones, and myself two and a half years later. There were people from workshops and friends of Tony's from Oxford. A lot of them came to nothing. Kenneth Haigh, the original Jimmy Porter, never really sustained any reputation on the stage, though of course he has done pretty well on television. Later on, Peter O'Toole and Albert Finney came and went; Peter arrived from rep in Bristol, Albert from Birmingham.

The next big success was *The Entertainer* (1957), not a very good play, with no real development or power in the last act, although it was a huge success for Laurence Olivier as Archie Rice, the seedy music-hall entertainer with a leering gap-toothed smile and an eerie, puppet-like deadness behind the eyes. That was the crucial factor, Olivier's alignment of his great reputation and sensational talent with the new writing of Osborne and, by association, the whole Royal Court. It gave everyone the most tremendous lift, but the chief beneficiary was Osborne himself. John talked to me a great deal about the play before he wrote it, as I spent a lot of time with him. He saw the closing of the music halls as a sign of the diminishing of England and he got terribly upset about it all. Then, bang, he got this idea of a comedian on the skids. He didn't really think about Laurence Olivier until he put pen to paper.

My association with the play was fitful, but finally fateful. I understudied Olivier as Archie Rice and although I never had the opportunity of playing the role, the great actor soon became 'Larry' to me and from that time onwards, and for ever more, he was the great example and mentor of my career. He enjoyed the great success of the play, but always assumed that the third act, which limped along and spluttered to an unsatisfactory conclusion, would get rewritten before we transferred to the West End.

I was on the stage when he told Tony Richardson, who directed it, that he wouldn't go on with the play unless something was done about it. The message was relayed to Osborne whose response duly arrived: 'We'll get another actor, then,' which was the height of arrogance because Larry, in the cleverest twist of his career, had made the entire success of that play. And of course they knew full well he wasn't going to let it go. So they did nothing at all. We transferred to the Palace Theatre in September 1957, with Joan Plowright replacing Dorothy Tutin as Archie's daughter, Jean, and myself taking over the small part of Graham, who comes on with a few lines in the imperfect third act!

Before the transfer to the Palace, with Joan, George Devine and John Osborne all in the cast, we put on Nigel Dennis's second play, *The Making of Moo*, which was subtitled 'A History of Religion in Three Acts' and which was reviewed in one of the evening papers under the headline 'BLASPHEMY'. It wasn't a very good play, more of a bitty revue, really, and it wasn't particularly shocking, but I remember it most for the presence in the cast – up to a point – of Esmé Percy, the wonderful old Shavian actor who had played opposite Mrs Patrick Campbell. He had joined the company for *The Good Woman of Setzuan*.

He was an outrageous old queen, but a most interesting raconteur. He had played all the great leads in Shaw, and had a glass eye, which used to drop out and rattle across the stage with everyone frantically trying to find it or at least not tread on it. He took a very flattering shine to me and, I would have to say, was madly in love with me. I adored all his rambling stories of the old days, and if you went for lunch or dinner to his house, you would find hand-written menus with your *placement*; he was wonderfully stylish, eccentric and lovable.

Also, which made him just a little less lovable to some people, he owned a smelly old spaniel called Skippo, from whom he was inseparable and who had to be included in every show he appeared in towards the end of his life. Skippo was fed on an unchanging diet of plovers' eggs, smoked salmon and caviar, so he used to fart all the time and slopped around the place in the nimbus of a most appalling stench. But if you wanted Esmé, and most people did, you just had to put up with Skippo.

Esmé was originally French and had been trained by Sarah Bernhardt in Paris. When he was sixteen he had gone to see her and said that he would throw himself in the Seine if she did not take him into her company. She took him in. In later life, and prior to this last period at the Court, Esmé had a one-man show, *The Legend of Bernhardt*, and used to perform these incredible imitations of her: how she came along the corridor, after her leg had been amputated in 1915, with a stick – bang, bang, bang – and how the critics would sigh, 'She comes, she comes.' Esmé told me that Bernhardt always took her money *before* the play, otherwise she wouldn't go on the stage. She would stuff the notes down the front of her dress and keep them there throughout the performance.

He also had lots of stories about all the old characters: Ernest Thesiger, who fell in love with a doorman at the Savoy Hotel and used to go and lay lilies at his feet; Henry Ainley, so handsome and attractive, who would be declaiming one of his great dramatic speeches in *Hassan* by James Elroy Flecker dressed in a long coat, his back to the audience, and suddenly open up the coat in a grand gesture to reveal to the rest of the onstage cast that he was entirely naked beneath it, and the whole crowd of them would corpse and giggle helplessly while he recited magnificently onwards; and the tyrannical Basil Dean, bullying a young dancer during rehearsals for *Hassan* (which Esmé said was magnificent) and bellowing at her, 'Oi, you, what are you doing that for?' to which the she replied, quick as a flash, 'Two pounds ten a week, Mr Dean.'

After the First World War, during the 1920s, Esmé ran three theatres in Cologne. He asked Mrs Patrick Campbell – Shaw's original Eliza Doolittle in 1914 – if she would play a guest performance in one of them as Eliza. Mrs Pat was far too old for the part by then, but she agreed, and Esmé rehearsed the production in which he also played Henry Higgins. He said she was absolutely vile. Suede shoes had just been invented, so he wore a pair of suede shoes in the last act. Throughout the performance, and especially during Higgins's long speeches, Mrs Pat was huffing and puffing and tutting not too inaudibly, impatiently exclaiming 'Oh, get on with it', hardly under her breath. When Esmé came to the end of a particularly long speech in the last act, she exclaimed even less inaudibly, and not at all Shavianly, 'And he would never have worn suede shoes!' Esmé was more than mortified. He said he was heartbroken.

Before we opened *The Making of Moo* in London, we played a week in Brighton. Tarn was very good to Esmé and one day took him out for some oysters and down to the beach. He always wore a straw boater, and he asked her to go and fill it with sea water so that he might bathe his face. We were all staying in the Royal Crescent Hotel, of which a fair amount more later on. The next morning, Tarn went along the corridor to knock on Esmé's door to go down for breakfast. Skippo was howling. Esmé had died of a heart attack in the night, and there he was, lying face up on his bed in his black silk pyjamas, a copy of *Paris Soir* on the bedside table and his glass eye glinting in the morning sunshine.

Tarn went down to tell Tony Richardson, who was already in the breakfast room idly toying with a boiled egg. When Tarn told him that Esmé had died, he plunged his spoon right through the egg and impatiently said, 'Oh, Tarn, don't *do* things like that to me; I'm absolutely fuwious with you!' He thought we were pulling his plonker, but we weren't and he soon had to get moving and think about re-casting poor old Esmé's role, which fortunately wasn't a very substantial one. John Gielgud took care of all the funeral arrangements, but Tarn and I had no option but to take on old Skippo, who lumbered around Chilcomb and never stopped blowing off all over the place.

Skippo was with us in Glebe Place when he died a year or so later. Tarn woke me at about four o'clock one morning. 'Robbie, he is going,' she said, as this awful coughing was going on outside the bathroom. Thus Skippo departed this world, and I deposited the corpse in the garden. In the morning, I stuffed him into a canvas holdall, with his four legs sticking up through the handles, and jumped into a taxi with him to the vet, who finally disposed of him. If we had been in Chilcomb, I would have dug a nice big hole, but there was no room for him in the London garden, and I didn't fancy a journey down to Winchester, with old Skippo ponging away with redoubled pungency in the boot.

Although one has to thank the Royal Court for what we did, what we did was in fact very minimal. The English Stage Company was a fairly working-class outfit, I suppose, though again, it was not as different from what was happening elsewhere in the regional and London theatre as it liked to suppose. Alan Bates, who was in all the opening productions, made a great impression with his natural, tousled charm and unaffected Derbyshire manner. Joan Plowright was obviously of the earth, earthy, a magnificent actress and a genuine new star. And of course there was Johnny Osborne. George Devine himself was a plummy, rather gentrified figure.

The director John Dexter, who was as common as muck, came along in the second season, taking responsibility for several 'Sunday night without décor' productions, and then the first revival of *Look Back*. While I was on tour with the Caryl Jenner Company we went to the Derby Playhouse to see a Somerset Maugham play and there was this dreadful actor playing the juvenile lead with a great big long scarf around his neck – it was John Dexter, doing his best to be an actor, before he joined *The Archers* on radio to play a policeman. I used to enjoy reminding him of this.

I knew Tony Creighton, who had lived on a barge with John Osborne for about nine years and had co-written *Epitaph for George Dillon*, very well. He had been a gunner during the war and developed a terrible sinus problem, so he became a vegetarian. And John became one too, but when he was successful he went back to eating meat.

I find it hard to believe, as Tony has recently been saying, that they had a prolonged homosexual affair. Tony was certainly enchanting and he succeeded in turning John into a vegetarian. But a gay one? John was always rather camp and dandyish and had a pronounced feminine side to his nature, but I never saw any real evidence of bisexuality. He never stopped chasing his women around as far as I could see.

One day when I went down to the gents in the Salisbury public house, a notorious gay pub in St Martin's Lane, I saw a graffito, 'I fucked John Osborne'. I told him and he was furious. John did say to me coming off the stage one night during *Cards of Identity* that he much preferred the company of men to that of women and that you only found loyalty and trust with other men. Mutual understanding is much more difficult to achieve, he said, with women. I knew what he was talking about but I never took it to mean anything to do with homosexuality. It is certainly true that Anthony Creighton was dropped from his life very quickly after *George Dillon*, which may have meant that he wanted to delete or deny an aspect of his private life from that point on; or it may not.

This obsession with the private lives of public figures is really ridiculous because we all have elements of ambiguity and confusion in our sexual make-up, or at least most of us do. I hate all this speculation and digging up dirt, especially when the people concerned are no longer around to defend themselves; and it's just as bad when they are, because it makes life such a misery for them and all their friends and relations.

It's the same with the allegations that have been made about Danny Kaye and Laurence Olivier. In all the years that I knew Larry, and I knew him very well indeed, there was never the slightest hint that he might be actively homosexual. But, on the other hand, no one knew about his affair with Sarah Miles, which we now learn from her autobiography went on for all those years at the Old Vic in the 1960s. At the time, however, it was a very closely guarded secret.

5

Flying High in London and New York

Osborne had written *Epitaph for George Dillon* with Tony Creighton before *Look Back in Anger* and nobody took much interest in it until George Devine needed to drum up some more interest at the box office and thought that we might get away with it on John's newfound name and fame. Tony always wanted me to play George Dillon; John wasn't around, he was in New York or somewhere.

Tony Richardson, the director, was not all that interested in me playing a leading role and wanted to cast either Dirk Bogarde, or an actor called Gary Raymond. At this time I was still understudying Larry in *The Entertainer*, which was one of three 'new writing' successes on in the West End; that one, an Australian play called *Summer of the Seventeenth Doll* by Ray Lawler, and also a light comedy, *Janus*, with Googie Withers.

All three companies, therefore, were invited to a big party in the foyer of the Albery Theatre. Vivien Leigh, who was still married to Olivier, was there, and this was the first time I met her. Tony Richardson said, 'Oh, I dahn't think you knaow Robert Stephens, who's understudying Larry,' He had the most extraordinary floppy and arrogant way of talking, as though he were expressing limp wrists, very camp, very bitchy. 'Oh,' she said, 'it's you! Alfred Lunt and Lynn Fontanne came to see *The Entertainer* on Monday night and you were the only person they could talk about afterwards. Larry was so angry with you.'

I was flabbergasted. As Graham, I only spoke five lines right at the end! Tony Richardson, bluffing like mad and not wanting to appear out-flanked, said, 'Oh yes, and we've got a wonderful part for Robert' – and it was George Dillon. I'm sure that if it hadn't been for Vivien, he would never have committed himself like that on the spot. I met the

Lunts years later, in 1970, when Maggie Smith and I went to give them a special award at the Tony Awards in New York after we'd made the film of *The Prime of Miss Jean Brodie*; I told them that they were responsible for me being there tonight!

I opened in the title role of *Epitaph for George Dillon* in February 1958 and the play transferred, simply re-titled as *George Dillon*, to the Comedy Theatre in May. Tony had written the domestic scenes and John the big duologue scenes in the second act for the girl and George, which were the heart of the play and easily the best passages in it. George, an actor and writer 'waiting for success', gets the girl pregnant and has to marry her – rather as I myself had done with Nora Ann – so he's trapped. He's also suffering from tuberculosis. In the last act they give him a new typewriter for his birthday but he's finished, he's all washed up, he'll never write anything worthwhile.

This moment was a great acting opportunity, where you had to try to convey a sense of tragic waste, the idea that this fellow was a failure even before he got started. Years later, in his autobiography, John Osborne described my smirk, as I unwrapped the typewriter, as that of an arch-conjuror destined to tap out a lifetime of 'Telephone Tart' plays, trapping the audience 'in a trembling moment of heart's agony'. And Ken Tynan, correctly observing that the cawing note in my voice might have been modelled on Osborne himself, said that my George was both wolfish and wan and 'the cleverest portrait I have seen of a certain kind of neurotic artist'.

Another critic who became a great friend, Alan Brien, said that I evinced all the charm of a beaten-out teddy bear, which was intended as a compliment. Michael Redgrave wrote furiously to Alan saying that he had overstepped the boundary of personal insult, but he rather misread the piece. It was nothing comparable to Ken Tynan commenting, as he did on one unfortunate occasion, that Jill Bennett looked like Donald Duck.

Out of this portrayal of failure came my first real success. It was a fantastic breakthrough for me, just what I had been waiting for. The director was Bill Gaskill, who was a great friend and protégé of Tony Richardson and indeed came from the same Yorkshire village and followed him into the same Oxford college. I never had a flop with Bill. He knew his stuff and he always worked very hard on behalf of the actors. He had worked in television and had gone into the art of acting by directing students, studying movement and voice, and he took it all very seriously indeed. He was a wonderful friend and director to me, and I would say

I am fondest of him of all the people I worked with at the Court. I'm glad to say he is still very much alive and well and working. It's a little sad to think of everyone else from that era – Tony Richardson, Lindsay Anderson, John Dexter, and John Osborne – all popping off within a few years of each other.

John was away in America when the play opened. And when it transferred to the Comedy, the newspapers were on strike, so it didn't do too well. I got £35 a week at the Court, and at the Comedy we only ran for six weeks. We were followed in there by Peter Shaffer's *Five Finger Exercise*, for which Osborne could never quite forgive him.

But I felt that I had arrived at last. I found myself invited to parties, some of them a good deal swankier than our usual theatrical booze-ups in Glebe Place, though those could be pretty swanky too. In that year of *George Dillon* in London I shall never forget meeting Raymond Chandler at a cocktail party. Chandler, whose writing I love and revere, was near the end of his life, and in fact died the following year. He could not have been more charming and delightful.

I asked him which of the screen interpretations of Philip Marlowe, his most famous sleuth, did he like the best. He instantly replied, 'Dick Powell in *Murder My Sweet*, because he was a song and dance man and played the toughness of the detective with such devilish lightness and wit.' Bogart was great as Bogart, he reckoned, but not as the character he had actually written.

There was a very pretty, but not very bright, debutante at this party with whom Chandler then fell into conversation. He was totally unfazed by the fact that she had not read his books and indeed had not even heard of him before. They chatted away, he laughed and flirted, and he suddenly moved away and asked the hostess the whereabouts of the nearest bookstore. He returned with an armful of paperbacks by Raymond Chandler, all of which he signed and handed over to the debutante. It was all done with such grace and good humour.

A little to my surprise, *George Dillon* was bought for New York, and John Osborne's interest suddenly came alive. He appeared at the rehearsals and had a lot to do with cutting it and rejigging it. Over there, I was on $600 a week, which was a fortune. We opened first in a huge 1800-seater theatre in Baltimore in October 1958, with a fabulous actress called Eileen Herlie taking over the part played in London by Yvonne Mitchell. Bill Gaskill was our indispensable director, and the producers were Joshua Logan and David Merrick. I acquired a New York agent,

Peter Witt, whom I liked very much, and everything looked set fair for fame and fortune.

Tarn was working at the Northampton Rep. Although she took over from Mary Ure as Alison in *Look Back In Anger* and was frightfully good, she was not given much work by George Devine; he preferred to keep her as a friend and confidante, I think. We started writing to each other again during this period of enforced separation. There was a short try-out tour before New York. In Baltimore, I tasted my first oysters. This was it! My big breakthrough in a John Osborne play on Broadway. And, just for starters, a few oysters! The theatre in Baltimore was a monster, and in my letters to Tarn I poured out my worries over the play being heard in such a vast, unsuitable auditorium.

Nonetheless, we were all charged up with enthusiasm and excitement. We moved on to Atlantic City for a week, and played in another frightful theatre where we had to be miked; the audience was completely old and partially dead; they had had only four plays visiting there in the previous twenty-five years. Still, the swimming was great, both in the marvellous surf of the sea and in our hotel pool.

At last we arrived in New York, where I was booked into the Hotel Plymouth on West 49th Street, just a few blocks from our theatre, the John Golden, where *Look Back In Anger* had been such a hit in the previous season. The build-up to the opening was fantastic and we were fêted all the way. There were suppers in Sardi's, and parties given by Lee Strasberg, who ran the Actors Studio, and his daughter, Susan, and I nearly fainted clean away when I saw Greta Garbo and was introduced to Kim Novak on the same evening.

I noted all these names in my letters to Tarn, who was busy having Glebe Place redecorated with some of the money I was managing to wire home. I saw Robert Preston and Barbara Cook in *The Music Man*, which I absolutely adored, and Bill Gaskill and I were always bumping into the actor Christopher Plummer and the director José Quintero. Above all, I loved the food and the comparative cheapness and cleanliness of all the restaurants and breakfast bars.

Everything was going like a dream until the reviews. Unfortunately the critics just went on the attack, partly, I think, because John Osborne had had a go at them for not reviewing *The Entertainer* very favourably. Well, you can't attack the critics, you just can't. It's a stupid thing to do. Many of the reviews were wonderful, but not the one or two that really mattered, in the main New York papers. So I never made that much money, and anything I made I spent pretty quickly anyway. New York is a good place to have a bit of money to spare. Although the word of mouth was fantastic, the reviews were death. We were buoyed up on an uproar of indignation and shock among our professional colleagues at the short shrift dealt us by the critics.

Noël Coward saw *George Dillon* in New York and came backstage afterwards with Marlene Dietrich. This was the first time I met a man who, in my estimation, and affection, was second only to Laurence Olivier. And a very close second. I adored Marlene, of course, but I really loved Noël. Meeting them both was completely mind-blowing. Noël was kind, funny, heart-warming and terribly wicked. I don't remember anything in particular that he said on our first meeting, but he was extremely generous. He was like a strange louche Chinese Emperor, flicking out comments and remarks with a terrifying, automatic skill. But you kept receiving these wonderful signals of warmth and understanding in his eyes, and in the way he listened to you. I've never known anyone quite like him.

Years later, when we read his diaries, we learned that Noël put his finger on the problem of *George Dillon* straight away. He wrote: 'Mostly very good, but weak last act.' He was also very kind about me – 'a new young man called Robert Stephens, who is quite wonderful.' Some great figures – the playwrights Arthur Miller and Tennessee Williams, the director Elia Kazan and the brilliant revue artist Mike Nichols (later famous as a director), as well as Noël and Marlene – took an advertisement in the *New York Times*. They said it was a disgrace that this fine play was coming off. We opened on a Tuesday, the notice of closure went up the next morning, giving us just two weeks on the Broadway stage.

Marlene Dietrich became particularly active and won us a brief stay of execution. As Coward also reports, Marlene flew at the producers and campaigned for them to give us a couple of extra weeks beyond the closing date. In the same week as we opened, *Flower Drum Song* was opening under some of the same management team. We were invited to their party, so we all went along there, accompanied by Marlene, who had taken us all, and me in particular, under her wing. I told her that *George Dillon* was coming off, and she called over David Merrick, the producer.

Merrick was wooing her for the role of Frenchy in a new musical, *Destry Rides Again*, with music and lyrics by Harold Rome. She said to Merrick, 'David, I wouldn't even consider working for somebody who took off such a play as *George Dillon*; however, if you give it two extra weeks, I will consider playing Frenchy in your new musical.' They shook hands, and she got us two extra weeks. When he went, she told me she had no intention of playing in the musical: 'I can't sing like Ethel Merman, I'm a cabaret singer.' So in the end it was Dolores Gray who played Frenchy.

The play came off but another young and very enthusiastic producer whose name I have completely forgotten was determined to put it on again if a theatre fell vacant. He gave us $150 a week expenses and, after a break of two months, re-mounted the play at the Henry Miller for just six weeks. It was a strange time, hanging on for the play to be rehoused, hoping for a change in our fortunes and frankly touting around for other work as well.

When we finally re-opened at the Henry Miller, Gloria Swanson and her *beau* came backstage and took me out for a drink. Some wit in the company said that I would be found next morning floating face downwards in her swimming-pool! She asked me if I could sing, because they were thinking even then of making a musical of *Sunset Boulevard*, and I said that although I could not, for her I could learn. I also saw quite a bit of Tennessee Williams, who never stopped laughing, which suited me fine.

News began to filter back from London about Peter O'Toole's arrival at the Court in *The Long and the Short and the Tall*, Willis Hall's play directed by Lindsay Anderson. Bill Gaskill told me what a fabulous actor O'Toole was, and how he was the exact opposite of me as he played completely on technique. There was a possibility – in that limbo period when *George Dillon* was suspended between New York theatres – that I might play O'Toole's role on Broadway, but I felt committed to *George Dillon* and waited for our luck to change. Which it never really did.

I was also eagerly lapping up any news Tarn sent me about John Dexter, who had been prosecuted for an offence of homosexually interfering with a minor and sent to prison for six months. He had been auditioning teenage boys for a Sunday night 'without décor' production at the Court. He had cast one boy and taken him to a dressing room and interfered with him. Then he saw another boy, and fired the first one, who promptly told his parents what had happened and they had gone to the police. It was all such a ghastly and unhappy business.

John had become a really dear friend and was always round at Glebe Place. The night before he went to court, he stayed over with us and asked Tarn if he might sleep with me. I simply held him in my arms while he wept and shuddered through the night. I insisted he borrowed a pair of my shoes as his own were dilapidated suede things with holes in them. Tarn cooked him breakfast in the morning, and we all joked about the condemned man eating a hearty meal.

We never thought for one minute he was going to be convicted. But the minute he walked into the courtroom, Oscar Beuselinck, George Devine's lawyer, told him that the judge hated homosexuals. Devine made a special plea, but it was no use. In the end, John had a reasonably enjoyable time 'inside', he even produced the Christmas panto.

While I was in New York, Tarn used to visit him in prison and he used to beg her to turn up wearing loads of scent because the smell was so horrible in there. He was released after serving four of the six months, and he hosted a party for all his friends in Glebe Place – paid for, I think, by John Osborne – to thank them for standing by him. He stayed on with Tarn for about six weeks (I was still away with *George Dillon*) and was the perfect house guest. He was a very courageous and true-hearted man, for all his tantrums and occasional fits of black temper. And a brilliant director.

In prison, Dexter read Arnold Wesker's first play *Chicken Soup with Barley* which he was very fired up about, and he used to tell Tarn about all the real cooking he was going to have on the stage, assaulting the audience with a pungent smell of fried onions. Such a thing had never been done before, but when that play and the other two in the trilogy were done at the Belgrade in Coventry, Tarn drove up to see them with George Devine and the designer Jocelyn Herbert, and they knew something quite big was happening all over again.

George Dillon was succeeded at the Golden in New York by Noël Coward's *Look After Lulu* starring Vivien Leigh, a commercial presentation that was totally disastrous but absorbed, in a different production, into the English Stage Company programme in the following season in London, with an entirely new cast surrounding Vivien. Anyone who was anyone had been to see us in *Dillon*, either at the Golden or the Henry Miller, so I got a lot out of it in one way and another.

In New York, I was cast by the director John Frankenheimer as the young schoolmaster in a television production of Terence Rattigan's one-act play *The Browning Version*. Rattigan had written the play in 1948 and offered the role of the unpopular disciplinarian schoolmaster master, Crocker-Harris ('the Himmler of the Lower Fifth'), to John Gielgud, who turned it down with the nervous reply, 'They've seen me in so much first-rate stuff, do you think they will like me in second-class stuff?' Gielgud's real worry was not so much Crocker-Harris, as the role of a clapped-out old actor-manager in *Harlequinade*, the second short play on the double-bill.

The actor and his wife were alleged to be based on either the Lunts, or on Donald Wolfit and his wife, Rosalind Iden. Gielgud, typically, did not want to upset anyone, or indeed make himself look foolish, so he turned down the plays which were passed on to Eric Portman. But in New York in 1959, he played Crocker-Harris in that television version, and did so beautifully and very movingly. Margaret Leighton, eleven years my senior, was also in the cast, and we fell in love. At first I thought that she and John were expecting me to be terribly obstreperous and avant-garde as I came from the Royal Court. But as soon as they saw that I wasn't going to start taking cheap shots at the West End, Binkie Beaumont and Noël Coward, we all got along famously. I was bedazzled by them.

Maggie Leighton, who was both terribly funny and terribly common, was born in Worcestershire and reared in Birmingham, had been married firstly to the great German director Max Reinhardt. By the time I met her she was married to Laurence Harvey, who was also much younger than her. We had an affair in New York which continued fitfully over the next couple of years. We did a play together in London, John Mortimer's *The Wrong Side of the Park*, in 1961. She was always dressed from top to toe in Yves Saint Laurent, but she sent herself up rotten. She was adorable, an extremely beautiful, elegant woman.

I went to dinner at Mike Nichols's apartment. Mike is known nowadays as a first-class film and theatre director, but he was renowned in those days for his performances in revue with Elaine May, a sort of American combination of Fenella Fielding and Eleanor Bron. They were brilliant, almost the funniest thing I'd ever heard. I didn't really know who Mike Nichols was then, and although he asked me to call him, I never did. It became a joke between us that whenever I saw him in later years he would say, 'Don't forget to call.'

While I was in New York, I saw Nichols and May, as they were known, in a revue – just the two of them performing material they had written. They ended the show by promising to do a sketch in the manner of any playwright named by anyone in the audience. The night I went, some smart-arse tried to put a spanner in the works by shouting out, 'Pirandello.' I slumped in my seat, wondering how the hell they would get out of *that*!

Nichols merely said, 'Thank you,' and the two of them began a perfectly ordinary conversation about how they had played another sketch. A gentle bickering simmered away until it built into an intensely personal row, with various bitter, horrible truths emerging. The audience froze, obviously thinking they were in the wrong place while this ghastly private argument was going to be pursued apparently to the death. Just when you thought they were going for each others' throats, Nichols snapped round at the audience: 'And *that's* Pirandello!' I've never seen anything like it in my life.

I identify this whole rumbustious period of 1958/59 in London and New York, really, with my success in *George Dillon*, and it was just my luck that it didn't really lead on to greater things straight away, although it undoubtedly established me as a leading actor, for which I am eternally grateful to John. In fact, I identified George Dillon so much with John Osborne that Ken Tynan said I sounded like him with a nasal twang, though I hadn't consciously modelled myself on him.

I knew John so well, and poor old George sounded just like him, and of course he really is a lot more like Osborne than Jimmy Porter, with his ideals and sense of struggle. When I was playing it in London, the Moscow Arts Theatre came over and the director wrote a long article in *The Observer* in which he said that the one actor in London who came close to how the Russians performed – meaning with heart and emotional truth, without sacrificing the grand gestural sweep, I guess – was Robert Stephens as George Dillon.

And what followed success, of course, was the liberation and wild enjoyment of it all. I was, you could certainly say, off the leash when we took the play to New York. And that is when my second marriage started going off the rails just a little bit, although Tarn never once gave me any ultimatums on the subject of my various flirtations. The base of our marriage was quite solid.

But I was beginning to fly around a bit, and not just with Maggie Leighton, I am bound to admit. Albert Finney once told me that he was in a play in New York and received a call from a well-known actress in California. He had never met her in his life, but she called up and said, 'I'm coming to see you in the play, then I'm coming to see you.' She flew in to New York, saw the play, saw Albert, took him to bed, then flew back again.

Nobody ever flew that far for a night in the sack with me, but there were, inevitably, opportunities that came my way which were very hard to resist. If you are successful in New York, the world is your oyster and everyone is after you.

The girl in hottest pursuit of me was Miss Tammy Grimes, unhappily married to Christopher Plummer, who had just gone off on tour. Before he went, I must confess that I spent some marvellous evenings in his company – he's a superb pianist – and with Jason Robards. But I was romancing his wife at the same time.

I realised in the end that 'Grimey Times' only had this romance with me in the hope that her husband would catch her at some point, and that this was her revenge on him for his own infidelity. Amazingly, the scenario is not dissimilar to Molnar's *The Guardsman*, in which Maggie Smith played with Christopher Plummer on television years after our divorce. In fact, he didn't find out about Tammy and me until it was all over, when Tammy herself told him!

I was running fast and loose. Tammy Grimes was very keen on getting married. Her little foray of revenge had deepened into something more serious. But I had no intention of moving to New York, and no intention of getting any more deeply involved with her. I saw Marlene Dietrich again at a party. I hadn't seen her since the night she blackmailed David Merrick into keeping our play on for a couple more weeks. As I walked in through the front door, there was this staircase going up, and she was sitting on the stairs with her legs wide apart, visible in her tight woollen tights right up to her crotch. Later, we both went back to Ken Tynan's flat, where he was living with Elaine Dundy, his first wife, who got frightfully pissed and a bit abusive.

Marlene asked me to get her out of the Tynan apartment so we went back to the party. It was fairly obvious that that wasn't going to be the end of it, and that we were going to get down to cases. But the prospect terrified the life out of me. Marlene was still extremely beautiful, but I was too frightened. She was like a crocodile. She had this incredible quality, one she shared with Vivien Leigh, of making you feel that you were the most important and attractive person in the world for as long as she talked to you. But you also felt that if you succumbed, you would never escape. It was jail for life. So I blew it. I was too in awe of her, and didn't know where to begin . . . maybe I was wrong.

André Previn once told me that when he first went to Hollywood at the age of sixteen as a boy genius, he was playing jazz piano at a party, when suddenly Ava Gardner was looking down at him. She asked him to take her home and he said, terrified, 'No I can't, I've got friends here.' A year later again he was playing jazz piano and she came in and he said, feeling braver and hopelessly attracted, 'Would you like me to drive you home tonight?' She turned him down flat.

The moment had gone. As had mine with Marlene. I've seen her lots of times since, but never in a situation like that.

New York was marvellous fun then; not so much now. I remember outrageous characters like Robert Webber, a big butch American marine, an actor friend of Tennessee Williams, with a big rasping voice. He had an affair with Mary Ure. I finally heard that he had come to know himself and come out of the closet; he was a terrible old queen, really. You never could tell so easily in those days. Life was still full of surprises.

6

Adventures in the Screen Trade

When I came back from New York, I left Tammy Grimes behind. There was no question of leaving Tarn at that point. Tammy was merely a romance, that was all. Having sorted myself out personally for the time being, I then made one of the biggest professional mistakes of my life by appearing in *Look After Lulu*, very badly adapted by Noël Coward from Feydeau's *Occupe-toi d'Amélie*.

It was co-presented by the Court with the impresario Binkie Beaumont. So much for the hotbed of new British writing. This was the same version as Vivien Leigh had appeared in in New York, and she joined the company to repeat her performance as the eponymous cocotte. We opened at the Court in July 1959 and transferred to the New (now the Albery) two months later.

Lulu was the most awful garbage, but you couldn't get a ticket because everyone wanted to see Vivien Leigh. The only consolation, and a very big consolation, was my platonic friendship with the utterly adorable Vivien. I felt she had got me the part of George Dillon when she said in front of Tony Richardson how much the Lunts had liked my performance in *The Entertainer*.

We became very close friends. I used to escort her to theatres to see matinées when we were not rehearsing, and indeed after we opened. I think Larry trusted me to shield her from his affair with Joan Plowright, which he and Joan pursued with my connivance in the house in Glebe Place, while conducting their more physical assignations a little further along the King's Road in the house of Roger Furse, the stage designer.

Vivien must have known that something was amiss but she never once revealed the source of her desperate unhappiness. She was beautiful beyond belief, but she was strangely cold on stage. As Lulu, she had a love scene on a sofa with me, but she played it as though she were interviewing me for a job. She was too fragile, too delicate, and she knew she was no good in it.

But offstage, she had the most extraordinary, powerful personality I have ever encountered. Her fragility was so moving. It was like being with a moth, or a butterfly. You felt she could be blown away at any moment. And she had the most exquisite taste and the most impeccable manner, as well as a dazzling beauty and flirtatious wit. She was also keenly intelligent, much more intelligent than Larry. I have never known anyone more perfect.

We used to have lunch before we went off to see our matinées. I'd go over to the flat in Belgravia, and she would say, 'Shall we have a nip?' Her preferred poison was a pink gin (gin and angastura bitters), straight up, no ice. Then we might walk along to the Royal Court Hotel, if we were going to the Court, or across the park to the West End. To walk along the street with Vivien Leigh on your arm was like walking on air. And to sit opposite her at lunch was totally riveting. You had no defence; you were her prisoner. She encompassed you totally, and made you feel that you were the most important and interesting and attractive man she had ever met in her life. This was not a trick; she did it for everyone.

Of course it was impossible not to feel attracted to her, but the chance of any carnal intimacy was about as likely a prospect as being struck by lightning. In that respect, she was like royalty. One simply dared not make a move. I often wonder what might have happened if I had. She was too beautiful to touch, in a way. And yet she was deeply unhappy at this stage, knowing that Larry and she were drifting apart, although she did not yet know that he was indeed having an affair with Joan Plowright. And if she knew, she never gave any impression that she did, such was her control and superb sense of style in public. Looking back on it now, it is clear that she must have been walking on eggshells. And although I regret, professionally, being in *Look After Lulu*, I do not regret for one minute being exposed to the full blast of Vivien's charms.

At this time Joan and Larry used to come and have dinner with us in Glebe Place every Sunday night.

Glebe Place was on a corner with Upper Cheyne Row, so there were two entrances. When the press got wind of Larry's affair, he would turn up at one door, Tarn would hand him a thermos flask and a few sandwiches, and he would sneak out of the other one. He had a lovely little Morris Minor Coupé which they used as a getaway. The divorce with Vivien was finalised in 1961 and then he was free to marry Joan and start their family together.

Meanwhile, the Royal Court, whose 'right-on', 'idealistic' actors and directors had been so dismissive of Binkie Beaumont and the 'sold-out', 'bourgeois' Shaftesbury Avenue crowd for years, was suddenly putting on a play at Binkie's behest; but only for Vivien. Then I went commercial, too, in *The Wrong Side of the Park* by John Mortimer at the Cambridge Theatre with Maggie Leighton, directed by Peter Hall just before he founded the Royal Shakespeare Company in 1960.

This was an odd experience because Mortimer had written the play — which was very good — as a response to my performance in *George Dillon*. Maggie Leighton had told me in New York that John had written the play for her and for me. She played a suburban housewife, married to a dull income tax official, living with him, and her parents, in a large house in which I was the lodger, just as I had been in the Osborne play.

Whereas George Dillon was an actor, this bloke was an advertising consultant. I entered this house which I wanted to take over, and there was a very funny seance scene with the old father, brilliantly played by a superb character actor called Charles Heslop. It was supposed to be my scene, but Heslop won every single laugh, and there was nothing I could do to prevent him. Joyce Carey, Noël Coward's great chum, was in the cast, and so was Wendy Craig who had also been in *George Dillon*.

The play was fantastically well reviewed, Maggie was wonderful in it, but it only ran for about seven months, moving in that time from the Cambridge, around the corner to the St Martin's. Laurence Harvey left Maggie during the run, not because of me — he had no idea that we were having an affair — but because he wanted to marry the widow of a film mogul and thereby secure some serious money and improve his career prospects with the mogul's studio, which was Columbia Pictures.

Maggie was devastated, but she was well rid of Harvey. They were so peculiar together. They drank an awful lot, but they never ate anything. At home, or even if they went out to the old Caprice, they would have the finest food and spit it out. Steaks would be chewed and juices swallowed, and then the meat spat out into a napkin. God knows what restaurant staff made of all this carry-on. I'm convinced that it accounts for his cancer, from which he finally died in 1973, and her debilitating illnesses.

Harvey was an appalling man and, even more unforgivably, an appalling actor. He had been in *The Country Wife* at the Royal Court, which transferred to the Adelphi, and I noticed something quite unusual in him as an actor. He had not a single nerve in his body. Most actors make an adjustment in their nervous energy just before they 'go on'; everything jumps a gear, and you become nervous, excited, concentrated, and you attack the stage and your role upon it, in this state. You undergo a profound physical and, I daresay, physiological, transformation, which is all to do with 'becoming' another character, but also with the business merely of 'performing'.

None of this happened with Harvey. In the dressing room, and in the wings, he would be smoking his Pall Mall cigarette in a long cigarette holder and probably sipping a glass of Macon. He would amble around, stub out his fag, cough up some phlegm, which he would spit on the floor regardless of who was around, and then he would wander on to the stage and start acting. Except, of course, it wasn't acting. It was just an extension of his usual demeanour, but as he wasn't in the same class of personality as Gerald du Maurier or Ralph Richardson – great light actors whose technique *fooled* you into thinking that what they were doing was merely 'natural' – nothing happened as far as the audience was concerned.

During the run of *The Wrong Side of the Park*, while I was trying to cope with a distraught Maggie and keep my own home life going, I was driven to Stratford-upon-Avon to audition for Franco Zeffirelli, who was directing John Gielgud in *Othello*. They were having trouble casting Iago. My audition was unsuccessful, which irritated me greatly at the time. Franco explained that while he loved what he knew I could do with the role, he was looking for a different sort of quality, and the person he said would be most ideal to his purposes was unavailable because he was too busy: Peter Hall!

Peter was just taking over at Stratford and was already renowned for his Machiavellian ways. They would have been much better off with him, too, as Ian Bannen, who was already playing Hamlet and Orlando that season, took on Iago and never really got on top of the lines. It was a doomed production. On the first night, Sir John's beard fell off. And when the curtain came down, Peggy Ashcroft burst into tears and ran off the stage, she was so unhappy about it all.

Maggie Leighton was in a dreadful state once our play closed. She fell apart. I've never seen anyone so bereft or ravaged with anguish. She was drinking vodka all night and Fernet Branca all day and was obviously heading for disaster. I consoled her as best I could. It was desperately important that she continued working and, in order to keep her going, Binkie came to her rescue and presented, for no other reason than it contained a good role for Maggie, *The Lady From the Sea* by Ibsen.

The play is as dull as ditchwater. I was asked by Binkie to play the Stranger right at the end but I said, 'No, it isn't me. You need someone amazing, who makes an instant impact and exudes the power, without saying anything, of Marlon Brando.' Well, they got John Neville instead. The production only ran for six weeks. Nobody really wants to go and see a play like that. It's the most awful claptrap.

My relationship with the Court was still fluid; you were never placed on a contract there, but were hired by the production, so you were free to come and go, even though you were obviously considered a Royal Court actor. I am not reverential about those years at the Royal Court, nor particularly nostalgic. There was a lot of rubbish talked about not touching a word of the text, performing the plays as written, which led to all sorts of problems.

Of course, the authors took the director at their word and this meant that the actors could never change a syllable of anything or ask for any rewrites whatsoever. Actors are the suckers who have to deliver these plays every night, and they tend to know better than fledgling or even experienced playwrights what they can get away with.

When Coward wrote his plays, the first person he always showed them to was Binkie, who invariably told him the truth about them, structurally and so on. This kind of rigorous inspection never happened at the Court. The plays were simply stood up on the stage and most of them fell straight down again. The person who suffered most from this in my view was John Arden, an essentially magnificent writer.

There was no real continuity. Admittedly, Osborne was followed by Arnold Wesker, John Arden and N.F. Simpson. But good new plays don't come up very often. Michael Hastings wrote one good play, *Yes and After*, and then virtually disappeared until many years later, when he wrote *Tom and Viv*, about T.S. Eliot driving his first wife insane. Doris Lessing wrote one, *Each His Own Wilderness*. The Sunday nights 'without décor' were often the best things at the Court, and where one felt something different really was happening: new plays by untried dramatists were slung on with no scenery, no money, lots of energy and enthusiasm, and just two weeks of rehearsal. That's how Mr Dexter came on the scene, and Lindsay Anderson, too. And Wesker's biggest success after his trilogy was *The Kitchen*, in which I played Peter, the German cook.

The Sunday night presentation of *The Kitchen* was during the run of *Look After Lulu*. This was the best version of *The Kitchen*; it was a one-act play of about an hour and twenty minutes, if that, maybe an hour; just three scenes in this kitchen, with the lights fading in between, and it was a quick series of brilliant thumbnail sketches. It was so fast, and then it was all over, performed with just chopping boards and knives, plates, no food. The later elongation did it no favours.

Dexter directed it in two weeks. He took four days off in the middle because his father had died in the Isle of Wight, and he told me to take over; he had already arranged the brilliant choreography of the waitresses coming and going. Having worked in a kitchen when I was a student at drama school, I already knew what it was like. The beauty of the short version was that you couldn't delve too deeply into Peter's love affair with the married waitress; it was on the move, flying. When this was elaborated in the full version, everything was slowed down.

Dexter was always adorable. He only picked on people, or became malicious, if they were lazy and didn't come in with anything. Then they really got it in the neck. 'I'm not here to teach you how to act,' he would say. 'I'm here to direct.' He was a very good director but, unlike Bill Gaskill, he was not a teacher of acting. He was great on pace and audibility, the level at which you spoke, which is frightfully important. Only directors who don't know what they are doing start to bawl and shout.

People from Twentieth Century Fox had come to see me in *George Dillon* and, through an agent they suggested, I was signed up on a three-year contract. I was flattered and excited at first, but I very soon realised that I had made the most terrible mistake.

The only respectable film I made at this time was *A Taste of Honey*, which was nothing to do with anything Twentieth Century Fox or the agent did for me, but a job that grew naturally out of my Royal Court connections. The director was my *bête noire* Tony Richardson, and the producers Woodfall, the company he had formed with John Osborne and Harry Saltzman in order to make film capital out of Osborne's first plays (the name came from Woodfall Street, where John used to live).

Richardson wasn't a real film-maker like Lindsay Anderson – you only have to look at Anderson's *Saturday Night and Sunday Morning* to see that – or Karel Reisz. At first, he convinced me (wrongly, of course) that anyone can make a movie. All Tony Richardson did was come in and ask his cameraman what he should do. If you look at one of Woodfall's biggest successes, *Tom Jones* (1963), which was directed by Richardson, scripted by Osborne and which became a huge, fluke success, they had three separate cuts and three separate music scores before it was finally put together. The synching and continuity is just dreadful.

Everyone involved thought *Tom Jones* was going to be a complete disaster and it was made for fourpence; Hugh Griffith and Susannah York cost a bit, and Albert Finney got a few thousand plus a percentage so he became a multi-millionaire out of it. They all made a fortune, and it re-promoted Tony's film career; it was a huge success in America. But he then did a dreadful version of Evelyn Waugh's novel *The Loved One* which more or less killed off his film career. He was a useless, unpleasant creature.

I was paid £500 for five weeks' work on *A Taste of Honey*, and I had to give Woodfall a week for nothing. Dora Bryan turned them down three times before she did it, Rita Tushingham was paid nothing, she was a schoolgirl, an amateur. And it was shot for peanuts on location in London and Manchester.

It was totally shoddy and amateur and yet the film proved immensely popular.

There were these lavish dinner parties hosted by Tony in the Midland Hotel in Manchester, where the production office was situated for the benefit of the producers and visiting celebrities and his own self-promotion.

I went to one with Dora Bryan and we started with champagne in Tony's room, then anything you wanted to drink in the bar, and then a five-course meal with wines, then brandy and cigars. I remember thinking that he could have been paying some of this to his actors who were actually doing the work for him.

After my success in *George Dillon*, I felt that Tarn was perfectly satisfied with that as the *status quo*. She probably felt that I had gone far enough. But I was hungry for more, and I had no intention of sitting around just waiting for something to happen. Hence all these rather unsatisfactory adventures in the screen trade, although *A Taste of Honey* remained the only film I made with Woodfall. I would have loved to have gone back to the Court at some stage and played Uncle Vanya; that's what I used to tell Michael Hastings when Max Stafford-Clark was running the place, but it never came to anything.

Another unrealised Court project dear to my heart, and Bill Gaskill's, was Etherege's Restoration comedy *The Man of Mode*. I would have been the near-perfect Dorilant. I loved the scene where, during Dorilant's *levée*, a young man comes in and Dorilant says, 'My love, my joy, my darling sin,' and kisses him full on the mouth, whereupon an orange-woman remarks, 'What a filthy habit these men have of kissing one another!'

Dorilant was based on the character of the Earl of Rochester, and Bill always planned to incorporate some of Rochester's poems and songs, which are delightfully filthy, all about cunts and things. I was intrigued to see that Max Stafford-Clark, a great follower of Bill Gaskill, did the play in 1994, in tandem with another new piece about Rochester, with his new touring company, Out of Joint, and that the productions played at the Royal Court. I've no idea who played Dorilant; I couldn't bear to go and see it.

My Twentieth Century Fox contract implicated me in a few disasters, the first and worst of which was *The Pirates of Tortuga*, which took me to Hollywood for the first time. They announced a technicolour cinemascope pirate picture, in which I was to play Sir Henry Morgan, a buccaneer who was made the governor of Jamaica and knighted and who then went back to being a buccaneer again. Which I thought sounded all right.

I arrived in Hollywood in January 1961 and was at first booked into the Beverly Carlton Hotel at $14 a day; I quickly moved to a smaller but perfectly comfortable place called the Montecito for half the price. I resumed my letter writing career to keep Tarn up to date. She was pregnant with Lucy, our first and only child, and I was hoping to be back home within the month, in time for the birth.

I was supposed to be the handsome villain of the piece, buckling my swash and flashing my sword all over the place. The producer explained that they had all the out-takes of a movie called *Anne of the Indies*, so we were just going to shoot some dialogue scenes and put them in between the *Anne of the Indies* out-takes, with all these galleons boom-booming all over the shop. So there was to be no Douglas Fairbanks glamour for me.

The producer said: 'It's not a B movie, not even a D movie, but a Zee-movie.' It was ghastly and humiliating beyond belief. They had expected to find in me a cross between Wallace Beery and Robert Newton. I was just twenty-nine years old and very wet behind the ears. I ended up wearing a costume worn by Bob Hope in *Monsieur Beaucaire* – a long, Restoration bellcoat – with a big moustache, beard and wig. It didn't work at all; they wanted some gross fat character actor about thirty years older. I was there for three weeks, and it was like being in prison: the company took away my passport and my return ticket and said that I had to stay on after the shoot in order to 'meet with' other producers and directors.

There were minor compensations. I was taken out for drinks in the Polo Lounge of the Beverly Hills Hotel and I did catch a glimpse of Elvis Presley on a neighbouring set. Some of my impressions were curiously prim. I wrote to Tarn: 'The town is full of fags and weird people. I even saw a woman the other day walking down the street in tights. And the trousers here make mine look like Oxford bags.' One party I went to was in a house built on a hundred different levels, with food cooked by a Russian princess, concealed lighting, everyone falling over drunk and the conversation blue enough to embarrass a roomful of sailors.

Pleading Tarn's pregnancy, I managed to get away and have a few days in New York before I returned home. I didn't think I was juvenile film star material, I wasn't Jeremy Brett. And then in came Brando, O'Toole and Finney, and Jeremy Brett and his type were out, too. I came home to do the full-length version of *The Kitchen*, my last play at the Court. Little Lucy was born, and I'm afraid that I plunged immediately into a serious affair with the actress Judith Stott, the former wife of the Irish television comedian Dave Allen. I had first met Judith while filming a TV play with her during the run of *The Wrong Side of the Park*. She was delightful: small, blonde, immense fun, and more than prone to staying up all night in the cause of having a good time.

I suddenly found myself thinking of leaving Tarn in order to marry Judith. But I didn't and, shortly after our affair was over, Judith began an even more serious liaison with Albert Finney, which went on for a very long time. Then she went to Australia to play in the double-bill by Peter Shaffer of *The Private Ear* and *The Public Eye*, taking over from Maggie Smith. It was in Judith's apartment, during a party there, that I first clapped eyes on Maggie Smith, who was then going out with Ian Bannen.

After *The Kitchen*, Twentieth Century Fox landed me in the Burton and Taylor film of *Cleopatra*. I played Germanicus, the young German general with Rex Harrison's Caesar. For seven soul-destroying months. I never even met Richard Burton. I had a couple of scenes with Liz Taylor, but most of what you might laughingly call my performance ended up on the cutting room floor. There was a lot of 'Hail Caesar' and banging of breastplates. My girlfriend was played by Francesca Annis.

The time you spent hanging around on that film depended on how much the director, Joe Mankiewicz, liked you. There was a beautiful slave girl from Los Angeles whom he took against for some reason or other, so he had her poisoned. Every day I would read the script hoping I'd see myself killed, but no, every day, there I was, standing around in Rome yet again like a piece of wallpaper. The silly old sod obviously took a liking to me. It went on for months.

The script was unbelievable. My first line was, 'I wouldn't put it past Potheinus to send an assassin in Cleopatra's name'; and Mankiewicz ordered me to say it on this huge set full of people as quickly as possible! It was like trying to deliver a tongue-twister. Tarn and little baby Lucy had come out to join me by then and were perfectly happy to be in Rome while I was working. But I was dreadfully miserable, professionally and personally. There are many people around who settle for the things they have and seem to leap happily into middle age. Our life together had become too placid and I was finding the domestic constraints terribly dull.

I couldn't plan anything and I had to turn down Bill Gaskill's invitation to go and play Iachimo in *Cymbeline* at Stratford, which I would have loved to have done. Half way through the film I instructed my agent Maurice Lambert to get me out of this contract, or else; I was becoming suicidal. I'd gone to lawyers in Los Angeles and London asking how to get out of it, but I couldn't find a way. It was cast iron clad. And I was a nobody on a cattle contract.

They could drop you at any time, and if you suddenly made a success, they had you anyway for tuppence. The whole thing was a nightmare and I nearly went mad. All the other English actors on *Cleopatra*, such as Michael Hordern, Kenneth Haigh and Michael Craig, were making a fortune; they would work for three weeks and then not do anything for six weeks, go back for two days, and they were paid by the minute. When they finished they all went home and bought houses. I was on £50 a week, about the same salary earned by the Italian electricians on the film. After a lot of wrangling, they eventually doubled my pay, and paid my expenses. I only got out of the contract by agreeing to continue receiving the same pittance of a salary beyond the time when, according to the contract, it should have been doubled.

While Maurice was negotiating all this, he received an enquiry from the newly formed National Theatre on my availability. Laurence Olivier was the artistic director, and was starting up in the new Chichester Festival Theatre in Sussex in July 1962 before moving the whole shebang into the Old Vic. A century of agitation and preparation was about to become a reality. I joined, after some misgivings, in the second Chichester summer season before the official London opening at the Old Vic in October 1963.

Larry naturally wanted to involve as many of his favoured Royal Court colleagues as possible; in them, and presumably in me, he saw something of the future. Nonetheless, my first reaction was to say no. I was offered Horatio in O'Toole's *Hamlet* and Captain Plume in *The Recruiting Officer* and a few bits. I was still iffy, because, despite all the unhappiness on *Cleopatra* and the fact that I was in effect on half-pay, that income was still much more than anything the National was offering. I dithered.

On our way back from shooting *Cleopatra*, Tarn, Lucy and I were invited by Tony Quayle to visit him and his wife, Dorothy Hyson, on his yacht, which he had brought down to Alicante during the filming of *Lawrence of Arabia*. We had become good friends during *Look After Lulu*, when he had put me in touch with the gymnastic instructor Edward Bolton, who helped me correct my faults of posture and was to figure in my later life at the National.

Tony was a really lovely man, untouched by any of the bitterness, or deviousness, which sometimes characterises people who have run great companies (he had been in charge at Stratford, and instrumental in bringing Peter Hall there). He had trained as an Olympic swimmer and he'd dive from his yacht and swim to the shore, where a fellow in a jeep with a supply of fresh towels would take him off to his caravan on the film set.

Tarn and I would join him later in the middle of the Alicante desert and eat roast lamb and potatoes for lunch under the blazing sky. That holiday was such fun. We would just sail off into the blue horizon, Tony and his wife, Tarn, Lucy and I, and the skipper – nobody else – and we would drop anchor, go swimming, eat and drink and enjoy each others' company. Nobody knew where we were, nobody could reach us on the telephone.

When we arrived home, John Dexter rang to say that John Neville, who was supposed to be joining the National to play the Dauphin in *Saint Joan*, was going off instead to Canada, and would I add that to my list of parts. It was a most unlikely casting, but I was intrigued that they might be casting in such unexpected ways and so I agreed. Nobody else would dream of casting me as the Dauphin. *Saint Joan* was scheduled for the second Chichester season in 1963: we started in Chichester and went to the Edinburgh Festival. And when we came to the Old Vic, *Saint Joan* was retained as one of the opening productions in that first London 1963/64 season, joining the London repertoire after the Peter O'Toole *Hamlet* and *Uncle Vanya*.

7

National Service with Larry . . . and Maggie

When the National Theatre was finally launched at the Old Vic in the autumn of 1963, I was in Ibiza. I'd gone on holiday with Tarn and Lucy without booking a flight back, and they were suddenly all full. I love my holidays so much that I sometimes forget they must come to an end. So I missed the first week of rehearsals for *Hamlet*, the opening production, starring Peter O'Toole, which wasn't very clever of me. Horatio, anyway, is a most unrewarding part, and the prospect of playing him did not exactly put a spring in my step.

I received a terribly frightening phone call from Laurence Olivier, but there was nothing I could do; there weren't any flights. I knew Larry well enough not to be cowed. I had, after all, understudied him as Archie Rice and he was never anything but warmly encouraging towards me, though it was always difficult to squeeze a compliment out of him. He made his point, though. I was reluctant ever to let him down again although, towards the end of that significant and tumultuous decade, he undoubtedly felt that I had.

It is worth stating that the National Theatre, and the theatre of this nation, owes everything to Larry. It saddens me deeply to see him derided and vilified in books and television programmes by people who know nothing and are not worthy of tying his shoelaces. He was a giant, a perfectionist, a man of fantastic loyalty and abiding courage, who worked himself to a standstill for the theatre and at almost negligible material gain to himself. In that sense, he was a true public servant, and that idea of public service in the arts has become rarer as, over the years, the arts themselves have become short-changed and betrayed by mediocrities in politics and journalism.

Larry was good at rage, however. He could be as gentle as a kitten and then explode in the most frightening fury. He was the most glorious, charming company, but he was also like an electric storm in summer. One of the best outbursts I had witnessed was during the run of the 1961 production of *The Wrong Side of the Park* when I joined him and Vivien for dinner at Maggie Leighton's house after a performance. We sat in her ghastly, tasteless dining room – black table and gold knives and forks, dreadful! – then we went downstairs for a drink.

Laurence Harvey, Maggie's husband, started talking about Ralph Richardson and how eccentric he had become. His underplaying was so extreme, Harvey said, that you could hardly call what he did acting at all. Then he had a go at John Gielgud and started on Paul Scofield and his ridiculous honking voice.

Larry sat through it all quietly, then suddenly exploded. It was like a bomb going off. 'How *dare* you,' he screamed at the top of his voice. 'Call yourself an actor? You're not even a bad actor. You can't act at all, you fucking stupid hopeless snivelling little cunt-faced cunty fucking shit-faced arse-hole . . .' God, it was awful. Harvey was just flattened like a bug against the wall. A terrible, glacial chill settled on the evening and there was no way of recovering the party spirit. So we all left, and as I went with Larry and Vivien to their chauffeured car, he suddenly got very upset about what he had done. Which is what always happened. 'I shall send the little bastard two dozen red roses tomorrow,' he said (and he did), cross with himself and the way the evening had ended.

The National maintained its close links with the Chichester Festival Theatre, where it had been 'tried out', throughout that first decade. Larry and Joan Plowright, whom he had married after his divorce from Vivien in 1961, lived in nearby Brighton and later in the Sussex village of Steyning. Chichester was very good for morale, and for the work. As actors, we felt we had a country address and a town home. We could enjoy the seaside air and open Sussex downs, and we always had the busy, bustling city to return to.

And we had a lot of fun shuttling between the two, believe me. Jeremy Brett joined the company early on, and during the early Chichester seasons, he would stay with Tarn and me at the Manor House in Chilcomb. Tarn had stopped acting after having Lucy, and in London she would drive me over to the Old Vic every morning. Lucy was usually in the back of the car and one day, as I got out, she said, 'Bye-bye, Daddy. Have a nice sleep!' She only ever saw me when I was in bed.

I saw less of Tarn, too, as time went by and my whole life was consumed by the National. But Tarn was very good at looking after me. I was nearly screwed again over money but, thanks to her, she made Maurice Lambert get on to the National and draw up a better contract for me; she discovered that I was being paid less than some of the others on the original deal.

Between 1963 and 1970, my friendship with, and my regard for, Larry deepened with every passing day of our association. I idolised him and took him as my first example of how an actor should acquit himself, onstage and off. He was the perfect guide and mentor for all young actors at the Royal Court, and at the National, because while he was palpably *primus inter pares*, he was also one of us. Not for nothing had he played Henry V so well in his famous film. He rehearsed with us and he ate with us in the staff canteen. When I was at the National in the late 1970s, I saw Peter Hall three times in the lift. In a company, you have to see the person who's running it all the time. Larry knew and understood what made us tick, and helped us whenever he could. Which, usually, was always. He was onstage with us every night. That is why I believe our great national companies should always be led by actors. They know what the agony and the ecstasy is really like. Directors and intellectuals do not.

What was so clever about the National at the start was that there was no real split between the older actors and the new younger ones. Larry saw to that. He simply wasn't going to have a situation – partly, I think, because of his Royal Court experience – where someone like Donald Wolfit, or any other old-fashioned grandee, would be in the ascendant over the young people, and of course no one would ever have the upper hand with Larry himself. Larry was such a wonderful inspiration to all the actors because he himself worked so damned hard as an actor.

As with all great professionals, whatever their calling, if you listened, you learned. Larry used to say that if you pitched your performance on the green exit lights in the circle, keeping your head or eyes level with them, everybody, anywhere, will see you. Actors so often make the mistake of playing to the stalls, which means that the majority of the audience cannot see the play on your face, which is frightfully important. Why should anyone want to look at the top of your head? There are audience-shy actors who really should stay in their dressing rooms. And it is all great fun for as long as they are in the wings waiting to go on. The minute they get on a stage they mumble into their feet and forget to play to the audience.

Larry, in particular, did two great things for the actors at the National. He gave us full-time access to a gymnasium and showed us how to make our bodies ready for the challenge of the greatest roles. And he employed a voice coach at the Old Vic, Kate Fleming, because he wanted the best acting voices in the world. He believed that every actor should develop an 'orchestral' voice, with different sounds, and a thrilling trumpet.

He gave Kate Fleming a seat in the circle for every performance of every production; and she used to tell the theatre when she wouldn't be using it – because, for most of those opening seasons, in fact most of that entire era, seats were harder to come by than gold dust. Kate was under strict instructions from Larry to be frank about anyone who was going wrong, and he would take them out of rehearsals and send them to her for special tuition.

One day, Larry stormed into the dressing room next to mine in the most furious temper, with six pages of notes; they were all for him! According to Kate Fleming, he was speaking too far back in his throat and was over-enunciating all the time. He was almost screaming with rage: 'This is why people come to see me,' he wailed. So, he got what he asked for, but not what he expected! But Kate stayed on, even though he personally never acted on her advice. She was a great help to people who were over-straining; she once told me that I was over-compensating in *Much Ado About Nothing* in 1965 for someone who wasn't very good. Actors can do that when they are feeling responsible for the success of a performance. And she was dead right.

My own lungs were developed through years of playing those big parts, including Shakespeare, in rep. If you put your arms around Larry you could feel his ribs like an enormous steel cage. His body was his professional life. When you play a lot of Shakespeare, the intercostal muscles between the ribs expand to provide you with lung space, as they do with opera singers. You also need that volume of air. Esmé Church, my drama teacher in Bradford, had always insisted upon the importance in Shakespeare of shooting forward to the end of the thought, not the line. You learn to breathe, and your lungs fill, and your ribs expand. And that is how you acquire a voice for the theatre.

Larry said about three weeks into the run of the opening *Hamlet* that it was the worst production of anything he'd ever seen. And he was the director. I asked him why, and he replied, 'Because I don't have a Hamlet.' Nonetheless, O'Toole, who had shot to international screen stardom in the previous year as Lawrence of Arabia, was the most tremendous draw, and tickets were changing hands on the street outside for £60 a piece, a lot of money in those days. Peter simply walked through the role, and didn't really bother with it.

Larry said that he understood why O'Toole played it like that, because he was adamant about not playing it exactly as he himself had done; but I don't think Larry wanted the sort of athletic, all-action Hamlet that he had been, even though he did give him a lot of gymnastic things to do – hurtling down stairs, throwing torches and so on – which any other actor, perhaps, would have jumped at. He really wanted Peter's Hamlet and was disappointed that he never got it.

Peter was terribly out of condition; he kept losing his breath, so he played most of it standing stock still. You have to have some muscle on you to play Hamlet. So it was all ghastly. It is a wonderful part, but not one I've ever wanted to play myself, funnily enough. It's undoubtedly the greatest part ever written, but it's so complex. You can't really play it, you just give an opinion of it. King Lear is much simpler in its psychology. With Hamlet, it's every man rolled into one.

The Old Vic itself was in a terrible state when we opened because of all the repair work and refurbishment. The Old Vic governors had agreed to hand over the famous theatre in the Waterloo Road to the National until the new premises on the South Bank were completed (in the event, the National stayed in the Old Vic for ten years). The Old Vic Company itself, which had churned out Shakespeare and other classics in the wake of Lilian Baylis's populist, 'culture for the masses' seasons of the 1930s, had only ceased operations in June of that year.

All the work and alterations which were deemed necessary had been done in a most fearful rush. A large revolving stage was installed. A new sound system was fitted. Seats were replaced and re-upholstered, the interior repainted. But even on the opening night, the dress circle had not been repainted, and the stalls were only just about cleaned up.

One of the major structural alterations was the extension of the stage into the auditorium by ten feet. There was newly-laid concrete in front of the stage where one of the workmen had placed his great big boot before it dried. Larry said to Michael Redgrave, who was playing Claudius, 'Oh, I see Vanessa's been having a look round the theatre!' (Vanessa, who had already made her own mark as a translucent RSC Rosalind in *As You Like It* at Stratford-upon-Avon in 1961, was not petite.) And the production was over-elaborate. One of the reviewers said that Michael Redgrave had more costume changes

63

than Eileen Joyce, the concert pianist who was famous for changing dresses between sonatas.

Poor old Michael Redgrave wasn't at all well when he played Claudius. He suffered from terrible shakes and fits of amnesia due to the onset of Parkinson's disease, which everyone misread as alcoholism. He was never drunk onstage, although he used to pop a few pills and wash them down with a revitalising slug of whisky. Gertrude was played by the beautiful, adorable Diana Wynyard who died soon afterwards, during Max Frisch's *Andorra*, a rather tiresome allegorical drama. She was on those slimming pills and simply faded away. They were great stars, but we were all equal, with them, under Larry.

Saint Joan, with Joan Plowright marvellous in the lead, and Max Adrian, the grand old man of character actors, as the Inquisitor, effectively sealed this sense of democratic excellence between generations of actors. Frank Finlay, who was playing Stogumber, said that he was going to get contact lenses, because he is one of these totally myopic actors – others are Alan Howard and Vanessa Redgrave – who are always mooning around the stage with their eyes wide open, like silly-looking fish. He had the lenses made, put them in, walked on the stage and immediately saw the audience. He nearly died with fright. He dried and fluffed, messed up every scene. And he never wore them again.

As the Dauphin, I wanted to convey the contained and jerky nature of the character in gestures that were somehow constricted; Tarn made me a harness from webbing which I wore around my shoulders and chest and that gave me the physical platform for the performance. It is such a small part that you have to make an immediate impact. I sat in the field at Chilcomb and tried out various voices – I tried out even more voices than Joan heard in her ecstasy! – and I decided to play it round-shouldered, with bent knees, the harness, a long nose and no eyebrows. And I shook and shuddered all the time. It was the ultimate in make-up and character performance, and although I got away with it, I don't think I deserved to!

One of Larry's cleverest moves was the appointment of Kenneth Tynan as his dramaturg, or literary manager. Ken had written a blistering attack in *The Observer* on the opening National production of John Ford's *The Broken Heart* at Chichester, and was obviously angling to be consulted on the repertory by the actor whom he admired and respected above all others. Larry knew that Ken would never shut up about what he deemed to be the failings and inadequacies of the National Theatre, and so he effectively appointed him to silence his criticism. He used to say that he would rather have Ken on the inside pissing out than on the outside pissing in.

Ken only came in three afternoons a week, but he was at every board and repertory meeting and really was Larry's right hand. There may have been a lot of bullshit with Ken but none of it was to do with hierarchy or status among the actors. He was a real breath of fresh air, and terribly amusing and stimulating. Although Larry may have appointed him for the wrong reasons, and no one liked him very much, or even trusted him at all, he certainly made his mark and exerted an enormous influence, mostly, I think, for the good.

We all worked like absolute donkeys. You were either rehearsing or performing all the time. There was one rehearsal room over the theatre, and one in Aquinas Street round the corner, where all the Portakabin offices were. You couldn't avoid each other in corridors, in the canteen or on the stage, whereas nowadays you have to send out search parties on the South Bank to find anyone to talk to.

More unavoidable than almost anyone else, as far as I was concerned, was a certain Margaret Smith, or 'Madam Schmidt' as Tarn unkindly, but not unreasonably from her point of view, came to call her. She was not 'one of us' from the Royal Court: she was a big West End star who had made her name in revue and light comedy and took ten per cent of the box office gross home in her pay packet. She gave all that up, temporarily at least, much to the annoyance of Binkie Beaumont and the West End establishment, to accept the challenge of the National Theatre.

I had met her at that party of Judith Stott's and knew that she was now living with the writer Beverley Cross, having been rescued from the possibility of marriage to Ian Bannen and a simultaneous conversion to Roman Catholicism. She had impressed me then as being a miserable, rather forlorn creature. But she struck across my bows in those opening months of the National like a salt-sprayed sea breeze. She drove me mad at first in rehearsals, because she has an uncanny and persistent way of dictating the timing in any scene she plays. For instance, she will take your hand and squeeze it, which is a signal not to reply to the line she has just delivered until she lets go. That is part of her brilliance, and she always has the right instinct for the rhythms of a scene. We fell head over heels in love and there was nothing we could do about it.

Like me, Maggie came from humble stock. She was born in Ilford, in Essex, in 1934 (I was three years older) and was brought up in Oxford, where her family moved at the outbreak of the Second World War. Her father was a medical laboratory technician from Newcastle and her mother a rather grim Scots Presbyterian from Glasgow. She was strictly reared and imbued with both moral and physical puritanism. Amazingly, at the age of twenty-eight, even though she had had several boyfriends and was living with Beverley Cross, she was, to all intents and purposes, sexually naive and inexperienced.

As with all my other affairs – and as far as I was concerned, Maggie was going to be just another of those – Tarn knew nothing of my bad behaviour. But I seemed to kickstart Maggie's sexuality, and I was soon deeper in than perhaps I should have been. At the same time, being closely associated with so brilliant an actress did little harm to my public image or indeed, in the long term, my standing within the company. We were immensely clandestine and immensely clever, though when Larry finally got to hear about it, he was not at all pleased. He warned me about mixing with thoroughbreds, and I think he felt that his marriage to Vivien had been so unhappy, in its final phase, that I could make the same mistake myself.

Tarn was the perfect wife for anyone, and a very good hostess. Our marriage went along quite happily, despite my odd bouts of bad behaviour, and could well have continued but for my being netted by Maggie's wit, charm and talent. I loved Tarn, but it is fair to say that I do become easily bored. That's my fault, not anyone else's. I fell heavily under Maggie's spell the minute we started rehearsing *The Recruiting Officer* towards the end of 1963. We did not marry, nor was I divorced from Tarn, until 1967, when Maggie became pregnant. For several years, even though she at first suspected, and then discovered, what was going on, Tarn was willing to stick by me and wait for the affair to blow itself out.

Maggie had begun that first National year of 1963 in the West End, scoring a huge personal success in a play called *Mary Mary*. And the film of *The VIPs* was released, in which she played a show-stealing scene with Richard Burton. She had really arrived in a big way, and *The Recruiting Officer* was her first role at the National, which she had joined at the suggestion of both Larry – with whom she had appeared in Ionesco's *Rhinoceros* in the West End in 1960, replacing Joan Plowright in Orson Welles's production – and of the director Bill Gaskill, my beloved Billy, who rightly saw her as the only true stylish contemporary comedienne in the Edith Evans class.

I was playing Captain Plume who meets Silvia (Maggie) disguised in the play as a boy; he embraces her warmly and as he clutches her to his bosom, declares, 'Sdeath! There's something in this fellow that charms me!' And indeed there was. But I remember that at Lynn Redgrave's twenty-first birthday party in March 1964, only two people – Lynn, and her father's dresser, Christopher Downes, who had got to know Maggie as she had started rehearsing *The Master Builder* with Sir Michael – knew what was going on.

I was given plenty of warnings about becoming embroiled with her, none of which I was in any position to heed. One of the stagehands said to me, 'Watch out for her, she drinks like a fish and swears like a trouper,' all of which I soon found out for myself to be true, though the claims about her drinking were rather exaggerated. She was incredibly witty and funny when she felt like it.

Maggie, like Vivien Leigh, with whom Larry endured years of unhappiness, certainly was a throughbred. But I didn't listen to his advice of not becoming entangled with the species. And besides, after two years of carrying on, she became pregnant with our first son, Christopher, and I had no choice. 'About marriage,' said Larry, 'very easy to get into, very expensive to get out of.' And when it all broke up I realised what he meant. And it wasn't the expense of money so much as the expense of spirit that you go through.

It was not exactly lust at first sight. She was baleful, I would say, but always terribly funny. You could certainly say that I met my match with Miss Margaret. I think she had arrived at a crossroads in her life. Beverley Cross had disappeared to Australia to direct his own version of a terrible French farce called *Boeing-Boeing*. She was absolutely convinced, I learned years later, that I wouldn't, finally, marry her. I had no plans to at the start; I thought that this was just another backstage romance, though I had obviously never met anyone quite like her before. But somehow, it all loomed much more importantly for her.

8

Shining as the Sun God

Maggie's and my developing secret life together was inextricably bound up with our work. I shared a tiny dressing room at first with Colin Blakely, Frank Finlay and Robert Lang. In the next door tiny room, there was John Stride and Derek Jacobi. Larry used to send his favourite actors into our room, Dressing Room Number 6, which is the one he used to have many years previously with Ralph Richardson. We stayed there for a year until Sir Michael left and Albert Finney joined the company, at which point I moved into Number 2 with Albert, opposite Larry.

Albert was delightful company, always so funny and boyish, but a big star, too. In that first season at Chichester, he had acquired a Silver Cloud Rolls Royce and a chauffeur. We all used to stand outside the stage door waiting for him to arrive and then we'd give him the big sarcastic raspberry, or 'razeroo,' so eventually he had to get rid of it! We shared the same dresser, Christopher Downes, who had stayed on after Michael Redgrave left. Christopher and I really hit it off and became very close friends.

That friendship deepened into collusion when my affair with Maggie Smith took off. He had got to know Maggie well, separately, through her work with Michael Redgrave on *The Master Builder* in 1964. Michael had great trouble with his lines and Chris used to read them through with him and then liaise with Maggie about how Michael was feeling from one day to the other.

The friendship with Chris was, and remains, very important in my life. Maggie, Chris and I became virtually inseparable over that entire period at the National. Chris became part of the family and used to look after the business side of things for us, too. We even all went on holiday together, which some people found hard to understand!

Larry was indeed not as happy as Larry at the start of *The Recruiting Officer*. He was playing Brazen, whom everyone talks about for three acts before he comes on with the most tremendous élan. The bad news, as far as Larry was concerned, was that Bill Gaskill said we were going to improvise for two weeks, which Larry hates doing. He simply couldn't do it. Bill said that Robert and Derek, say, would read the first scene between them, then put down the books and do it immediately again in their own words, so that they got to the heart of the meaning in the scene. Larry immediately said, 'Sorry I cannot do that; I work from the outside in,' and so on. Give him a false nose or a curly wig and he could do anything.

And he sulked and he shamed himself before his own company and said that he would play it for a few weeks and then Robert Lang or someone could take it over. I said to him, don't be stupid, you've got the best part in the play. I asked him if he knew who had played Brazen. He didn't. I said David Garrick. So I had a go at him, and Bill Gaskill sent him up a bit – which was a bit disrespectful of him, I thought – but the people who were best at improvising in that cast were Maggie and Max Adrian, because they both came from revue.

Anyway, to his eternal credit, Larry found his own way of negotiating this purgatory of improvisation and was of course brilliant. He just had a little bit extra about his coat, a few blue ribbons in his periwig, the swagger stick and he made this great subliminal first entrance where he merely walked across the stage at the back, looking at the river and finding that his pockets were a bit empty – and went off, to a huge round of applause!

Then we had a scene where he comes on and says, 'My dear!' and I say, 'My dear!' and we meet in the centre of the stage and we embrace and kiss. 'Give me a buss, my dear,' 'Half a score if you will, my dear!' Well, the audience screamed with laughter which we didn't expect on the first night. So, with our lips locked, Larry muttered, 'Don't move, don't move,' and then lifted one leg up behind him, and the laughter just went on and on.

In the interval, Larry called Colin Blakely, Maggie and me into his dressing room and opened a bottle of champagne, which is something I never saw him do during a performance either before or after that first night. He knew we had a hit, and he knew that he was a huge success in this wonderful role. It was a superb production by Gaskill, and everyone adored doing it and everyone adored watching it.

Maggie scored a great personal success as Silvia, and her following two roles, as Desdemona to Larry's Othello and Hilde Wangel opposite first Redgrave, then Larry, in Ibsen's *The Master Builder*, really set the seal on her claims to be considered an all-round classical actress, and not just a comedienne. I was hoping to be cast as Iago – my performance at the Library in Manchester had, after all, received a glowing notice from Bernard Levin in, of all places, the *Daily Telegraph* – but Larry had other ideas. He decided instead on Frank Finlay, and I couldn't argue with that because, in Wesker's *Chips With Everything*, he had been simply brilliant as this dark, ghastly sergeant. I thought he would be equally brilliant as Iago but, as it turned out, he wasn't.

Frank had never played Shakespeare before. But that wasn't the reason he failed. Larry made sure that he played it in such a way that he didn't win over the audience. He knew very well how Iago can come along and steal the play; he's charming, funny, has the ear of the audience, talks to them all the time. There's a good essay on the role by one of the Booths, the American acting dynasty, where it is argued, rightly, I think, that Iago should be so convincing in his reasoning that the audience should truly believe he is in the right.

He has, after all, been done out of a job, and he's served very well, so he's going to get his revenge, anyone else would do the same in his position – these are the sort of lines to be thinking along as Iago. The trick with the part is to play it differently with every character. With Othello, you are honest Iago. With Roderigo, you are a convincing go-between. With Cassio, your face is conciliatory.

Larry insisted to John Dexter, who was directing, that he should have an Iago who was an NCO, a Non Commissioned Officer. This idea was rooted in his war-time experience of serving with the Fleet Air Arm. Larry was in barracks with another private, who could hardly believe he was sleeping next to the man he knew on the silver screen as Heathcliff in *Wuthering Heights* and Maxim de Winter in *Rebecca* (both films were released in the first two years of the war). He told his wife, who got very excited, and invited Larry over to his house in the country for the weekend.

This fellow was then promoted above Larry, to corporal, or sergeant, and started treating him abominably, sneering at his acting and narking him at every opportunity. Larry was determined to get his own back.

Iago-like, he thought of the bloke's wife who had been so impressed at meeting him. He got himself invited over to the house again and took the wife out for an extremely long walk, lasting about six hours, all around the neighbouring farms and churches, back to the village, popping into pubs and into every shop, buying stationery, cigarettes and flowers.

When he returned, laden with these purchases, he kissed her hand in front of her husband – she had, of course, been utterly bedazzled by his charm – and did everything to imply to his host and superior officer that he and the lady had been out in the fields having a splendid fuck. Larry said that this performance completely destroyed his condescending adversary, and that he never dared speak to Larry again.

Subsequently, casually and *en passant*, Larry would say to this bloke, 'And how is that darling girl of yours?' Now *that* is Iago, totally, and brilliantly. *Othello* could just as easily be called 'The Handkerchief'. And that is why Larry asked John Dexter for an NCO. He identified with Iago too easily and knew what a great and dangerous role it was.

More controversially, Larry convinced himself for the purposes of this production, and in order to justify the neutralisation of Iago, that Iago doesn't make Othello jealous: Othello makes *himself* jealous! He talked to me about this, and I said, 'But what about the huge temptation scene where Iago pours it all in?' He overruled me by saying – ridiculously, in my view – that Othello is lost to his hysterical passion at the first mischievous hint of Desdemona's infidelity, at the very minute Iago lays the first false trail. By that cock-eyed reasoning, you don't need Iago at all. So Larry never gave poor old Frank a chance.

He certainly didn't want me or Albert playing Iago, and he didn't want some cocky young fellow either; he wanted an ordinary actor who hadn't done much Shakespeare, whom he could just push out towards the corners, leaving the centre of the stage clear for him to prowl and prate in. Larry always treated the stage like a bullring, or a boxing arena. And there was no way he was ever going to lose a fight or even begin to look like losing one.

Larry told me on the train from Brighton one day that he had learned the whole of the part, seven months before the first preview. I advised Frank to learn Iago, too; it's the longest part in the canon, longer than Hamlet. But he didn't, so he got pushed from pillar to post. He sounded a bit like Olivier, a bit like Frank Finlay, a bit North Country, a bit not North Country. He didn't stand a chance. Larry just blew him off the stage. His preparation was phenomenal.

He went to the gym, he deepened the lower register of his voice by an octave, he trained as if for a prize fight. Bill Gaskill used to say that you could stop that performance at any point in its duration and you'd be able to tell immediately what the character was thinking; that's a sign of the containment and control. That's how faultless and structured he was. He left nothing to chance. He never gabbled through anything, which is a great lesson for any actor. Everything you say must have a point and a purpose.

Larry never really liked John Dexter, whom he found too saucy, too full of himself, too conspiratorial and back-stabbing. The falling out started when they were on the road in Cardiff with *Othello* and John asked them all to stay on the stage afterwards. He then gave them the most almighty bollocking, saying that the evening had been the dreariest he had ever spent in a theatre, anywhere, and that they were all, without exception, boring and second-rate.

Larry was furious. He summoned John to his dressing room and said, 'You are never, ever, to talk to my company like that again.' And John made a terrible mistake. He turned round and told him that it wasn't *his* company, it was the National Theatre Company. From that moment, John was always about an inch from being fired.

John and I were in Larry's dressing room after *Othello* one night when he was showering off his body make-up. He always covered himself, top to toe, in three layers of this blue-black body make-up, so he looked like a Nubian slave. Standing in front of the mirror, he suddenly looked at himself and said, 'What a tragedy that such a very great actor should have such a very small cock.' There's not a lot you can say to that apart from, 'Well, not bad,' but you certainly wouldn't offer to swap your own for his.

Oddly enough, Larry never presented any great evidence of sensuality or sexuality in person. I never saw him coming on strong with any woman. Never. I suppose he was very feminine in that he left them to make the running. The only running he did was running the National, and although it undoubtedly wore him down, you never really saw that. He was like a dog. He would never give in. This competitiveness did invariably lead to problems, certainly with Maggie, who can give anyone a run for their money. Things were fine between her and Larry in *The Recruiting Officer* and *Othello* – she was a perfectly sweet and charming Desdemona and did nothing too much to upset him – but they never really liked or trusted each other all that much.

In *The Master Builder* she was too fast for him and he didn't like the fact that she could give as good as she got. He was infuriated by a review which said that she had acted him off the stage and he gave her a ticking off, saying she was too slow. Well, that was like a red rag to a bull. She went on that next night and tore through their scenes so fast he could hardly get his lines in.

She made him look like a complete monkey, and not many people ever did that to Larry and lived to tell the tale. No one, in fact. So that was that. Larry swore never to work with her again, ever. Nor did he, except in that terrible film Beverley Cross wrote, *Clash of the Titans*. He had originally promised to play Antrobus in Thornton Wilder's *The Skin of Our Teeth* with Maggie in the Vivien Leigh role of Sabina. But he pulled out of that, saying she was too competitive to work with.

Larry's Othello made a profound impression on me, even though he played a Negro instead of a Moor. The performance was one of animal vitality and remarkable technical virtuosity and it really threw down a gauntlet to anyone with aspirations towards true distinction. His example influenced my performance as Atahuallpa in Peter Shaffer's *The Royal Hunt of the Sun* in 1964, which was undoubtedly my greatest personal success since *George Dillon*. I knew that if I wanted to give a performance even remotely comparable to Larry's Othello in excitement and style – which I did – I had to work my arse and bollocks right off.

Atahuallpa is an Inca sun god who is tracked down by the Spanish expedition to Peru led by Pisarro, who was played by Colin Blakely. The play is the story of their friendship and the betrayal of Atahuallpa by Pisarro. Derek Jacobi was originally cast as Atahuallpa but luckily for me John Dexter changed his mind and cast me. I went to the gym, as Larry had done for *Othello*, and as I was now in the habit of doing anyway.

In addition to Kate Fleming, the voice expert, Larry insisted that the gym instructor, a wonderful man called Edward Bolton, with whom I had first worked during *Look After Lulu*, was at our permanent disposal. I took advantage of this excellent facility throughout my time at the Old Vic, but never more so than in *The Royal Hunt of the Sun*. Nobody knew what an Inca god sounded like and so, whatever Peter Shaffer may claim now, I had to make it all up. But it was like a conjuring trick: once I had found the way of playing it, and worked hard in the physical and vocal preparation, it became the easiest part I had ever played in my life. The performances themselves took nothing out of me at all. Larry had one

My mother Gladys in 1966

My father Reuben in later years

A rare picture of me as a baby

With mum, aged 3, outside 34
Priory Road, Shirehampton

Aged 5 at Priory Road

BELOW LEFT In my teens, acting with the National Association of Boys' Clubs

BELOW In one of my first productions – *The Hewers of Coal* – in which I played a miner

ABOVE LEFT Nora Ann
Simmonds, my first wife

ABOVE My first son
Michael with his uncle,
Nora's brother

An early publicity shot
aged about eighteen

Tarn Bassett with Claude Hulbert (left) and Sonny Hale in *Not a Clue*, 1953, the play in which we first met

The 'Have a Cigarette' *Othello* with myself as Iago to Brendan Barry as the Welsh Moor in Manchester, 1955

My wedding to Tarn with Jeremy Brett as my best man, in London, April 1956

LEFT John Osborne in his Kent garden with my daughter, Lucy

The great old character actor, Esmé Percy, with his beloved Skippo (Michael Wagen)

BELOW With Wendy Craig in *Epitaph for George Dillon*, my breakthrough at the Royal Court in 1958

First night of *George Dillon* in New York; celebrating with an unknown admirer in Sardi's

Relaxing at Monthawk Bay with Tarn during my first New York stay

Kissing Dora Bryan in Tony
Richardson's film of *A Taste of
Honey*, 1961

As Peter the cook, with Alfred
Lynch, in Arnold Wesker's *The
Kitchen* at the Royal Court, 1961

Two great and glamorous stars: my beautiful friend, Margaret Leighton, and
Noël Coward, my colleague and idol (PA News)

The 1964 National Theatre production of Noël Coward's *Hay Fever*. Left to right: Lynn Redgrave, Robert Lang, myself and Maggie Smith (Angus McBean)

With Laurence Olivier in *The Recruiting Officer*, National Theatre, 1963 (Lewis Morley/Akehurst Bureau)

piece of advice: 'Be careful of your voice.' And he asked me, in that shy, retiring manner of his, if I could possibly make love to Maggie after playing in *The Royal Hunt of the Sun*. Of course I could. He said he couldn't rise to anything after playing Othello, and I said it was an entirely false comparison: Othello was much more demanding than Atahuallpa.

The worst part was standing unseen for twenty-five minutes behind this back wall which opened up like a sunflower to reveal me in all my godly splendour. It is really quite a small role, despite all the grandeur. Marc Wilkinson, who composed the music, had been to Paris and found all the Peruvian bird noises in some sonic museum, and we assimilated that and also the accounts of how the Incas spoke – they hit consonants very hard, but their vowel sounds were like floating sighs.

A friend in the music business gave me a record of some Bolivian Indians singing in the jungle, and that corroborated how the Peruvians might have spoken. One day in Glebe Place, where I was still living despite my still semi-furtive affair with Maggie, Tarn was cutting up some of the bird tapes, and the place was reverberating with all these odd squeaks and squawks when a policeman knocked on the door; someone had complained that we were mistreating a dog. The words I was given by the playwright were along the lines of 'White man speak with forked tongue' – utter crap – but I somehow elaborated it all into the dying exhalation of a doomed kingdom on the top of a bloody great mountain. The heart of Shaffer's play, the relationship between Pisarro and a primitive king who believes he is the son of God and will rise in the morning if he dies, was fine. But there is no description of Atahuallpa at all in either Shaffer's play or *The Conquest of Peru* from where he took the story.

Shaffer wrote a sort of love story. But he didn't help at all in how people spoke or looked or behaved. And of course Dexter's production was a work of sheer inspiration, sparked off by the famously unhelpful but challenging stage direction of 'They cross the Andes'. So it was a good play only in the sense that it was a great gift to the actors' and director's resources of invention and imagination.

Because there was nothing of that in the text, I appeared as close as dammit to a god as I could manage: shaved, buffed, my two prominent front teeth to the fore, with a dancing movement and an invented language. I had to take the audience into that kingdom of the Incas, take them on that trip through my imaginative efforts. With my Aztec profile, swept back hair and curious balletic movement, I was hardly surprised when one critic said that I reminded him of Margot Fonteyn, though I've always thought that I looked rather more like Maria Callas!

I loved working with Colin Blakely, and I loved him as a friend, too. I'd first seen him walk on the stage at the Royal Court as a collier in *Sergeant Musgrave's Dance* in 1959 and I couldn't believe he was an actor; he looked like a collier, he was terrifying. I didn't know him then but I got talking to him in the pub afterwards. We liked each other enormously. He was such a big man and I always think there's a lot of him in Gérard Depardieu; big and bear-like, a real Belfast bruiser, but such a gentle soul, too, and great fun to be with.

Colin was a colossal drinker, and often went on the stage totally pissed. During *Volpone*, a few years later, he would bounce along the walls of the Old Vic corridors, but the moment he stepped on the stage, boom, he was completely in control. In that role, he had to climb up a fake ladder in order to get to a girl's room, and she repulsed him at the top; he came straight down and was caught by the crowd. I was convinced that he would break his neck one day, but he never put a foot wrong.

Colin played rugby. He had so much muscle on him – although short of limb, he was in fact built like a tank, so he seemed huge – that he effortlessly absorbed all the alcohol. Built like that, and built to a certain extent as I am, you never get so drunk that you can't speak, as opposed to someone like Peter O'Toole in his drinking days, who was constructed like a sparrow, so he appeared pissed if he'd had three drinks.

Colin was a man of true valour and ritual. He always wore a medallion around his neck that his wife, the actress Margaret Whiting, had given him. In the dressing room, he would observe the same routine every night: he would remove his watch, then his rings, and finally his medallion, which he would kiss and place meticulously in front of his mirror, without fail, before every single acting performance of his life.

On the *Royal Hunt of the Sun*, which was an enormously elaborate, if not totally exhausting, play to do, the three of us in the dressing room – myself, Bob Lang and Colin – had a little wooden mouse, and when the mouse was on your place, you had to send out for six bottles of Guinness, which was almost our company tipple, at the Old Vic. The mouse was moved around between us by Chris Downes. On a matinée and evening day of the *Royal Hunt*, that mouse went round like a creature demented. But everything we drank was lost in sweat.

When we moved on to the Queen's Theatre for a season, Colin switched to brandy and coffee. But Bob Lang and I stayed on the

Guinness, so the mouse worked just as hard but on a shorter route. At Chichester, we used to go out wining and dining a great deal after the show. Colin was a great trencherman. He liked his steaks. One evening at a restaurant in Midhurst, some toffee-nosed Welsh prat at the bar who had overheard our no doubt raucous conversation, shouted across to Colin, 'Give us a song there, Paddy!' Colin was muttering that if he shouted this once more, he would go across and break his jaw. He would have done, too. We finally left and, at the door, Colin turned and loudly said, 'Goodnight, Taff!' and made it sound like the vilest insult you've ever heard.

Colin's father came to see *The Recruiting Officer*. A vile man, his father, but Colin, who was very respectful of both parents, poured his father a whisky when they came round before the show. Then he carried on getting changed. His father drained this drink and sat there with an empty glass, then threw it on the floor. Which is what you do, apparently, in Belfast. I thought this was terribly bad mannered. As Colin bent down to pick it up, his father kicked him. Colin said nothing. But I heard later that he was at home when his father was being nasty to his mother and he suddenly punched his father on the jaw and broke it, landing the old boy in hospital for a month. It took a long time to push Colin too far, but when he was pushed, he stayed pushed.

9

Crowd-Pleasing with Noël . . .
and Franco

1964 was one of the best years of my working life. I was gloriously happy playing Atahuallpa and spending so much time in Maggie's company, although I was still living in Glebe Place with Tarn. The complications of this deceit were never anything I worried about too much. Maggie was still to all intents and purposes living with Beverley Cross in her flat in Eldon Road, Fulham. Tarn was a full-time mother with little Lucy who was a delightful three-year-old. She accepted the fact that I was rehearsing all day and playing in either Chichester or the Old Vic at night. She accepted lots of other things as well. Life was too hectic to worry about the details, and I just went with the flow.

Our next play together was *Hay Fever*. On the first day of rehearsals, Noël Coward said: 'I'm thrilled and flattered and frankly a little flabbergasted that the National Theatre should have had the curious perceptiveness to choose a very early play of mine, and to give it a cast that could play the Albanian telephone directory.' Coward was out of fashion at this point, and no one had thought seriously about *Hay Fever*. It had been written in 1925 as a vehicle for Marie Tempest and subsequently forgotten.

The play, we discovered, was both barbarically simple and hysterically funny. Absolutely nothing happens. Each member of the Bliss family – Judith the actress, David the novelist, their two grown-up children – invites a guest down to the house by the river for the weekend. Charades are played after dinner. The guests leave in the morning before breakfast, having been either embarrassed or put out. The Blisses are last seen squabbling among themselves over a map of Paris and a topographical detail in David's next novel.

Edith Evans played Judith Bliss, although she was far too old, and she made life very difficult for everyone. She simply couldn't learn her lines. What was interesting about her, though, was that she insisted on rehearsing on the stage, with all the furniture and props. She would sit on one side of the stage, entirely alone, and no one else would be allowed there, unless you had to make an entrance, and even then you had to walk all the way around her and cross to the other side. This ridiculous rigmarole must have been what Marie Tempest did, but I've never known anyone else carry on like that.

Noël had been offered Coral Browne as Judith at first, but he said she was far too common. But I think he was wrong; Judith Bliss *should* be common; she's not a duchess, she's just an actress and, what is more, a touring actress, like Arkadina in *The Seagull*. Like Arkadina, she evinces all these airs and graces.

You could see with Edith that she was going to blame everybody else for anything that went wrong with her performance. Nothing was ever her fault. The only way she could make the production work as far as she was concerned was to pull rank and frighten everyone else to death. She deliberately trod on everyone else's lines and pretended that the other actors didn't exist; all the young actors had a terrible time – Derek Jacobi and I, Louise Purnell and Lynn Redgrave. The only person she didn't frighten was Maggie, who hated her. Altogether, she was a bloody nuisance.

She also insisted on saying in rehearsal, *à propos* of the weekend cottage's situation on the Thames in Cookham, 'On a very clear day you can see Marlow.' Finally Coward could stand it no longer and yelled from the back of the stalls: 'Edith, the line is "On a clear day you can see Marlow." On a *very* clear day you can see Marlowe *and* Beaumont *and* Fletcher.'

There was another problem. Louise Purnell replaced Sarah Miles as Sorel during rehearsals. Larry had employed Sarah Miles, with whom he was having an affair (although none of us knew it), for *The Crucible* which he directed, and for *Hay Fever*. They had met while making the film *Terms of Trial*. Half way through the *Hay Fever* rehearsal period, it became clear that Noël simply wasn't getting on with Sarah, and that he very much disliked her developing performance as Sorel. We now know that he was on the point of firing her; and also that he, almost alone, knew of her affair with Larry – and he didn't approve of that, either.

Suddenly, almost conveniently, Sarah gagged on a chop bone while eating dinner at home and was rushed to hospital for a minor operation. She was told to rest her severely scarred throat. So she was replaced. I never liked her very much because of her dirty, schoolgirl quality; she was always boasting about bodily functions, and going on about drinking her own urine. But Colin Blakely, for instance, who appeared in *The Crucible* with her, fell head over heels in love when she joined the company for the very same reasons that I disliked her.

No one fell in love with 'the dame', as we called Edith Evans. Noël had wanted us to be word perfect at first rehearsals, which we were, with the exception of the dame. And she could never learn the part. Before we opened at the Old Vic, we played a week at the Opera House in Manchester. We all stayed at the Midland Hotel. Noël summoned Maggie and me to his suite and told us that the dame was refusing to go on. She had told him that she had a dropped stomach and no saliva.

He had shaken her 'like a rat' and told her that she was a disgrace to the acting profession, and to Christian Science (like the critic Harold Hobson, she swore allegiance to that odd organisation), and that she had to go to the fucking theatre and go on, or else. The doctor, Noël said, had visited the hotel and tried to persuade her to take a bromide. 'Bromide!' exclaimed Noël. 'What she needs is a firecracker up her arse.' He then sat down at his grand piano and played a smart, bouncy version of 'All things bright and beautiful'.

Noël was hysterically funny, and everyone adored him. Apart from the dame, of course. By this time, things had gone from bad to worse. On the Sunday night of the final dress rehearsal in Manchester, she sat quivering in her hotel room with her friend, the actress Gwen Ffrangcon-Davies, who was trying to help her learn her lines, and Noël delivered his master-stroke: he announced that the dame's understudy would go on as Judith Bliss. The understudy was Maggie Smith, or 'the little Smith girl', as the dame disparagingly called her. Although Maggie played the lesser role of Myra the vamp in that production – brilliantly – she already had her eye on Judith Bliss, and she played it, as you might expect, to the manner born that Sunday night.

Word got back to the dame and she miraculously recovered and opened in the role on the Monday. She certainly didn't want Maggie to steal her thunder, as she could easily have done. The dame, great actress though she was, resembled a gifted amateur. She didn't really know what she was doing. What she had was an infallible instinct for the turn of a speech, or a line, and what she did was entirely instinctive, and executed without much thought, imagination, or guile.

Hay Fever, despite all that, became one of the National's biggest ever hits, and stayed in the repertoire for some years. A kind of sorcery went on with Noël Coward: you couldn't tell he was directing us apart from the obvious fact of his very powerful presence. On the other side of that Christmas, we opened Franco Zeffirelli's madcap Italianate version of *Much Ado About Nothing*, with Maggie as Beatrice and myself as Benedick. That, too, became a block-busting crowd-pleaser, with people queueing for hours to get in, and buying tickets from touts on the street outside.

Much Ado may have looked all right – in fact, it looked stunning – but it was a misery to do, because it was so uncomfortable. Our costumes made us look like Sicilian toy soldiers and we were trussed up and pushed around like clockwork dolls. Maggie wore a red dress and an orange blonde wig and I was tottering around in huge dark glasses, my hair slicked back with a ton of pomade.

I had a few days' holiday before we started rehearsals, and learned the whole of Benedick. At the first read-through, Franco said: 'That's very good, but it's no good for my production.' It wasn't Italianate enough for him. The trouble was that, having given that general piece of direction, he then couldn't help me any further. His 'Italian' text simply did not correspond at all with what Shakespeare had written.

I was in a dreadful state about it. Franco wanted Benedick played like a temperamental Italian, full of himself and strutting about all over the place, whereas the part is in fact written as a man who is deeply indecisive about his emotional impulses and defensively fending off the truth of his feelings towards Beatrice. I begged Maggie to help me. I didn't know *what* I was doing in it. She said she couldn't. 'How do I make it funny?' I asked her. 'I don't know,' she said. *She* was funny all right, but then Beatrice is quite a small part. She is talked about an awful lot, but she doesn't actually come on much. Also, she was excused being Italian by Franco because of her colouring. I think she would have refused, anyway.

When I had to walk around the garden talking to myself, Franco wanted me to bark gruffly at the leaves on the trees, which went totally against the grain of the text and the meaning. I realised in the end that the trick was not to *try* to be funny at all. But I could never reconcile what I knew about the character with what we were required to do in the production, and I was never happy with it. Peggy Ashcroft later told me that John Gielgud had told her how awful it was, 'with Bob Stephens wagging his arse at the audience all night'.

Eventually, Joan Plowright took over from Maggie. She'd been to see her in it about twenty times and was worried that she couldn't do it. She started by copying her but, as by now I had taken over the direction from Franco, I could tell her to forget all that. She was really much more suited than Maggie to Zeffirelli's idea of Beatrice, and she looked more Sicilian. But she was desperately unhappy in it.

The night before Joan took over the role I took her out to an Italian restaurant. I knew what she was going through – we'd all been through the same wringer. Franco had been given six weeks' rehearsal but he'd chosen to do it in only three. He directed the play like an opera and he didn't help the actors at all. He just produced the dressing around it and you had to find a way to fit into it.

Even the great Alberto, aka Albert Finney, solid as an oak tree, was undermined. He walked on carrying a great big cigar, about a foot long, and it was shaking in his hand like an electric eel. At the dress rehearsal, Frank Finlay took off his hat and stamped on it in rage. On the first night, half the audience booed and half cheered, and everyone walked on not knowing what they were doing. And yet the whole thing was a triumph!

Despite appearances to the contrary, we all hated doing it, and rather agreed with Bernard Levin who said the production was one of the most excruciating evenings currently obtainable this side of Hell. But of course when I saw it from the front, when I was re-directing it, I wept, it all looked so beautiful. And Larry always told us not to worry about it; for the audience, he knew, it was magic, full of high spirits and twinkling away with coloured lights. My old Royal Court friend Bill Gaskill violently disapproved of this production, and you could hardly blame him. It was a travesty of the play and of all the pure work on text we were used to in Sloane Square.

John Osborne had written a wonderful new play in 1965, *A Patriot For Me*, and I was desperate to play the leading role which John told me he had written with me in mind. But I was fully commit-ted at the National Theatre. I went with Larry to see the play in a preview. Maximilian Schell played the role I coveted, Redl, the colonel of humble background in the Austro-Hungarian army, whose ambivalent sexuality leads him into an underworld of blackmail and spying for the Russian army. It's a really great part, and Larry said to me that there were only two actors who could play it: 'You or me.'

At the end of the first act, Redl is discovered in bed with a boy, who leaves him and then he's beaten up. His curtain line is 'Why did I wait – so long?' That is, to express his homosexuality. Max Schell merely whispered the line. I went backstage afterwards and said to Max, who is a fine actor, that, on that line, he should have taken the roof off the theatre. I certainly would have done. And Larry, no question, would have removed not only the roof, but the lagging and the rafters, too.

Alexander Cohen, the American impresario, asked me if I could possibly make myself available to play the part on Broadway. But Anthony Page, who had succeeded Tony Richardson as Osborne's favoured director, was holding out for Richard Burton, Marlon Brando or Cary Grant. The whole idea was ludicrous. Larry at this point said that I could leave the National, but Tony Page buggered around so much that the opportunity slipped away. Max Schell played the role in New York as well, but not for a few years thereafter.

The production that was potentially one of the best ever at the National was John Arden's *The Workhouse Donkey* in 1963, which was part of the opening season in Chichester. It was an extremely amusing musical play which would have been infinitely better if it had been taken apart and really worked on. Frank Finlay was brilliant in it as the Lord Mayor. There was a wonderful gang, all friends, who went there from the Royal Court – Dexter and Gaskill, the directors, and Colin Blakely, Frank Finlay and Joan Plowright. Arden, in my view, should and could have been the most brilliant writer of them all. But nobody did any work on his plays. They were just left to fend for themselves.

In the new Chichester season of 1965, I was in another of Arden's plays, *Armstrong's Last Goodnight*, an essentially dazzling piece, written in an ersatz Scots dialect, which nobody understood. It was a disaster. Everyone worked like demons on it, including Albert Finney in the title role; on the first night, Ken Tynan suddenly produced a glossary to put in the programme. Well, that's no use to you while you're sitting there trying to follow the play in the dark. I was lucky, I was playing the diplomatist Lord David Lindsay of the Mount, I could speak very clearly. I had been sent from Edinburgh to see about these bandits in the Lowlands.

In the first speech, I had to say, 'I'm Lord Lindsay, king of arms, and I'm here to tell ye a lang story anent Johnny Armstrong.' In rehearsals, I had asked, 'What does "anent" mean?' They said, 'About.' 'Well, why can't I say "about"?' They wouldn't hear of it. But 'anent' wasn't a word in common usage, and people thought I said 'went' or 'dent' or 'lent', 'bent' or 'Kent'. The whole show was riddled with these problems of comprehension. Bill Gaskill and John Dexter, who both directed it, were from the Royal Court and because of the old sacred respect for the text as written and handed down like tablets of stone to the humble poor buggers who had to try to make it work on the stage every night, they wouldn't change a thing.

We might just as well have played it in Japanese. It was simply awful. Albert had said, 'I'm going to blow the top off this theatre, and Larry'll shit himself,' and indeed he was magnificent, but you couldn't understand a word he said. He also chose to make his first entrance eating a leg of lamb, so he had not only this terrible accent, but also a mouthful of meat . . . *and*, on top of that, a speech impediment! Which impediment, half way through the play, he loses: another key point in the play 'anent' which the audience remained entirely bloody clueless. The critics, not surprisingly, laid into the play, the directors and poor old Albert.

That 1965 season was incredibly difficult. At one point, our great leader 'El Laurence' went to Moscow on tour with *Othello, Hobson's Choice* and *Love for Love*. He took half the company with him. Every one of the leading company members had gone apart from Maggie (Billie Whitelaw had taken over as Desdemona by this time), Albert, myself, Derek Jacobi and Bill Gaskill. We had a meeting about the repertory and our long-term plans, during which it emerged that Gaskill was intending to return to the Royal Court.

We were all a bit unhappy at Chichester, and we rang John Dexter, who was directing an opera in New York. Dexter had heard that Bill was leaving the National and he said that he felt he could no longer handle Larry by himself, so he was going to leave, too. But we begged him to come over and take charge of things at Chichester and be there for perfectly good directors such as Michael Elliott, who was directing *Miss Julie* with Albert and Maggie. Dexter knew the tricky Chichester stage inside out, and had had many successes on it. So he came.

Soon afterwards, Maggie and I went on tour and were playing *Hay Fever* in Glasgow. Larry had returned from Moscow and flew up to Scotland with Albert to see us and have supper. We had a wonderful time. Larry was on top form. And he invited us all back to his hotel suite, telling the porter to bring up a bottle of brandy.

The door shut. And he started. About John Dexter coming to run the

Chichester season. He gave us the most *terrible* bollocking, language you never thought existed, let alone ever heard. All about how dare we do this and go above his head. We all said it was for the company. He went berserk. You have never seen such a performance in all your life. He played every single part you've ever seen him play, from Heathcliff to Henry V, shouting in that rasping tenor voice. Maggie came back at him on every single point. So then he started to cry. And we were pleading for John Dexter's job.

He quietened down and he said, 'Who made the call to John in New York?' I said that I had. 'You cunt,' he screamed. 'You cunt! And it cost £62 on the phone in my dressing room!' I really thought he was going to kill me. He jumped on top of me in a rage like a tornado. He was totally out of control, though he didn't actually hit me.

Anyway, we managed to talk ourselves out of it. And he did get us more leading actors for Chichester, but he warned us never to do anything like that again, and that if we ever wanted any help we should go to him and never to anyone else. He was right, in the end. But we had acted in total innocence, not in any devious way, and in the best interests of the company, we thought. But this was a preview of the more serious falling out a few years later.

Other than that, Larry was always very nice to me. I was sitting in his office one day and he suddenly said, 'You have one very serious flaw in your acting personality, you know.' 'Oh,' I said, 'what's that?' 'You are the most terrible flirt on the stage.' 'I agree, I am,' I said. 'And I learned from a master.' 'And who was that?' he piped. 'You!'

He really was the most terrible flirt, with all his guile and chucking under the chin, and winks and winning ways. Onstage and off. But at that big row in Glasgow, Maggie matched him emotion for emotion, so when he shouted, she shouted, when he cried, she cried. He could never get one over her, and that was his trouble and why they never really got on.

In the following year, 1966, during the tour of *Armstrong's Last Goodnight*, I was in Manchester with Albert, and Maggie was in Rome making *The Honeypot*, that terrible remake of Ben Jonson's *Volpone*, with Rex Harrison. She flew over one weekend. I said I had some fantastic news for her, but I waited until after my evening performance and we'd had a couple of drinks and sat down to dinner in the French restaurant in the Midland Hotel.

Then I sprung it on her: Beverley Cross had married someone else, a model called Gayden Collins. Instead of being delighted, as I expected her to be, she burst out crying and was inconsolable for the rest of the weekend. I didn't understand it. She'd left the man to be with me, written to him to tell him it was all off between them – she couldn't bring herself to tell him to his face – and now that he'd gone off and married somebody else, she was carrying on like a tragedy queen in the last act.

Still, we muddled through and I thought about finalising a divorce from Tarn. Obviously the whole business was very hurtful as far as Tarn was concerned, but she really believed that my infatuation with Maggie would blow over and that our own marriage would be resumed. She knew about the affair, but assumed it would not lead anywhere. For myself, I was in no great rush to marry Maggie, but the possibility was more practical now that Beverley had married someone else.

One of the highlights of 1966 was an Old Vic gala night to raise money for the George Devine Award for new playwrights. This was an evening of extraordinary magic and, on the personal front, high drama. John Osborne, who was taking part in the gala, alongside Larry, Alec, the dames Edith and Sybil Thorndike, Noël, Albert, Peter O'Toole, Maggie and me, everyone, in fact, cruelly told his wife, Penelope Gilliatt, that he was leaving her for Jill Bennett. John and Penelope had taken a house in Positano for the summer – he was writing a new play – and had returned especially for this occasion. He was talking with Jill Bennett in her dressing room when Penelope, who was sloping around backstage as she was wont to do, knocked on the door. He opened it and said, 'I've left you. I'm going away with Jill.'

Backstage, this carry-on quite overshadowed everything else. It was a celebrity night of bits and pieces: Larry gave his Archie Rice, Alec his Ionesco (*Exit the King*), Albert his Luther and Peter his coruscating Bamforth from *The Long and the Short and the Tall*. The whole evening ended with a shortened version of the first act of *The Kitchen* in which the waitresses included Vanessa Redgrave and Rita Tushingham, the cooks were John Osborne and myself, the head waiter was Larry and the manager, the 'Master', appropriately enough, was Noël. All Noël did was walk around the stage and say how hot it was in here in an accent that sounded so ludicrous you felt he must be sending the whole thing up. But he wasn't. He said later that he was speaking in 'stage common'.

Afterwards, Maggie and I were on the street outside waiting for a taxi, when Penelope found us. She came back to Eldon Road with us and I made spaghetti carbonara, but in my haste to keep everyone happy, I poured all the pasta down the Tweeny in the sink as I transferred it from pan to colander. It was one of those evenings. Penelope stayed the night and said that she was going back to Positano without John: there were still a couple of weeks on the lease of this wonderful house. Maggie and I were free in the National's repertoire, so we took a snap decision and went back to Italy with her. We could therefore be loyal friends while simultaneously enjoying a comparatively cheap holiday. Somehow, Penelope got through the pain of it all by drinking whisky – not just from noon to night, but also from dawn to dusk.

One day, Maggie and I were walking around Positano when we bumped into Peter (aka 'Ruby') Shaffer and the actor Victor Spinetti. Ruby was in a state of high excitement, having spotted Tennessee Williams at a distance. As I knew Tennessee from New York, I told Ruby to calm down and promised to effect an introduction. (Victor Spinetti, incidentally, had been given a copy of Neil Simon's *The Odd Couple* with a view to its London production, and when he read it to me I thought it was one of the funniest plays I had ever heard; I still do, though Victor, who is a wonderful camp actor, was entirely the wrong casting for the mousey little heterosexual fellow, the Jack Lemmon role, who goes around tidying up in his pinafore.)

I tracked down Tennessee. He was staying in Italy in a great house looking right out over the sea and keeping to his usual routine of writing from nine o'clock in the morning until one. Then he would start on the vodka Martinis, have about ten of those, followed by lunch with wine.

He would then go to the beach. In the middle of the afternoon he would go in the sea and swim underwater for about an hour. By packing so much oxygen into his lungs, his brain would be fired and his entire system restored to a state of utter sobriety. At five o'clock, as the boat from Capri came around the rock, Tenn came out of the water, sat on the beach for another hour, then went up to the house to change for dinner and launch once more into the vodka Martinis at 6.30 pm.

I therefore advised Ruby to be on the beach between five and six one afternoon. He sat in a deckchair next to Tenn and delivered the most extraordinary and gushing tribute to a man he described, quite rightly in my view, as 'without doubt the greatest poetic dramatist of the century'. But he did not leave it at that. He went on and on, quoting from the plays and almost turning into Blanche du Bois herself. He was virtually on his knees, prostrate in obeisance. Tenn, who was the most perfectly mannered of men, dripping with refined and tactful Southern elegance, listened to all this and looked at Ruby with a raffish twinkle in his eye and finally said, 'I think you're up to no good!'

Towards the end of 1966 Maggie became pregnant, and Tarn had finally had enough. She gave me a real dressing down and told me that she was going to sue me for divorce. She was terribly upset, and very angry. I could hardly blame her. She had to resort to private detectives and endure the humiliation of hearing them stand up in court and describe our various movements as though we were characters in a Feydeau farce. Only because Maggie was pregnant could the divorce be expedited as quickly as it now was. There was a lot of unpleasant publicity, none of it instigated by ourselves. I kept mum, and so did Maggie, and Tarn was looked after by Joan and Larry. Lucy's primary school teachers in Chelsea were very considerate, too.

Tarn began taking Lucy, and Albert Finney's little boy, Simon, down to Brighton at the weekends to play football with Joan and Larry's children, Richard and Tamsin. They all formed quite a useful little team by the sound of it. Tarn was heartbroken by the failure of our marriage, and I've always felt bad about what happened. But there was nothing I could do. We'd enjoyed a most wonderful love affair, and now my life had changed. Tarn had quite rightly had enough of me. She couldn't sit there and warp her woof for another five or six years, like Penelope waiting for Odysseus, hoping I would get tired of Maggie Smith.

After our decisive break-up in 1967, Tarn went to see Ralph Richardson's Shylock in *The Merchant of Venice* at the Haymarket with our friends Howard Sackler and his wife. They introduced her to an American cancer specialist called Dr Gresser, with whom she went to live in Paris, where he worked, taking Lucy with her. She married Dr Gresser, had two more daughters with him, and eventually separated and divorced.

Tarn acted a little bit while she was in Paris, and did a little teaching work, but she returned to England in the mid 1980s to re-establish her nationality and put her two younger daughters through university: one is reading natural sciences at Cambridge and the other read Politics, Philosophy and Economics at Oxford. Lucy is a successful lawyer, having studied both in London and at the Sorbonne in Paris, and is married with a three-year-old son and another baby on the way. So they've all done very well, and I'm as proud of them as I am of the way Tarn has brought them all up: she puts their success down to the quality of French education.

Tarn still lives in Chilcomb. She gives a big summer barbecue every year which I can never attend because I'm always working. Maybe next year I will. During the girls' school holidays, Tarn became interested in helping old people remember their life stories. She started compiling geriatric memoirs, and has concentrated recently on those of one particular very old lady, who's almost blind and deaf, who lives just about forty-five minutes' drive from Chilcomb. Tarn is employed by her to annotate an immense private library. It is odd to think of her doing that. But I am glad she has found peace of a sort. She put up with an awful lot from me, that's for sure.

I moved into Maggie's flat in Eldon Road. As usual, I travelled light. I had no possessions and was not really bothered about my clothes. I'd had some beautiful suits made while I was in Italy, and Tarn kept asking me to go back and collect them, but I never did. She finally gave them to some gypsies near Chilcomb, so for a time there must have been some incongruously attired tramps, roaming over Hampshire dressed by Gucci and Armani.

Maggie and I carried on our punishing schedule at the National. Whatever the quality of each production, the public wanted to see almost everything we did. Except, I have to say, John Osborne's version of a Lope de Vega piece, *A Bond Honoured* (1966). This was one of the National's most spectacular disasters, and I was lumbered with the leading role. A very long play was condensed down to one act, and I played one of the biggest anti-heroes ever written, which is where Osborne came in. I turned myself inside out to do the damned thing and it didn't work.

I played Leonido, a poor benighted creature who has raped his mother, blinded his father, seduced his sister, assaulted a priest and renounced Christianity. There were not a lot of laughs. I tried desperately hard to be Spanish and spouted away non-stop as the rest of the cast tried to suppress their giggles in the background, moaning and groaning away, which was Dexter's way of trying to get an interesting production going. Instead, it all looked completely silly and trite. John Dexter announced one day in rehearsals that we were going to have some music – a sure sign of desperation – and something called 'Leonido's song'. I now knew we really were in deep trouble.

We rehearsed it for ten weeks, and we lost ten days of performances because of a bad finger injury I sustained while rehearsing one of the endless fights and jumping through a pair of scimitars. I was in every scene and never stopped shouting and stabbing people. We played to no houses at all as the curtain-raiser to Peter Shaffer's *Black Comedy*, a very funny short farce in which a stage full of people bumbling around in a power cut was seen by the audience in full stage light.

We went off, changed our costumes and make-up, and came back: the place would be packed! But, for my pains, I did at least receive marvellous notices. The wretched thing only played for an hour and twenty minutes. I begged Dexter to convince Osborne that he should rewrite my last speech, where the character is crucified like Christ. He wouldn't, or he couldn't, and he agreed that it was a lazy piece of writing. The critics crucified the play. On the second night, Osborne was in a rage, saying he was going round to Irving Wardle's house to throw a brick through his window. I said, 'Why? They're not disagreeing with you or attacking you. They are simply saying what you already know: that this is a lazy piece of writing.'

Larry was always mightily relieved not be appearing in a flop, though he was sympathetic when it happened to the rest of us. His best performance at the National – better, in my view, even than his Othello or his Solness in *The Master Builder* – was another tornado, the Captain in Strindberg's *The Dance of Death*, which was raw and performed totally without guile. It had tremendous contained power, that sense of whatever note you hit there are about a thousand more elements to come. He never varied the performance from night to night; it was incredible to be on stage with him as he recreated an exact replica of what he did in the role on other nights but made it sound as if he had just thought it up.

He was totally in control. Acting for Larry was never about 'letting it all hang out' or irradiating some specious, untethered emotion. I think he dug deep within himself to find the pain and the anguish of his marriage to Vivien Leigh in the Strindberg, but he never wallowed in it. He was always citing the example of Sarah Bernhardt who was reputed to give ninety-five per cent and keep five for herself, which is exactly what he did in that role.

Peggy Ashcroft saw that production, and came round afterwards. She and Larry had appeared together in Gielgud's production of *Romeo and Juliet* in 1935 (Larry and John alternated in the roles of Romeo and Mercutio), and it was reasonably well known that he had harboured an unrequited passion for her ever since. They embraced charmingly and exchanged extravagant, bravura compliments and she had barely shut the dressing room door behind her when Larry said, 'She's had more cock than you've had hot dinners.'

He could be so cutting, and I dread to think what he used to say about me when I turned my back. He never showered you with compliments, but when I played Molière's Tartuffe in 1967 in a disastrous production by Tyrone Guthrie, he did tell Maggie that I was brilliant and that he would never, ever, have thought of doing the part in that way, which is I suppose at least a back-handed compliment!

Guthrie, like Olivier, was a source of golden nuggets of information about one's craft and he directed one of my very long speeches in the Molière as if it was an operatic aria; he made me deliver it as though I was not drawing breath, though of course I was, and he helped me technically. He was rather nervous and behaved accordingly. But he was another great director who expected you, as an actor, to work out your own performance.

He was always famous for concentrating more on the dustman who comes on with three lines than the bloke who is playing Richard III. Larry was relieved not to be in *Tartuffe* because of that, but I found Guthrie enchanting throughout, a genius. Working with Guthrie or Olivier, you never talked about emotional memory or motivation, or what you felt when your dog died, or any of that nonsense. You talked about technical, practical matters and the art of acting at its most basic and essential level.

10

The Unhappy Private Life of Sherlock Holmes

Maggie and I were, for several years, blessed in our relationship. We were living through heady times. Our first son, Christopher, was born in June 1967 and ten days later we were married in Greenwich registry office. We wanted to avoid the glare of too much publicity and so Virginia Fairweather, the National's press officer, fixed a license in Greenwich because one of Maggie's twin brothers, who were both architects, lived nearby in Blackheath.

We moved from the flat in Eldon Road into a 1902 villa on four floors on a little estate in Queen's Elm Square near the Fulham Road. It was a very pleasant house – Maggie still lives there – with plenty of room to be noisy and entertain when we felt like it. We enjoyed the friendship of Albert Finney and Colin Blakely and so many others at the National. The ever loyal Chris Downes, young Christopher's godfather, often came back after the show and we cooked and we drank until dawn, and Chris would stay over and sleep on the sofa. Chris's partner, Illtyd Harrington, the former deputy leader of the Greater London Council, was incredibly busy during this period with the Tourist Authority, and he was also teaching, so Chris had plenty of time for us.

Illtyd, too, became a great friend and I have always relished the fact that we both share exactly the same birthdate. It became a ritual, in fact, that we would all have a lunch party and then a dinner party to follow. Some of these occasions would become very high-spirited indeed.

Everything was marvellous between Maggie and me – living and working together, never out of each other's sight. We were like Siamese twins, day and night, joined at the hip, and without realising it at the time, we were suffocating. And finally we had nothing to talk about except 'You trod on my laugh in the middle of the second act' and that was about it; we'd done it all together all day at work.

Until we started work on the film of *The Prime of Miss Jean Brodie* in 1968, the hit National shows continued in the repertoire, we managed to fit in a couple of television plays together and the good times rolled. Maggie was completely brilliant in *Brodie* and deservedly won the Oscar, and I was doing quite well. And of course if somebody suddenly goes cold on you – as she certainly did – and I had done nothing wrong, well, something's bound to happen. I had not been philandering up until that point. I didn't have time for a start. And I never had the opportunity.

When we started on *Brodie* Maggie went to a doctor and told him that she had very low blood pressure and had to find so much variation in this picture – she was in nearly every shot. She was worried about lasting the course of twelve weeks' shooting and asked for something to keep her going. He proscribed Drynamil and said that if she took one at six every morning, the effect of it would expand over the following twelve hours. It is an amphetamine rather like speed, so you are in fact speeding all the time. It also makes you terribly impatient with everybody else because your mind is working at twice the pace of anyone else's. The Drynamil saw her through the film all right, but in order to sleep at night, she was also on sleeping tablets, Mogadon. It was a very common scene in the Sixties, and I do not wish to blame Maggie for the steps she took to keep going. Even Michael Redgrave washed down his pills with whisky to get through his performances at the Old Vic. Everyone in the theatre was on something or other in those days. But the effects, in Maggie's case, were disastrous, and they finished our marriage almost as soon as it had begun.

A medical friend was horrified when he found out about the Drynamil, threw them down the lavatory and prescribed Valium instead. But Maggie just went spinning on with these Drynamil and it affected our lives. When Maggie was in New York with *Private Lives* much later on, in 1975, she had a minor breakdown of some sort and when the doctor saw the medication, he said that Maggie had become an addict to Drynamil and had been poisoned over the years. They couldn't take her off it straight away, but they weaned her off it gradually. Nowadays, she won't even take an aspirin. But that's what began to screw up the marriage.

She soon became intolerable to live with, snapping all the time, because she was speeding. I took a Drynamil once when I was exhausted, and the effect is extraordinary. You just take off. It didn't matter so much during *Brodie* because we hardly saw each other except on the set; we went through our lines together, or I went off to the National, and then we'd go to bed. But afterwards, we went on holiday to Italy, and she was behaving very oddly, very cutting all the time.

It was like living with knives. She was always ratty and nasty, and for no particular reason. She wasn't the same person I had met six years earlier. She was always sharp-witted, but she became too sharp. There was a change. It was like living with a person who was not just extraordinary to start with, but abnormal in addition. I do think that if it hadn't been for those blasted pills the break-up would never have occurred.

Although I had looked after the production of *Much Ado* after Franco went away, I had not really done any direction, and I thought it was time to have a go. In 1968, I directed a Victorian curtain-raiser for two comedians called *A Most Unwarrantable Intrusion* in 'An Evening of British Comedy' devised by Ken Tynan for the National. Derek Jacobi played a comic in the old style of touring actor's make-up, rubbing red off a brick and hot black (a cake that you spit on, and it's just like a much heavier mascara) on his eyelashes. Maggie came to watch the dress rehearsal with an invited audience.

Derek didn't get one laugh. Disaster. Mystery. Because he's quite a funny actor when he wants to be. I even heard he was quite funny, though unintentionally so, in the RSC *Macbeth* recently. But there's only so much you can do in directing comedy; you can't be funny for them. And it didn't require much. It was good light farce, needing some high comedy playing. He should have been perfect.

Maggie, Derek and myself were going to dinner in Covent Garden. Derek was upset at the cold reception to his performance and he was crying his eyes out; all the hot black was running down his face. I asked Maggie to go on ahead with him to the restaurant while I sat and watched the final part of the triple-bill – John Lennon's *In His Own Write* – and came on later. When I arrived, Derek had calmed down and was all right. I said we'd have a quick run-through tomorrow afternoon before the opening and he went home.

I thanked Maggie and asked her what she had said to him. She had told him that, basically, he was mean and stingy in life, and that his performance was similarly mean and stingy; it wasn't coming beyond the footlights, but stopping dead. There was no generosity. She told him he was too tight-arsed and that he had to give it out. He took all this in good part and his performance the next night was transformed; he came forward and he gave out, and he was very funny. Marvellous, in fact. Now, I can't imagine Maggie ever being a director for one moment, but she certainly knows how to put her finger on what's right and what's wrong in a performance.

As we started filming *Jean Brodie*, it began to make economic sense to think of a second home, a place in the country, and Maggie turned to her brother in Blackheath for advice. This fellow had a practice based in Guildford, Surrey, and he and his wife wanted to move nearer the office. The plan we hatched was for him to find a house big enough to split down the middle with Maggie and me.

He found Tigbourne Court, an 1899 house of considerable interest and quality designed by Edwin Lutyens, situated at Witley, one and a half miles from Chiddingfold and a few more from Guildford. It had a huge garden, designed by Gertrude Jekyll, and walls of Bargate stone, drilled with lead, with red bricks in the chimney stacks and window surrounds. It was all very impressive, and I absolutely loathed it.

The place terrified me. It was like Buckingham Place, as far as I was concerned. Nobody but a complete idiot would have thought of buying it. My father came to see it and he was horrified: 'Nobody today could afford to build this house,' he said. It was like a white elephant which had to be heated, carpeted, furnished. It was unsuitable for the children. It was too big to make cosy, we were never there long enough to enjoy it, and we hardly ever had enough people to stay and make it worthwhile.

I remember, when we had finished making *Brodie*, Maggie was on tour and called me from Yorkshire to say she was going to have another baby. So I thought that's what this is all about, she's building a nest. Miss Brodie was now Miss Broody. But I began to lose touch with what she was really up to, and how our relationship was supposed to develop. Six weeks after Toby, our second son, was born in April 1969, she went straight back to Chichester to appear in *The Country Wife* and I started work on Billy Wilder's film *The Private Life of Sherlock Holmes*. I hardly saw her over the next few months, during what proved a very difficult period of my life. Maggie, the boys and a nanny moved down to Tigbourne Court, while I was left to bang around on my own in Queen's Elm Square.

It was not an ideal arrangement from my point of view. I was fully committed to twenty-nine weeks with Billy Wilder, which was like being put through the meat grinder every day. He was obsessed with perfection. He said he didn't want the film to be good, or very good, but perfect, and he didn't care how long it took. He used to say that the cheapest thing of all on a film was film itself, so he didn't care how much he used. The experience was to prove a turning point in my fortunes, and my marriage.

One important factor in all this was that Maggie had been stung into action by a major rebuff at the National, where Larry had asked her to choose between Viola in *Twelfth Night* and Rosalind in *As You Like It*. Athough, for a few years, our partnership was exploited in the casting at the National, I think Larry was beginning to resent our notoriety as the new 'Lunts'. He messed Maggie around. When she indicated that Rosalind might be the part she should play – and she really should have – Larry announced an all-male production of *As You Like It*. So she played neither role at the National and only ever played Rosalind when she went to Canada ten years later.

Larry did, however, make me an associate director at the National in 1969 because he wanted other actors to feel they could go and talk to an actor about anything. If the problem was not serious, he wanted me to resolve it so that he could deal with everything else. But he was always there, like a long stop. When Charlie Kay joined, for instance, he (Charlie) wanted to buy a house but he couldn't afford a mortgage. He asked me if the National could help with a loan, and so I arranged a meeting with Larry and of course they did.

I also advised Ronnie Pickup to have his teeth fixed, because he had awful gaps in his mouth, he was losing air out the side of his mouth, and he didn't smile properly. I arranged for his bridge work to be done by a dentist friend for as cheaply as possible and docked five per cent of his salary every week until it was paid off. And the dentist gave him a cut price anyway.

When I started work on *The Private Life of Sherlock Holmes* I missed this sort of camaraderie, though I did have Colin Blakely alongside me as Doctor Watson. Billy Wilder couldn't bear going to the theatre, because he couldn't say 'Cut!' He was always terrified that somebody was going to dry, or the scenery would fall down. He told me how somebody had dragged him reluctantly to see *Oh What a Lovely War* in New York one night. He was in a terrible state about going, very nervous, and he sat there just wishing the theatre would catch on fire. Believe it or not, he had been sitting there for just three minutes when a man walked on to the stage and said, 'Ladies and gentlemen, would you please all leave the theatre as quietly and quickly as you can.' It turned out there *was* a fire!

No one was more surprised than me at getting the part. Billy Wilder had nursed this project for some years with his scriptwriter, I.A.L. Diamond, and was at last in a position to cast and shoot it. He had never met me before but had heard about me and seen a couple of my films. I was summoned to meet him at the Connaught Hotel. We had one drink. I didn't read anything, or do an audition. We chatted, and I left. I had lunch with a playwright friend, and when I got home, there was a message for me to ring Maurice Lambert, my agent at Film Rights. Billy Wilder wanted me to play Sherlock Holmes. I was more elated than I had ever been in my life.

I think he had already made up his mind to cast me, because after we had chatted for half an hour or so, he simply said, although I could hardly believe it, 'Well, now, we've got our Sherlock Holmes, but you can't have Laurel without Hardy, so we have to find our Doctor Watson.' He had seen three actors that day and couldn't decide between them. However, when he told me that the third one had left the room and said, 'God bless you,' I knew that must have been Colin Blakely, because it's what he always said. I explained that I already had a working relationship with Colin and that he couldn't do better than cast him.

Colin didn't much enjoy being directed by Billy Wilder, but he seemed to cope with it better than I did. I admired Billy Wilder tremendously, still do, but that kind of obsessive perfection can make an actor feel terribly inept a lot of the time. He used to make you time the putting down of an object at the exact syllable in a word and he never stopped within a millimetre of what he wanted; he only stopped when he got *exactly* the action and the word on the beat together, and that would be one tiny thing in one scene with a million other pieces of direction going on.

I met Jack Lemmon when we went to Hollywood with the National and Billy Wilder threw a party for us, principally for me, as I was about to start work on the film with him. Jack said how much he adored Billy Wilder but that he drove him crazy with all that Germanic regimentation and matching of action to the slightest inflection. This was before I started, so I should have been warned. Walter Matthau used to have a bad time, too. Matthau sort of shambles round a script, with his 'ums' and 'ahs' and 'wells', which drove Billy mad with rage; every word was precious. Izzy Diamond was at every single *Sherlock Holmes* rehearsal, poring over the script as if it were the Dead Sea Scrolls.

Colin Blakely put up with this obsessive exactitude for hours on end and would then say that he couldn't go on any longer. Then Billy would change his mind and say, 'Forget all that, now do it like this.' We would spend hours on a line such as 'If the study door was open . . .' which meant nothing at all, changing the emphasis, banging a gavel or an ashtray on the desk just as we said one or other syllable until the whole thing was squeezed completely dry and you felt like running, screaming, off the set. Which is more or less what I did.

Billy was, and is, an effortlessly witty man, it must be said, as witty, I'd say, as Oscar Wilde or Noël Coward. A real stickler for detail. He told me that the film was a spoof and that I was never to try to be funny. He told me to play it as if I were playing Hamlet and that he would make it funny in the editing. He didn't, as it happens, because I know people who see the tape now still think that the implied homosexuality at the end between Holmes and Watson is meant seriously.

We started off all right with the studio shoot, though in retrospect I was not in the best of health. I had lost a lot of weight at Billy's insistence: he wanted a lean, mean Sherlock Holmes, and I thought this was a good idea. But my strength was sapped after a crash diet. On top of which, we had completed a very exhausting location shoot in Scotland – most of which was finally scrapped – before we started at Shepperton. Billy adored Christopher Downes, who was looking after me and Colin, and bringing in food for us so that we didn't have to go to the ghastly canteen at Shepperton. So good was the fare and the company that Billy and Izzy Diamond never went to the canteen; they always came to our caravan. They were keen on pink gins, and there was always wine to drink.

The whole project became like a prison sentence to me, when it should have been my ticket to stardom. I was hoping the film would do for me what *Lawrence of Arabia* did for Peter O'Toole, or *Tom Jones* for Albert Finney, but I could see from day one that this was going to be very unlikely. Doctor Watson describes everyone who comes in to Baker Street. But there's no description of Holmes except that we know he's very tall, plays the violin, is terrible with women, lives alone, takes cocaine, describes himself as a thinking machine, and has a brother called Mycroft who is much cleverer than he is and works for the Foreign Office. He's an enigma. A totally amorphous creature.

In the middle of shooting, I suffered the most terrible crisis of confidence. The film was getting on top of me, and the demands Billy was making seemed to me increasingly severe. He wasn't sure how we should play Holmes; the film was meant to be an affectionate, light look at the character, but he had asked me not to try to be funny.

He wanted me to be as thin as a pencil, and I wasn't to put on a pound in weight.

I was shooting all day and every day at Pinewood. It is a very lonely life shooting a picture. I was coming home to the empty house in Queen's Elm Square, getting my own food, learning very complicated dialogue for the next day's work. And it had to be learned to the comma, because he would rehearse the scene with his co-writer Izzy Diamond lurking behind him on every shot. You'd do the scene and Billy would say, 'Cut! Are all the words there, Izzy?'

No scene was ever finished or wrapped until every word was exact. Irene Handl played the housekeeper Mrs Hudson. Irene was a Cockney, so of course she translated all Izzy's lines into her own words. But if just one tiny phrase or word did not correspond exactly to the script, Billy would cut and we'd go again. Irene would protest that a Cockney landlady would never say such and such; Billy would say that he couldn't help that and off we'd go again. Then Irene would say that she was a writer herself; Billy would say, yes, he had read her books, they were all wonderful, but that he had taken nine years writing this script and that he wanted it done the way it was written.

There is a sequence in the film – dawn in Baker Street. There was only one time we could shoot that, in what is called 'the magic hour' at dusk. Towards you comes a policeman, swinging his truncheon. He sees something, behind the camera, and steps into a doorway. Past him comes a horse and cart, which is washing the streets. The whole scene had to be set up with enormous care. Billy did it twice with an actor called Bob Todd as the policeman – a very funny actor who was a stooge to Benny Hill – and it went wrong.

Billy wanted it exactly right. He'd lost Bob Todd by now, and so he turned to Chris Downes and hauled him in! Colin popped by and gave him a huge a glass of vodka. But it didn't help. Billy treated Chris like he treated everyone else: he had to get his first foot on this step, his second on that one, avoid that lamppost, swing his truncheon at precisely that moment! He directs, as Shirley MacLaine once said, down to the last eyelash. Chris survived, just about, and you can catch the tiniest glimpse of him swinging his truncheon in the early morning light of Baker Street.

It was all so much more complicated than *Jean Brodie*, and I was working with a genius who knew exactly what he wanted. Billy didn't care how much film he used, even if one little scene took thirty-five takes, it simply didn't bother him. He'd say, 'Listen, I don't want very good; I want it exactly as I want it. I don't have to show the rushes to anybody. I am my own master. We can take as long as it takes.' But it was too long for me.

The endless weight of all this, going in at six every morning, working twelve hours, coming home to an empty house, took its toll. I wasn't drinking particularly heavily; I had no time to. But I found it difficult to cope with by myself, doing my own cooking, trying to learn the lines. I suffered a frightful crisis of confidence. I had been to the same doctor as Maggie and I told him that the film was getting on top of me. He gave me some sleeping pills, enough to kill a horse. One night, mixing them with a bottle of whisky, I was sure I had enough to kill myself.

The next morning the driver taking me to the studio could not get any answer, as I had passed out in the sitting room. The second assistant director rang Chris, who took a taxi over to the house, found a ladder and got in. He rang the studio and I was quickly whipped off to St Stephen's Hospital. They just caught me in time. I had simply had enough, although I hadn't really planned to commit suicide. I did not leave any notes or make any marks. I just drifted away from everything with a bottle of whisky and a pile of pills while watching the television. It was, I dare say, a personality crisis.

I later realised that I was physically debilitated. I had contracted pneumonia three or four months previously at the National, and I had been on some serious medication. My marriage was in disarray. Curiously, when asked for my address at the hospital, I gave them 38 Glebe Place, so poor old Tarn had the press on her doorstep once again. Larry intervened to keep the story out of the newspapers and, once again, he proved a great friend to me, and to Tarn. Billy Wilder's insurance people would not have been too thrilled if the incident had been plastered all over the media. The budget was $10m, which was as big a budget as any film had in those days.

My crisis held up the film for two or three weeks. Billy was terribly upset and said that it was all his fault. But it wasn't, really. It was a culmination of things, and I was terribly embarrassed to return to the shoot. To their eternal credit, Billy and all the team and crew carried on as if nothing had happened, and I was immensely touched by that. He came and said that we'd carry on and finish the picture and that we'd go a little slower and not hurry things. But of course, when I returned, it was all exactly the same! I felt a bit stupid when I went back, but everyone was very kind and I just got on with it. I've never felt like that about anything before or since.

The irony is that although the film was a failure at the time, it has recently been reassessed, and you can now see the full version, with an hour of extra footage that was edited out on the first release. The latest edition of the *Radio Times* film and video guide, for instance, gives the film four stars (five would be 'brilliant') and comments:

Wilder on great form in this revisionist . . . tale of the Conan Doyle sleuth. Stephens and Blakely are excellent . . . more serious and haunted than Rathbone and Bruce would have recognised . . . It's a complex affair involving spoof, homage and reinterpretation – for this is a Holmes obsessed by cocaine and the violin, who plays up to his public image, and flirts with rumours of his relationship with Watson.

11

Shadows of the Evening

Larry was not quite finished with myself and Maggie yet. After this traumatic period, we were invited to rejoin the National on tour to Los Angeles early in 1970 with *The Beaux' Stratagem* directed by Bill Gaskill, and Larry's own production of *Three Sisters*. René Allio, who had designed *The Recruiting Officer* for Bill, also designed the second Farquhar, just as exquisitely. Maggie was given an olive green dress, however, with a very flat, starched front, which looked rather puritanical. She objected to it on two counts: the colour, she felt, was wrong for comedy; and also, her tits were not showing.

Allio argued with her, saying that a lighter colour would not fit with his scheme. So she had another designer in to do her costumes. She won. And she was quite right. She was brilliant as Mrs Sullen. The long speech before the interval about an entitlement to divorce from her ghastly husband had been played by Edith Evans for lots of laughs. Gaskill thought it was more moving than that, and made Maggie stand quite still and just say it. And she did it like that, and was really heart-breaking.

On the first night in Los Angeles, where we played for three weeks before coming to London, she was suffering from an ear infection she had picked up in Jamaica where we had been visiting Noël Coward. So she was taking the Drynamil, and something for her ear, and the drugs interreacted so that she spoke terribly slowly, as if in a kind of dream. But as the evening wore on, the drugs wore off, and she picked up the pace and was absolutely fine.

We had visited Noël lots of times in Switzerland, but never before in Jamaica. That was the first time. Noël had built a holiday house there in the mid 1950s which he named Blue Harbour, and he spent more and more time there as he grew older, writing and painting, cossetted and cared for by his immediate 'family' of his close companion, Graham Payn; his right-hand man, Cole Lesley; and any permutation of four overpowering women – the actress Joyce Carey, the designer Gladys Calthrop, Noël's secretary, Lornie Loraine (Lornie and Gladys were both widows), and Clemence Dane, the playwright. It was an incredibly tight-knit little group which I always found rather sinister. Everything was geared to treating Noël, 'the Master', like some sort of god who had wandered on to earth by mistake.

The routine was that you got up in the morning and had your breakfast and stayed down in Blue Harbour by the pool. At about midday, you were driven up to Firefly, Noël's little one-bedroomed outpost and working 'shack', with a fantastic view over the island. There you would lay about on the lawn – Maggie used to like to stand on her head – have a few drinks and light lunch and at about three o'clock he would say, 'Now, darlings, fuck off.'

And you would indeed do just that and return to the main accommodation down in the bay. At about six thirty, you would go up again and start drinking again. The shuttling back and forth was usually done by Graham Payn, who recorded how Maggie would look at the smiling faces of the locals as we passed by on the unmade track and enquire, in a tone of acidulous mock-concern, 'What strange religious ceremony do the natives believe we come here to observe?'

There was only Graham and Coley in the house when we were there. It was a house rule that all the boys swam in the nude, while the girls were expected to keep their costumes on. This was just as well, because you would never have got Maggie to prance around in the buff. It didn't worry me. Everyone measured up splendiferously, especially Noël; they all looked as though they had weights hanging at the end of their cocks.

Noël used to surprise you sometimes with his vulgarity. I remember that when John Dexter had been sent out to Switzerland a few years earlier to show him the model of the set for *Hay Fever*, and the costume designs, he was flabbergasted to be suddenly asked, in the middle of dinner, 'Do you take it up the arse?' John was quite puritanical and working class about these things, so he stuttered and blushed a bit before saying, 'Well, yes, I do as a matter of fact.' 'I don't,' replied Noël. 'Far too small.'

He always used to say of me, in that fluting, cut-glass way of his, 'I have never, ever, seen Bob Stephens give a bad performance,' which, let's face it, was a line to cover all circumstances. Bernard Shaw used to have a similar ploy when compelled to visit friends in dressing rooms after disappointing plays: 'Good isn't the word!' he would cry as he advanced towards the trembling thespian. And Ivor Novello, I'm told, used to storm every dressing room he entered with his arms wide open, yelling at the top of his great Welsh voice, 'Isn't it *marvellous*?!' Noël was genuinely fond of me, I think, and he adored Maggie, whom he once accused, not disapprovingly, of being even more common than Gertie Lawrence, his favourite leading lady.

I loved his stories about Maggie Leighton and Vivien Leigh staying there when their affairs and relationships broke up; they cried and drank so much, he said, that there was dew on the carpet in the morning. He wouldn't tolerate Maggie's moaning about Laurence Olivier in comedy, about his being too heavy, and a bastard. 'I've seen him be terribly funny in comedies all my life. I won't hear you say these things about him. But,' he said, 'I admit he does have one fatal flaw. He is incorrigibly jealous. Years after he was in *Private Lives* with Gertie and me, he admitted that the demon operated even then, and he was eaten with envy of me while enjoying a much needed success!' But the thing about Larry was that he was jealous of everyone, whatever they did, if he felt they did whatever they did better than he could. This gnawing dissatisfaction made him terribly unhappy all his life.

Soon after that visit to Jamaica, Noël was in London, staying at the Savoy Hotel. He was not very well and was confined to his bed. His doctor told me that he had an infection of the anus caused by years and years of wearing very tight shoes. If you wear tight shoes, your legs are in a permanent state of tension, and your anus perpetually contracted. It sounded a bit far-fetched to me, but there we are.

Noël made me promise to go and see him every day after rehearsals, which was easy enough to do as we were just over the river rehearsing *Hedda Gabler*, and we never worked for more than three or four hours each day. Noël also made me swear to take him a present on each visit. I took chocolates, a handkerchief, cologne and one of those riddle rings, very popular at the time, which fell to pieces when you took them off. He loved his gold riddle ring.

But he was even more thrilled when, one day, I took in Twiggy as his 'live' present for the day. She was about to make the film of *The Boy Friend* and was learning how to tap-dance. Noël insisted that we rolled back the carpet in his suite and that she tap-danced for him there and then. Which she did, very well. He absolutely adored her.

Looking back on it now, I think Maggie and I were best together in *Hedda Gabler* in 1970, directed by Ingmar Bergman in which, again, she was absolutely brilliant. Larry had wanted to cast me as Tesman, the dull husband, and Jeremy Brett as Loevborg, the lover. But I persuaded him to switch us round, so you had something more unexpected and original. Jeremy was a wonderfully quiet and watchful Tesman and I suppose my Loevborg made a change from the usual Byronic wreck. I tried to play him as someone who really might write a great book one day, unlike poor old George Dillon, for whom the gift of a typewriter in the last act of Osborne's play was obviously superfluous to his future.

Larry had initially asked Ingmar Bergman to direct *The Dance of Death* but had received no reply. He went to Sweden and saw his production of *Hedda Gabler* and was determined to have it in the National. So he wrote to him and offered him Maggie Smith and the rest of us, and still got no reply. He telegrammed, telephoned, left messages, wrote more letters. Still no reply.

One day, Larry found out that Ingmar was staying at the Savoy Hotel, so he went and banged on his door. And he agreed to direct *Hedda Gabler*, though he didn't really want to. 'This man, Lord Laurence' – he always used to call him that, long before he was a lord – 'this man, is a warlock. I didn't want to do it. We went to lunch and on the way into the Grill I was saying no, and on the way out I was saying yes. He's a warlock.'

He was busy with a new film but he agreed to do a week of rehearsals and then Larry would take over. But in that first week, Larry kept chipping in with ideas, and Ingmar turned them all down and eventually banned him from the room. He then went away for a month and we rehearsed on our own, then he came back and polished it up. But I was the one who had to go and tell Lord Laurence that he was fired from Ingmar Bergman's production!

Ingmar was adamant that we rehearsed every day between eleven and three and that was all. We knew we couldn't change anything because if we did, we would be in the dark. He lit the play like a film, and it was an unbelievably complicated lighting plot. He surprised Maggie by asking her if she'd ever had any lesbian feelings, because of the scene where she suddenly makes a remark about Mrs Elvsted's hair and pulls at it quite savagely. He made her touch it, caress it, much more gently, which was much more terrifying. But Maggie wasn't having any of the lesbian suggestiveness.

We all loved the way the rehearsals were so concentrated, even when he wasn't there. No one else was allowed in the room, there were no newspapers, no distractions, no fooling around, no leaving or coming back in. The door was locked. And that suited Maggie down to the ground. You would think that Bergman was a very humourless, grey kind of person, whereas the truth is exactly the opposite. He was the most enormous fun, very witty. He insisted on the actor always being there for the whole of the act he was first in, so that he knew what he was going into. Also, he had to know what happened after he left.

He couldn't get anywhere with the girl playing Auntie Julia, and I told him that it wasn't his fault, she was just miscast. 'Do you think it would help if I went up and tweaked her bosom?' he asked. Every single woman just fell for him. He had an extraordinary understanding of women. I like to think I do, too, but I'm afraid that's more hope than certainty.

I introduced him to Mia Farrow, whom I had known since the days at the Royal Court, when she and André Previn, to whom she was married, were regulars on the 'Swinging Sixties' party circuit along the King's Road. Ingmar was totally beguiled with her. We all went off together to see a television film I'd made of *The Seagull* because she was thinking of playing Nina and the BBC arranged a showing. Ingmar explained why the last act didn't work because it had been played as Nina's return rather than as Konstantin's farewell before he shoots himself, and he talked and laughed and took us all back to his suite in the Dorchester.

He ordered beers to be brought up. Mia was saying she had to get back to the country and her family, and Ingmar insisted everyone stayed, but I managed to whisk her away to Victoria Station. Mia said, 'That man is extraordinary. He's a magician. If I had stayed another five minutes, I would have stayed all night.' He knew every trick in the book.

During the run of *Hedda* I had my fortieth birthday. My date of birth is exactly the same as that of Chris Downes's partner, Illtyd Harrington, and we always tried to celebrate this double occasion together. Our shared birthday parties were an essential part of our lives. Some were enormously successful, and some less so. This one was a real catastrophe. I booked a table on the patio in the Meridiana in the Fulham Road and invited Chris Downes and Illtyd, Jeremy Brett and Nicola Pagett, Dave Allen and his ex-wife Judith Stott, and various other people, including our dentist, Brian Kanarek and his wife, a not unattractive but rather stringy woman, who made a pass at me while we were studying the menus and later accused me of making a pass at her.

Chris was sitting next to Nicola Pagett and I told him to give her a kiss. So he turned around and kissed her on the lips. She promptly put her tongue in his mouth, which gave him the most frightful shock, especially as he thought she was actually Jane Merrow and had been animatedly discussing her performance in *A Lion in Winter* with her just beforehand.

It was absolutely freezing cold. The waiters were not at their best. The food was not hot. Jeremy at one point popped over the road to Queen's Elm Square to bring a pile of old sweaters for everyone. Maggie was in one of her foulest moods, not without good reason, as Illtyd, Chris and I had been merrily drinking away all day and we were already becoming quite noisy.

We all went back to the house to warm ourselves up and drink some more. Jeremy Brett put on his own record of *The Merry Widow* and was kind enough to start singing along with himself. Maggie was very cross indeed as we all got drunker and drunker, and the boys were asleep upstairs. So there were reverberations from that evening for a while.

Our married life was going downhill and I found the responsibilities of the associate directorship very worrying, too. I was surrounded by accomplished, deadly politicians like Larry and Ken Tynan, and I was not a political animal. I'm not a wily, scheming or manipulative sort of person and I suppose I had been placed in a situation beyond my strength. It was a dangerous time for me. Whatever my shortcomings, I'm a straightforward innocent abroad. There was no question of them undermining me, though Larry was certainly toying with both Maggie and me by then.

It was more a case of me failing to see how I might be upsetting them when I suggested productions that might be suitable vehicles for Maggie and I which they didn't really want to have anything to do with. The misunderstanding arose that in some way Maggie and I were planning to set up our own shows in Los Angeles and New York on National Theatre notepaper. Nothing could have been further from the truth, but Larry eventually became convinced we were out to get the better of him.

The upshot of all this misery and misplaced doubt was that I was drinking too much. I used to drink in the offices in Aquinas Street and was often the worse for wear on stage during *Hedda Gabler*, though luckily it never showed. I was even morbid enough to keep a gun, admittedly only a pellet gun, but a gun all the same, in the dressing room, which was a rather gloomy Ibsenite touch.

As an associate director in 1969, I was given an office and a telephone and I always said to Larry, 'If there's anything I can do, just let me know.' But he never wanted to be made to look as though he depended on anyone. Basically, one just said yes, yes, yes. If you said no, you got the frosty eye. I went very quiet, for instance, when he came up with the idea of doing *Guys and Dolls* and him playing Nathan Detroit. It was a terrible idea, encouraged by Ken Tynan.

None of us could sing or dance. Joe Mankiewicz, who had directed the film, heard about it from Maggie and thought we'd all taken leave of our senses. He told us that he hadn't even wanted Frank Sinatra as Nathan because he wasn't a good enough dancer. His choreographer, Michael Kidd, had got hold of twelve of the best dancers in America and rehearsed them for three months.

You used to hear people like Geraldine McEwan wafting around singing 'A poison could develop a cold . . .' It would have been ghastly and although I gather it was okay in the end when Richard Eyre *did* do it at the National, they brought in singers and had pretty lightweight casting in the leads. I felt very strongly about it and organised a round robin asking who wanted to be in *Guys and Dolls* which perhaps I shouldn't have done. Nobody did, apart from understudies and small part players and Geraldine McEwan. I wasn't going to have anything to do with it. Broadway musicals require a special technique and we don't have it here, or at least we didn't then. The musical was dropped.

Joan Plowright then accused me of ganging up against Larry and I was mortified. Unlike Frank Dunlop and Ken Tynan, I did not go around joining partisan factions and whispering in corners. So she then delivered what she thought was her *coup de grâce*: 'Well, what were you doing having lunch in the Savoy with Lord Chandos?' Chandos was the chairman of the board of governors. I said, 'Because he asked me and Mags to lunch. The National Theatre was mentioned. Twice.' At this time Larry was becoming increasingly paranoid and thought I was after his job. We had been to Los Angeles with *The Beaux' Stratagem* and *Three Sisters*, and we'd had a triumphant success.

But what riled and worried him was that, as a result of that visit, we forged a separate working possibility with my old friend Mike Nichols, whom I had first met when I played George Dillon in New York. While we were in Los Angeles, Mike rang up and invited me over. I was thrilled, because I knew he was slated to come to the National to direct *Long Day's Journey Into Night* with Larry playing the father, Celia Johnson playing the mother, and myself and Ron Pickup playing the brothers.

Nichols turned on me and, inexplicably, attacked me for letting him down, and not telling him the truth. He went on and on, and I had no idea why. Apparently, the production was now off, but this was the first I'd heard of it. Larry had read the play, I later discovered, having first agreed to do it without reading it, and had chucked the script across the room saying, 'I'm not playing some loud, foul-mouthed drunken Irish cunt,' and that was that. But only Nichols had been told at this point.

So as we talked further, we agreed to work with each other, anyway, on a production in Los Angeles a year hence of Noël's *Design for Living*, with myself and Maggie. I arranged the rights with Noël, had all the costumes made in England, and I employed Ingmar Bergman's set designer, Mago. The idea was to produce the play in Los Angeles and then take it back to Larry, and the National repertoire, at the Old Vic. It was probably terribly naive of me to think that I was doing the National a favour by operating in this way, but I genuinely thought it was a good idea.

A few months later I was in Venice when I received a call from Mike Nichols's lawyer saying that the money we were paying Nichols wasn't enough. We were only doing a six week run, and he wanted a huge sum, plus a split of the profits; well, we were only doing it because we thought it would be fun, and worth doing, whereas Mike, I now realised, did not really do anything without counting the dollars – in millions. He simply didn't work for less than ten million dollars.

And so finally he pulled out. We employed Peter Wood in his stead and confirmed that the production would open at the Ahmanson Theatre in Los Angeles and then enter the National repertory. At this point I went to Larry and presented the whole idea to him. He made out he was happy, but insisted that the Ahmanson paid $100,000 into the production before it began. This was an unreasonable demand. The theatre had no such money to guarantee. The subsequent row between Larry and myself over this point marked the real beginning of the end between us.

Everything was coming to a point of no return. It was clear that Larry was trying to exclude us from the future of the National. He considered that we were ganging up on him and maybe felt that I was after his job. Nothing was further from my mind, but I did want to ensure my own acting reputation and felt I had *some* grounds for taking the initiatives that I had. I was, after all, supposed to be an associate director. However, Joan always felt, I later discovered, that I was betraying Larry by even talking to Mike Nichols and suggesting a link-up between the Ahmanson and the National. But I was only operating within parameters set by the

National's already established association with the Ahmanson. We had been there, and scored an enormous success, in 1970.

After Larry's demand of $100,000 fee upfront proved impossible to accept, the Ahmanson decided to go ahead anyway by forming a company with Bobby Fryer, the Ahmanson's director, Maggie and myself. The company was called BMB – ie, Bobby, Maggie, Bobby – and *Design for Living* was our only production. We got off the ground and promptly fell to earth. Bobby had been an executive at Twentieth Century Fox when that company had been setting up the film of *The Prime of Miss Jean Brodie* and had been instrumental in persuading them to cast Maggie in the title role over their preferred choice of Deborah Kerr. The show was never going to be a National project by this stage, but I concede in retrospect that Larry, paranoid as ever, must have thought we were trading on our National credentials. We were simply protecting our lives as actors.

Ironically, of course, by this time, Maggie and I were getting fed up with each other and I used to say why don't you write to Paul Scofield asking him to do a play with you here at the National, or in the West End? Apart from anything else, he would be enormously flattered. And it's always best to work with the best. Otherwise she should have been teamed with Colin Blakely, or John Stride, to make a change from me. I wondered, too, how my career was going to develop. It was obvious that I should be playing Leontes, Antony, Macbeth, and the realisation dawned on me that Larry was never going to offer me those parts at the Old Vic. As far as he was concerned, I had grown too big for my boots.

He felt that I had betrayed him. The golden age was coming to an end.

12

Tangled Webs and Trick Cyclists

I used to think Maggie fell out of love with me and in love with her career but that wasn't quite right. It was a combination of many factors. The pills seemed to trigger everything off. The house at Guildford did not help matters much. And the closeness of our working lives, together with Larry's increasing frostiness, combined to exacerbate the overall unhappiness. For me, it was particularly hard to bear the sadness of being cast out by my mentor. But that is essentially what happened. Maggie was never going to be affected in the same way.

We had really good times on the whole. Maggie, when she chooses to be, can be as gregarious and sociable as anyone. We would often go to the West End together, and she was always going out with our friend Christopher Downes if I wasn't around. We weren't terribly good at holidays together because I love the sun and splashing around in pools and she much prefers the shade and a good book. Her skin's too fair. She'd often just be sitting in the bedroom reading while I sauntered along the promenade or the beach.

We may well have looked like an ideal couple to the outside world. And to a certain extent we were. Until after we made *Brodie*. She did very well and she got what she wanted. She had left the West End, where she was a huge, highly paid star, against all the advice of her pals, to join the National. She took certain decisions, I feel, with cold deliberation and when I came along she decided it was time to get married and start a family. So we got married, had a baby, bought a house and everything was going according to plan.

If I'd realised earlier the effect the pills were having on Maggie, and in consequence on me, maybe something could have been done to avert the break-up. But I daresay the fact that I didn't know, and she didn't tell me, reflected on the state of our deteriorating relationship anyway. And when she went cold on me it was hardly surprising that I started to look around elsewhere. I was treading on very thin ice, and it was only a matter of time before the truth of what I was getting up to got out.

Over the next couple of years, 1971 and 1972, everything was very tricky. I played Rasputin on the television, in a huge two-part drama, and the role required a very complicated make-up, to put it mildly. I stipulated the best make-up girl possible, because I wanted to make myself up as I would for the stage and then have it adapted for the camera. So, along with the wig and the beard and the moustache, came this adorable make-up girl called Daphne.

I was then going to play Oberon, King of the Fairies, in *A Midsummer Night's Dream* on television, for the same producer, Cedric Messina, so along came Daphne again. I felt, because of Oberon's row with Titania over the Indian boy, the make-up should be Oriental. I had lipskin tied on with lace on either side of my eyes, so that my skin was pulled back from my eyes. When the lace was removed it created a startling Eastern effect. It was all very complicated. Well, not surprisingly, over this long period of several months, I fell in love with this make-up girl, who was married but not happily married. It was my television studio romance.

Also, working for our dentist, Brian Kanarek, who was a great friend, and one of the most distinguished dentists in London, there was a very beautiful girl, a receptionist called Carmen. Carmen 'Rollers' was Maggie's name for her, when the truth was out. Carmen was also the dentist's girlfriend, but she was extremely flirtatious. I asked her if she was having a fling with Brian, but she assured me that it was all finished. Meanwhile, Maggie was in Spain making one of her more dreadful films, Alan Pakula's *Love and Pain and the Whole Damn Thing*. He should have been making a film about us, with that title. So I called up Carmen and suggested a trip to Paris the following weekend. Off we went.

However, Carmen kept on about Brian, saying he was very possessive. Then a few weeks later she telephoned and said that Brian had gone away again to Majorca. I insisted that I was not going to see her again if there was still anything going on with Brian. He was a friend of ours and I didn't want to cause any trouble. She said that there wasn't anything lingering in their affair, so we carried on having a good time together for ten days or so. A few weeks later, Jeremy Brett was giving a party in his flat in Notting Hill Gate, and Carmen and I arrived in a taxi cab. And there was Brian Kanarek standing on the doorstep.

Well, he went bonkers. He drove her off down the road in a fury and the next day I got a call from Carmen saying that if Brian found me within the next twenty-four hours, he would kill me. Jeremy Brett panicked and said I should go and stay in a shop in the New King's Road where he was a partner, pointing out that Brian Kanarek had been a boxing champion at school and was also a karate expert. He insisted, although I protested that he was being silly and that we weren't in a Warner Brothers gangster movie. I refused to go to ground in this melodramatic fashion and instead went along the next morning to see Brian in his surgery to talk the thing through, telling him that Carmen had assured me that there was nothing going on any more between them.

Brian said, 'Okay, I'll swallow that. But you've got to tell Maggie.' I said, 'I can't possibly do that,' and he said, 'You've got to be honest for once in your life and tell her exactly what's going on.' I reminded Brian that Maggie was a puritanical Scots woman and that any such news would finish her off, and ruin my marriage. I said I couldn't do it, and what's more, I wouldn't do it. And he said, 'If you don't do it, I will. I shall call her tonight. And besides, she's got an appointment next week and I can't have all this hovering in the air between us.'

And he did. Things went from bad to worse because I'd taken the make-up girl, Daphne, along to see Brian to try to work out something with her on the right sort of teeth to go with the make-up, which was another horrendously complicated job, for a film I was going to make with Glenda Jackson about Queen Isabella of Spain (it never happened). The king, whom I was supposed to be playing, was an incredibly ugly man, so this entailed another major prosthetic job. I wanted a second set of teeth to go over my own and change the entire shape of my mouth.

This was a bit stupid of me, because of course Brian twigged immediately what was going on between me and Daphne and he told Maggie about that as well. And indeed, when Daphne, ironically enough, turned up soon afterwards on the BBC *Merchant of Venice* set in which Maggie played Portia, they had to keep hiding her in cupboards because Maggie would certainly have killed her, had they come face to face. As Maggie told Alan Bennett at the time, after everything had come out in the wash, that the quality of mercy was very, very strained whenever Daphne appeared on the set.

Brian arranged a big show-down. He, Maggie, Carmen 'Rollers' and

I had a summit confrontation in his surgery in Devonshire Place. On top of all *that* torture, Maggie and I had a secretary called Sheila Pickles, a real middle-class respectable Yorkshire girl from Halifax. She had worked for Franco Zeffirelli at the big agency, London Management. Then Franco pinched her to go and work for him as his secretary in Rome and Positano, when she was about eighteen. She was a gorgeous creature.

Franco bought her a flat in Rome and a huge pile of children's stories in Italian, so she learned the language by reading these simple books. I had known her for ages. Working with Franco was driving her mad, and she used to burst into tears about it every time she saw us in London. I told her that she had to get out of Franco's household with all those evil old queens screaming and shouting at her all day before it was too late and she turned into a dumpy old frump. So, with Franco's full agreement, she left him and came to work for us in London. He knew it was time for her to go.

I was very attracted to her and when I had to go over to Los Angeles to finalise the casting on Peter Wood's production of *Design For Living* in 1971, Maggie said, 'Take Sheila with you.' Which was rather silly of her. She knew that Sheila was no angel. Maggie, being not that way inclined herself, loved to sit and talk for hours on end with Sheila about her past affairs. Maggie said it would be a nice break for Sheila, someone to travel with, and that we could see to the production, sort out the house we'd rented on the beach at Malibu and stock it with food. I protested that Sheila should stay with her and the nanny and the children. But she insisted.

Finally, Sheila and I flew to Los Angeles and were met at the airport by Bobby Fryer, the co-producer at the Ahmanson where the play was going on. He drove us to this house at Malibu, stopping for something to eat en route. We arrived at that house after midnight, it was a wonderful evening, we walked out on to the beach and – la-la-la – of course, it happened. We had an affair for a week but of course we kept it to ourselves, because if Maggie had so much as sniffed anything she would have gone nuts.

Later in the same year, I had to go to Switzerland to see Noël Coward about *Design For Living* and then to Positano to see Franco about some other projects we were hoping to plan for the future. And Maggie said, 'Let Sheila take you in the car to Montfleur and then drive you down to Italy!' I couldn't imagine what was going on in the back of her mind and even began to wonder if she wasn't scheming my downfall in her own eyes.

I had already been on my own in a beach house for a week in Malibu with a girl I'd known for years and years, and to whom I was already very close. And she knew that Sheila put it about a bit. And now this! So we drove to Paris and stopped overnight and, naturally enough, we jumped straight into bed with each other and it started all over again.

And of course it all came out at once. Maggie found out about Sheila Pickles because we were all in the same house at around the same time as she found out about Carmen 'Rollers' and the make-up girl. It was all terribly unfortunate. Mind you, I've no idea how I managed to keep all three of those delightful women going at the same time, but I did, just about.

Brian Kanarek's contribution to the developing catastrophe was to suggest that I go into a nursing home, which was really some kind of glorified private mental hospital in north London. I had certainly behaved badly, but I don't think I deserved to be talked to like a madman, which was how they talked to you in this place. It was a private hospital and, by being there, of course, you are earning a lot of money for them. I was in there for about two or three months; and the trouble is that, once you are in one of those places, you start to believe that there really *is* something wrong with you.

The only really constant friends I had through all of this were Christopher Downes, whom Maggie did like very much, and Jeremy Brett, whom Maggie did not like at all. They really were my life-savers. Everything seemed to be falling apart. Larry had convinced himself – quite wrongly – that Maggie and I had set up that Los Angeles production of *Design for Living* on National Theatre notepaper. Our days were numbered there, and I had offended my mentor, my greatest friend and hero. My private life was a shambles. I was at rock bottom.

Jeremy took me to the nursing home, where they wouldn't accept me at first because I was drunk; I was so desperate I had found a bottle of vodka in Jeremy's flat, where I had stayed the night before, and swallowed most of it. But they eventually took me in and gave me a shot of sedatives. Two nights later I skipped out and went to find Jeremy at his theatre – he was appearing in John Mortimer's *A Voyage Round My Father* at the Haymarket. I was very unhappy, and in a terrible state. But I went back into the nursing home until I could stand it no longer.

At this point Jeremy took me home and looked after me. People often assume that we must have been lovers, but our friendship, forged in those early days in Manchester, went far deeper than that. I'm afraid that the idea of jumping into bed with a hairy-arsed sailor, let alone Jeremy Brett, who is an immensely attractive man, fills me with horror.

Christopher Downes, whom Maggie and I knew equally and of whom we were, and are, equally fond, was in a rather awkward position during this period. I think Maggie gave him a pretty tough grilling and forced a lot of details out of him. It got to the point – he shouldn't have said it, but he did – when he clearly implied to Maggie that if she wanted to know what was going on she should ask Sheila Pickles. Well, the poor girl was working in the house, and was also Maggie's closest confidante and friend.

When Maggie turned on her, she was understandably backing up in terror against the wall, and she said, 'Oh well, it only happened in Paris . . .' And of course when I was alone with Maggie, I told her it had only happened in Malibu. So it was all a terrible mess. Funny when you think of it in farcical terms, but a terrible mess all the same!

When the shit hit the fan, we were in the bedroom in Queen's Elm Square and Sheila Pickles was downstairs in the drawing room. Maggie's reaction was to go into the bathroom and vomit. Which I thought was extraordinary. And she said that she would either forget and not forgive or forgive and not forget, I can't remember which, and started punishing Sheila Pickles.

Maggie didn't fire Sheila Pickles. She stayed on, although her life became miserable. There was an awful lot of coming in and banging of doors and 'Oh, what's going on here, then?' sort of remark. Sheila was finally offered another job back at the agency on the literary side, so she left.

Christopher Downes told me that Maggie was driving somewhere in town with him in the car one day when they suddenly saw Sheila Pickles crossing the road. Maggie half-jokingly muttered out of the side of her mouth, 'Shall I run her over?' This was the aside not of a Joan Crawford but of a wounded wife being witty. She's brilliant behind the wheel, Maggie, quite literally; she's a very good driver indeed. Whereas I don't drive at all. Never saw the point of it and it never interested me. I said once that if it bothered her I would buy a very fast MG sports car and that would be the end of it. Which it certainly would have been for anyone unfortunate enough to be in the car with me. But she told me not to bother.

The marital squabbling continued without respite until Binkie Beaumont suggested we did *Private Lives* in 1972 and called us into his office on top of the Globe in Shaftesbury Avenue to ask us who should direct it. Maggie affected indifference and said that she didn't care, though of course she does when it all starts going wrong, as it did for her years later, in 1993, on *The Importance of Being Earnest.*

Our performance together in *Private Lives* was the last-ditch attempt to salvage something from the marriage, and Binkie was the broker, just as he had been when he tried to help Maggie Leighton after she had been deserted by Laurence Harvey. He had always been very annoyed that Maggie had joined the National soon after she had established herself as a West End star, but Binkie was now coming towards the end of his life and was feeling magnanimous. Within the year, both he and Noël would be dead, popping off within a few months of each other in 1973. This was to be their last big splash in the old-style West End together; and it was the end of Maggie and me.

Maggie refused all the directors she was offered by Binkie – Bill Gaskill ('No'), Lindsay Anderson ('No'), John Dexter ('No'), Peter Wood ('No, no, no, no, no!') and finally Binkie said, 'What about Johnny G?' And she said 'Yes,' and John Gielgud said to us that we didn't really need a director for Coward, we needed a conductor. There's no action (apart from the second act fight), just the music of people talking. And the fight, he said, we had to do ourselves because he was no good at comic business. So we did. And we thought that the show might save the marriage, but of course it didn't.

However, we played to capacity business at the Queen's Theatre and audiences seemed to enjoy the production. Coward himself unwittingly stated what was going on in our real private lives, when Maggie's character, Amanda, says: 'I think very few people are completely normal really, deep down in their private lives. It all depends on a combination of circumstances. If all the various cosmic thingummys fuse at the same moment, and the right spark is struck, there's no knowing what one mightn't do. That was the trouble with Elyot and me, we were like two violent acids bubbling about in a nasty little matrimonial bottle.'

That tragic dilemma of two people who love each other too much to be able to live together was horribly appropriate. I learned much later on that Gielgud had misgivings over my performance as Elyot, but that may have been because I dug quite deeply under the surface. There's an awful lot going on in that play, and I must say, having come back from the brink of suicide during the filming of *Sherlock Holmes*, I could appreciate the call to triumphant triviality.

There is a quality of savage hedonism about Elyot which no doubt reflected the last-gasp quality of my life with Maggie: 'Let's blow trumpets and squeakers, and enjoy the party as much as we can, like very small, quite idiotic schoolchildren. Let's savour the delight of the moment. Come and kiss me, darling, before your body rots, and worms pop in and out of your eye sockets.'

Elyot is indeed defined in the play as Amanda's first real love, a man who drinks and knocks her about and to whom only the worst part of her was attracted. I have never been physically violent in my personal relationships, but there was something here that fitted rather well. I remember one night in the wings, before going on, Maggie spoke to me gravely in the style of the play we were performing: 'You know, the problem is, Robert, I love you, but I don't think I like you very much.' Or it might have been the other way round. 'Snap, snap, snap, like a little adder,' jeers Elyot. 'Adders don't snap; they sting,' scoffs Amanda. It was just how we talked to each other at home.

The show was not at all well received by the critics. Harold Hobson, in particular, accused Maggie of resorting to the same old bag of tricks, so she was in nearly as unhappy and insecure a state as I was. At around this time we both went to see a half-German psychiatrist called Krauppell Taylor who, in his youth, had been a favourite pupil of Jonathan Miller's father, who was a distinguished child psychiatrist. He wanted to know why I had told Maggie about all the romancing, and I said that Brian Kanarek had advised me to come clean. He thought that I'd made a big mistake.

His advice to me was, 'In your life, be circumspect. Don't act on instinct. Think before you jump. You must never say to a woman that you have been unfaithful to her. Never. They are creatures too delicate to handle it. You may think women are stronger than men, they have babies and so on. But they are not. If you are unfaithful, they assume that you are telling them that they are either ugly, unattractive or getting too old. None of which need necessarily be the case. But that's what they think. So keep your lip buttoned when you play around.' I have followed this advice almost religiously ever since.

Binkie Beaumont, increasingly distressed by our bickering, rang Jeremy up to ask if he could do anything to help, and I moved out of Queen's Elm Square and went to live with Jeremy in Notting Hill for about six months.

Again I was desperately unhappy and there's no doubt that the booze was within me and I'd lost my way. But the booze was only a painkiller. My career was at the crossroads, my marriage had failed and there seemed to be nowhere for me to go.

I left the production – Maggie was joined in the cast by John Standing as Elyot – and went off to the Chichester summer season of 1973 to play Trigorin in *The Seagull*, directed by Jonathan Miller. This was the one and only time I really made good use of Tigbourne Court: I lived there, and had the boys there, and I used to invite the company over. When you had the place full with twenty-five people, it worked. Otherwise, it was a waste of time. A tremendous amount of drinking went on. Tony Hopkins came over and played Skryabin endlessly and brilliantly; he's a concert class pianist.

Maggie Leighton returned to my life a little during that season. She and Michael Wilding, to whom she was now married, had a place near Chichester called Gauntlet Cottage, known locally as 'Vodka Villa'. They came to the show and invited me out for dinner afterwards. In the theatre, she and Michael, who were with the actor Charles Gray, were all drinking quadruple vodkas. When she came round afterwards, I heard her say to Irene Worth in the dressing room next door: 'You've got a fucking big voice, why aren't you using it?'

Then she came in singing 'Daisy, daisy, give me your answer do', and Charles Gray was brick red and cross about something in the production, and Michael Wilding droned on for about half an hour about how boring everyone in Chekhov was because they just droned on for so long. It was like being in a nightmare. Maggie suddenly turned on Charles and accused him of getting them off on the wrong foot that morning by making the Pimm's with cider. In the restaurant, Maggie started singing again, 'Chase Me, Charlie', and Charles was incredibly rude to the waiters and started drinking stingers, which are crème de menthe and brandy on crushed ice – lethal – and making a fuss about his potatoes, in that enormously loud voice of his.

He was playing a very rude character in some television sitcom at the time, and as we left the restaurant, he apologised loudly for being a bore but said that one just had to take him as one found him. I said, 'Not at all, Mr Gray, it's a pleasure to see you and to experience at first hand the fact that you can be as rude off the television as you are on it.' Which shut him up for five minutes, anyway. We all went back to 'Vodka Villa' and stayed drinking until dawn.

The following Saturday, I went over for lunch. They were all pissed again and it was barely midday. They were serving gimlets – vodka and lime juice – in glasses the size of flower vases. Chris Downes was locked in conversation with Michael Wilding, who spoke slowly and softly because he suffered from *petit mal* by then, and needed prompting. I congratulated Maggie on how well and happy she seemed with Michael. She said how much she adored him, how charming he was, adding, in a very loud voice, 'And he's got the most enormous cock.'

Maggie retained all the style, exuberance, beauty and cheerful vulgarity of our first days together in New York. She was a true spirit and I loved her deeply. Within two years of this Chichester reunion she was dead, one month short of her fifty-fourth birthday. She had a great career, culminating in the CBE in 1974 and her last London stage appearance, in Ivy Compton Burnett's *A Family and a Fortune* just months before she died. Still, you sensed that she hadn't really done herself justice by dying so comparatively young. Despite suffering dreadfully from multiple sclerosis, she went rollicking to her grave with a song in her heart and a glass in her hand.

Jonathan Miller had tried to insist that Trigorin is a mediocre writer, which he may be, but I could never play him if I believed that. He says of himself that when he dies people will pass by his grave and say, 'Oh, there lies Trigorin; he was a good writer, though not as good as Turgenev.' He's self-deprecatory. Whereas in fact we all know that Chekhov was a much better writer than Turgenev, and all the things said of Trigorin were said about Chekhov himself.

The only way I could play the man was in the firm belief that he was the best writer who ever lived. Trigorin is a mediocre person, but that has nothing to do with his talent. If he's running around with Arkadina, and his works are published, it must be the boy, Konstantin, who lies about his worth. Trigorin is a careless dandy, with scuffed shoes and the band still around the cigars he smokes.

In the second act, in his speech to Nina, he gives the greatest statement about being a writer, or indeed any artist at all, in dramatic literature. He says, in that enormously long speech, 'The moment I've written something down I hate it and wish I hadn't written it at all,' which is not necessarily the confession of a mediocrity. All great writers are riddled with self-doubt. 'Then I see something and a big ball goes rolling around in my head, and that's another story, and I have to sit down and write it . . .' He is enslaved to his talent, not depressed by it.

My second big breakthrough as the sun god, Atahuallpa with Colin Blakely, in Peter Shaffer's *The Royal Hunt of the Sun*, NT, 1964 (Angus McBean)

With Maggie Smith in the Franco Zeffirelli production of *Much Ado About Nothing*, NT, 1965 (Zoë Dominic)

Maggie Smith and I together on film in *The Prime of Miss Jean Brodie*, 1969

Opposite Maggie again in Ingmar Bergman's production of Ibsen's *Hedda Gabler*, NT, 1970 (Zoë Dominic)

Off to Los Angeles with Maggie and our first son Christopher

As the great detective in Billy Wilder's film of *The Private Life of Sherlock Holmes*, 1970

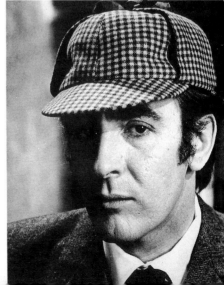

Patricia Quinn as Magenta in *The Rocky Horror Picture Show*, 1975

ABOVE With Bob Hoskins and Gawn Grainger in Charles Wood's *Has Washington Legs?*, NT, 1978 (Michael Mayhew)

MIDDLE As Maskwell in *The Double Dealer* with Ralph Richardson, NT, 1978 (John Haynes)

BELOW With the great Richardson again in Eduardo de Filippo's *Inner Voices*, NT, 1983 (Alastair Muir)

On tour in Brighton with *Murderer*, 1975, with Patricia Quinn, Christopher Downes and the late Sydney Edwards

As Falstaff with Michael Maloney (Prince Hal) and Rob Edwards (Poins) in
the RSC production of *Henry IV*, Stratford-upon-Avon, 1991 (Donald Cooper)

Relaxing by the River Avon
between shows in 1991 (Roy
Jones/Evening Standard)

As King Lear in the RSC production,
1993 (Donald Cooper)

Wedding bells with Pat in Camden Town, 1995, attended by Illtyd Harrington (left) and Christopher Downes

My son Toby as Coriolanus with the RSC in 1994/5 (Alastair Muir)

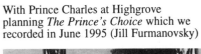

With Prince Charles at Highgrove planning *The Prince's Choice* which we recorded in June 1995 (Jill Furmanovsky)

Newly knighted and facing the future at home in Regent's Park (Chris Barham/Daily Mail)

It is a flawless role, and I really loved playing it. He is such a demure man. He doesn't want any trouble. But I simply cannot see him as a mediocre writer. Nobody ever reads anything he's written, so you don't know the truth. After that season, Jonathan asked if I would play it again at Greenwich in 1974, as part of a season titled 'Sons and Lovers', in which we also did *Hamlet* and *Ghosts*, with the same core company in each play: Peter Eyre as Konstantin, Hamlet and Oswald; Nicola Pagett as Nina, Ophelia and Regina; Irene Worth as Arkadina, Gertrude and Mrs Alving; and myself as Trigorin, Claudius and Pastor Manders.

It was a great idea and a very good season indeed, highlighting the links in the Freudian tapestries of the plays. It diverted me a little from the domestic agonies with Maggie and convinced me finally that we had no future together. A sense of failure overwhelmed the particle of success I had achieved on the stage. For me it was a third failure in marriage, and I was deeply upset about it all. I hadn't been so affected by the split with Tarn, but she was pretty cut up and annoyed about it all and I can hardly blame her. From this point on, I saw little of our sons Chris and Toby.

Maggie herself immediately rebounded into the ever-ready and welcoming embrace of Beverley Cross, who was unhappily married to old Gayden Collins. He proposed again and this time Maggie said yes. So that was that. Divorces all round. Our divorce was finalised in April 1975. She married Bev in August of the same year and off they went to Canada, where she shook the dust from under her feet in the classical company run by Robin Phillips at Stratford, Ontario. It was very romantic of Bev to wait all that time. I was left with nothing: no house, no sons, no possessions, no status. The boys went to Canada with Maggie and Bev, and they used to come back once a year. For no reason at all they were a bit nervous about seeing me. Bev would bring them up to London from wherever they were and I would take them out to lunch and then Bev would take them back again.

When they were smaller I was never mentioned. Toby once asked, apparently, 'Where's my father? Is he dead?' I don't blame anyone for that. In a way it was wrong that they never talked about me, but I daresay it was all a bit difficult for Maggie and Bev. It was probably best to keep me out of the picture. I wasn't upset at the time, because I didn't really know about it. But, in a strange way, my loss of security and domestic dignity contributed towards my identity crisis. Life became very difficult.

13

Oh, Oh, Antonia!

During that 1974 Greenwich season, the actor Peter Eyre, who is a charming fellow and who knows absolutely everyone, was visited backstage by his great friend, the writer Antonia Fraser. She was and is a very beautiful woman, handsome, elegant, not large exactly, but certainly big-boned. I thought she was one of the most attractive and glamorous people I had ever seen and she took great trouble to say how much she had enjoyed the performance.

She was beautifully dressed, her blonde hair glistened, her eyes sparkled and she had a perfect and ready phrase for everyone and everything. I was instantly smitten. It is ironic to reflect that when she was riding around Oxford University on her bicycle in the early 1950s, the veritable Zuleika Dobson of her generation, Maggie Smith was sweeping the stage as an assistant stage manager at the Playhouse.

Antonia came down to see all the plays at Greenwich. I knew that she was married to the businessman and Conservative MP Hugh Fraser, but I also knew that she led a pretty independent life within that marriage. Everyone knew that. She was a genuine live wire. I said to Peter afterwards, straight out, that I would like to have an affair with her. He said that it was about time she had a bit of rough trade! He promised there and then to arrange a dinner for the three of us and that he would contrive to leave at the appropriate moment.

I had not been having much fun at all. There had been one rather odd encounter with Vanessa Redgrave during the run of *Private Lives* a little earlier. I had arranged to have supper with Jeremy Brett who was appearing in a television series with Vanessa. He arrived in the restaurant with Vanessa, who was in floods of tears. She'd had a frightful row with the director and they had just finished the recording.

I tried to comfort her, telling her it was only a play and they couldn't shoot her, only the film, and I put my arm round her and kissed her on the cheek. We left the restaurant at half past one in the morning. Jeremy dropped us off at Vanessa's house in St Peter's Square, Hammersmith, and of course we ended up in bed together. Vanessa had long since divorced my *bête noire* Tony Richardson, and had not yet taken up with Timothy Dalton, so she was a free agent. I think she took pity on me because I took pity on her. There was nothing else to it.

I left her house early the next day, in the dark. There was no one around. And then in the *Daily Mail* the following Monday a gossip item appeared about me and Vanessa. Nobody could have possibly known except Jeremy Brett. And he wouldn't breathe a word. It must have been someone in the restaurant who called Nigel Dempster, the *Mail*'s gossip columnist, and told him that I had been there and had kissed Vanessa Redgrave.

This was a very peculiar time in my life. I was banging around with no great sense of purpose or direction. Before my impulsive obsession with Antonia Fraser took hold, I remember having a buck-up session with Ken Tynan, who had been very upset at being shown the door by Peter Hall when he took over the National from Larry in 1973. Tynan was a great critic and writer but he was also a great back-stabber, so he could hardly complain about receiving a few blows himself. I never really got on with him all that well, partly because he was so damned clever and I felt a little out of my depth.

But we kept in touch, and I went to see him because he was a bit low. He said that he'd written a film script and that he wanted me to play the lead. It was wonderful stuff, but you could never shoot it. Basically, there were two girls hitch-hiking in the South of France and a man stops to pick them up. They speak in French, but he suddenly says, 'Why don't you speak in English, I know who you are. You are wanted by the police. You are drug-pushers and if you are caught you will go to prison for twenty years. I'll give you a choice: you can either get out now or come to my château in the hills and in six months time I will put some money in a Swiss bank for you and you can leave. But you've got to do exactly as you are told in that six months.' So he's there in this castle with his wife, and these two girls, and then the show begins.

There was every kind of perversion in the world. It was terribly well written, elegant pornography, just like the Marquis de Sade. Ken wanted Romy Schneider to play my wife. I said, 'That's all very well, but I doubt if she'll do it.' Ken, who had a famous stutter, said, 'Do you th-th-th-think that M-M-M-Miss Schneider would object to having her a-a-a-anus licked?' And I said, 'Well, no, it's not her tongue, is it?' I couldn't believe what I was nearly getting involved with, and I went to the loo and just screamed with laughter. Ken had it all set up, including the château in the South of France with a big pool; we were going to have a party and shoot it all on location. But of course it never got made. He never got the money for it.

I was intrigued and bewitched by Antonia Fraser. She had been conducting an affair with Jonathan Aitken – who was unmarried and newly elected to the House of Commons – which she wanted to hit on the head. So, as promised, Peter Eyre arranged a dinner with me and her at a restaurant in the Fulham Road, the Meridiana, literally one hundred yards from where I lived in Queen's Elm Square. Peter eventually buggered off, leaving us alone. And I didn't really know at this point what to say. The bill came, we found ourselves on the street and there were a million taxi cabs coming up the street. I had to be quick or the bird could have flown.

I panicked. I had to say something. So I said, 'I have to say something to you.' 'Oh, what's that?' 'I would like to have a romance with you.' And she said, 'Oh, that's very sweet, and I would like to have a romance with you, too.' We went back to Queen's Elm Square. There was nobody there apart from the nanny, though I didn't know that at the time; Maggie, with whom I was barely on speaking terms, and the boys were all away in Carlisle visiting relatives. And that was that. La-la-la.

Maggie did not know that I was having an affair with Antonia, though she may have suspected it. On the first night of *Hamlet*, Antonia gave a party at her house. Maggie was in *Snap*, a terrible comedy about venereal disease, in the West End. She suddenly said to Chris Downes, who was with her, that she hadn't done anything about my first night, and he told her that Antonia was giving a party.

We were hardly speaking by now, but Maggie was feeling mischievous and decided to come and crash the party. Sir Hugh Fraser opened the door to Chris, and when he saw Maggie over his shoulder, he invited them in straightaway. Antonia's face when Maggie walked in the room was a real picture. She almost turned to stone. Maggie went home quite early, leaving Chris and I in the house of my lover, and we ended up staying the night. We both fell asleep on the sofa.

I received very good reviews at Greenwich and, according to Harold Hobson, walked off with *Ghosts* as Pastor Manders, which was quite an achievement considering it is the most boring part in the world bar very few indeed. All he does is tell the plot. A week later I was reading the reviews of *Hamlet*, and I came very well out of that, too. I felt reasonably elated and I turned to the nanny, Jan Clark, and I said, 'Where's Maggie?' And she said, 'She's gone to see her lawyer about the divorce.' I was shattered, though frankly I don't know what else I was expecting to happen. So I simply went upstairs and packed and moved out there and then into the Porchester Hotel for a couple of nights.

When the Greenwich season was over, I went to Tuscany with Antonia for a couple of weeks, to stay with Lord Lambton, one of her former lovers, and when I came back to London the divorce proceedings were going ahead. I heard, months later, that Maggie's lawyer, Michael Oliver, suggested that they get private detectives on to me, while Antonia put me in touch with Lord Goodman because she said he was the best lawyer in Britain. What she meant was that he was the best for people he had heard of, and any friend of Antonia's was a friend of his. Goodman rang Oliver and said, 'I understand you are considering putting detectives on Mr Stephens. I'm sure we can settle all this quite amicably,' and that was the end of that.

I finally changed my residence from Queen's Elm Square to a basement flat which became available in Regents Park. Basement flats are very depressing. I fell into a state of terminal melancholia; I realised fully the consequences of what I had done and everything hit me. I had nothing. I was back to square one. I was overwhelmed by a desperate sense of failure and the unmitigated sense of depression was ghastly. Unbearable. I was still seeing Antonia but I felt I couldn't share anything of what I was going through with her because it didn't really have anything to do with her. To me, she was the diversion, the bubble in the squelch and squeak of daily life, someone who thought of me still as a famous and glamorous actor. She kept me going and she cheered me up.

But the minute I was on my own, or down in the dumps, things got worse and worse. I had to get out of doing some television thing that I had agreed to do. I couldn't concentrate on anything with this great weight on my mind. And I was drinking more than usual – and it's fair to say that my 'usual' is quite a lot anyway – which didn't help. I said to Christopher Downes that I couldn't live by myself and that I would have to go and live with him and Illtyd, and he said, certainly, by all means. So I left the basement flat and went to live in his flat off Lissom Grove in Marylebone.

By now, I was in a terrible state. I called Jonathan Miller. We had always got along really well, and that Greenwich season had been particularly enjoyable and worthwhile. He had noticed that I had been flying a bit high during the season, and had sent me to someone for some pills that brought me down a bit. Which they did.

It was the separation from Maggie even within our marriage which had finally pushed me over the edge. I still loved her and needed her, but we had grown irreconcilably apart. It made me realise where I was, which was nowhere. I hate having to be dependent on people, and the confession of needing help is immensely humiliating. But I did need help, and I knew that Jonathan Miller would understand. I went to see Jonathan and his wife, Rachel, who is a general practitioner, and I explained everything to them. They said they would try to arrange some medical supervision for me.

The very next day, I went to have lunch in Soho with Tony Shaffer, Peter's playwright twin, and Michael White, the producer, about Tony's new thriller, *Murderer*. The play would not prove my economic salvation, but the actress eventually cast opposite me would prove my emotional and personal salvation. In the middle of that lunch I received a call from Rachel Miller, telling me to go that afternoon to the mental hospital adjoining the Hospital for Tropical Diseases in Camden Town. I was in no position to ignore the instruction. I left the restaurant, went home, packed an overnight bag and reported to the hospital.

They were expecting me there, and I was told to put on some pyjamas. They gave me a big shot in the arm and – 'boomph' – I went straight out for about thirty-six hours. They kept me in there for about ten weeks. Although I was unaware of the fact, I was in the middle of undergoing a serious nervous breakdown. They put me on all kinds of medication and I saw a psychiatrist which obviously, as far as I was concerned, I didn't need.

During my stay there, I learned the whole of the part in *Murderer*. The divorce was finalised half way through the run of that play, in April 1975. With me, everything just spilled over all over the place. Maggie, on the other hand, is very contained and keeps herself to herself. She says she only feels she comes alive for two and a half hours each night on the stage, which I think is crap. I never understood that, and I suppose you could say that I never really understood her at all.

But we had proved, finally, to be incompatible. The fact is that we were gloriously alive together in those few years at the Old Vic, working with Larry. I suppose I can't help being alive every minute of the day, and it is bloody hard work sometimes. Being on stage is a job that I take a pride in doing well, but it is only part of everything else, the company of friends and of people I like and admire.

I was very grateful to Jonathan Miller and I'm very fond of him. He helped me through a bad patch and thought nothing of doing so, never expecting any favours in return. He can be a bit undergraduate, though. For instance, when we were doing *The Seagull* in Chichester, Tony Hopkins turned up, visiting backstage, and I said to Jonathan that it might be a good idea if I played Othello and Tony played Iago.

Jonathan was keen and said that he would direct and set the whole thing beneath the Cyprus walls. We could have tents with mosquito nets, and Othello would have decorative insignia, or pips, on his shoulders. 'Excuse me,' I said, 'what about the Turks coming back and all the rest of it? The play has very little to do with Cyprus, it's about the Venetians fighting the Turks. Nothing to do with the English in Cyprus.' It was obvious that Jonathan had just thought about Cyprus and had become temporarily possessed with an anachronistic idea of military occupation. He just picked the idea out of the air. I love working with Jonathan, but you have to keep your eye on him.

When I was in hospital, Antonia was fantastic. So kind and so sweet. She came to see me every day. But it was a sexual romance, and romances of any sort do not last for ever. An actor's life is hedged around with what I choose to call romances. They mark his progress, define his days. Antonia was a very special person to me, but a romance, nonetheless.

I left the hospital and started rehearsing *Murderer*. Whenever I called her, Antonia would say she was too busy to talk to me, so I stopped calling. Something was going on. Eventually I received a letter from her in which she apologised for not having been more solicitous. 'The truth of the matter is,' she said, 'I have fallen in love with another. A writer. Nobody you know. And he has forbidden me to see you ever again. Sexual jealousy, I should imagine.'

I rang her up and said, 'Look, it's not fair; I could go on and play the violins, and say that you had broken my heart, but it's not true. The world is not coming to an end. It was only a romance, and they don't last for ever.' I had fallen anyway by then for the beautiful actress Patricia Quinn, but she didn't know that. I poured out my heart to Pat during rehearsals. When we finished work each day in the hall in Church Street, Kensington, I would pop round to Queen's Elm Square to see the boys, just to say hello, really, and then I would meet up with Pat in a pub nearby. I found her immensely sympathetic and for some reason – possibly because I was trying to seduce her! – I told her about all my affairs, all the women I had known.

I am an extremely possessive person and immediately felt so as far as Pat was concerned, which was hardly reasonable of me as she was married to somebody else and I was in a jealous state over Antonia, although I pretended not to be. I pressed Antonia about the identity of this new lover of hers, and she caved in, admitting it was Harold Pinter. My old understudy! At the Royal Court in 1959 Harold was still working as an actor under the name of 'David Baron', and he had understudied me as George Dillon, the failed writer. At that time he himself was, of course, poised between the commercial failure of *The Birthday Party* and the great critical success of *The Caretaker* in the following year.

Fully aware of the vindictive, difficult nature of the actress Vivien Merchant, Harold's wife, I said, 'Do you know Mrs Pinter?' 'Not really, I've met her.' 'She is a monster. She will tear you to pieces.' Which is what she did, with all those remarks about Antonia's feet being big enough to allow the couple to share the same shoes. But Antonia was now inextricably involved with Harold, and would remain so, happily ever after; I was her last bad boy.

While preparing for *Murderer*, I decided to do Edward Albee's extraordinary short play *Zoo Story* in the Open Air Theatre at Regents Park, very near the zoo, as a lunchtime diversion. The monologue I delivered to an impassive bystander, played by Michael Gambon, was a torrential suicide note about the ugliness of existence, the squalor and misery of the downtown apartment block where the character lived, and a general outpouring of unassuaged anguish. The critics were very complimentary. But I doubt if they knew how much of my real inner self was in that performance. It was a truly cathartic experience.

I walked on to the street of the Park's inner circle by the stage door one afternoon and a very handsome man congratulated me on my performance, introducing himself as Nigel Dempster. 'Oh, we meet at last!' I said. There had been so much about me in his columns – 'seen at the opera with Antonia Fraser', that sort of thing. There was no point in telling him to get lost, he said, because he was putting the finishing touches to a two-page spread about the loves of Antonia Fraser including Lord Lambton, the King of Greece, Harold Pinter, myself, and two other people, with a big picture of Antonia climbing into a taxi cab, to convey this hectic life of rushing between social appointments and romantic trysts.

So I said, 'You ask me what you want to ask me and I'll tell you what I want to tell you.' He was perfectly sweet, and he didn't get anything out of me. All I remember about that column is the great quip attributed to Antonia while giving Clive James the brush-off at a literary party: 'I only sleep with the First Eleven.'

Which only goes to show that you blow your nose in public at your peril these days. Not that any of all that bothers me. I tend to go with the tide and be philosophical about gossip and bitchiness. Nothing is really more trivial or serious than anything else and in that respect gossip can be quite a healthy outlet and a useful deflationary device. Some people, especially actors and other nonentities, do get frightfully grand and ludicrously self-important about it all.

The gossip columns only became a problem, if that's the right word, during *Private Lives*. But I've never minded them particularly. All's fair in love and war, and I dare say they have a job to do. But suddenly something appeared in the *Hollywood Reporter* saying that 'Robert Stephens is recovering from a dental operation because his wife Maggie Smith discovered his affair with Antonia Fraser and punched him on the jaw.'

It was all nonsense, except for the kernel of truth about the affair and the damaged jaw. I'd gone to a gymnasium during *Private Lives*. The instructor gave me a weight heavier than I was expecting and, as it fell, it hit me on the mouth, so I went to the dentist straight after the play. The crucial point is that, until that moment, I'd had a rather distinctive pair of long front molars. It's amazing how such things get in the papers, but what nobody ever commented upon was the transformation of my appearance by the dentistry required as a result of the accident. My face was always long, and it seemed longer with the long teeth. My mouth was now less vertical, my smile less ghoulish, my teeth more even.

My romance with darling Antonia was bound to be noted because we used to go to the opera, which I absolutely loathed. I never understood what was going on and would frequently prowl the bars and foyers after the first act, waiting for the curtain and Antonia to emerge in splendour from the stalls. Antonia always used to say that we were reasonably safe because the papers would never print anything about the wives and families of members of the House of Commons, of which Hugh Fraser was an upstanding member. As far as Antonia was concerned, I was an upstanding member, too, though not in the House of Commons. Luckily for us it was all twenty years ago.

Things have got a little out of hand these days and I dread to think how stories about the West End actor and the politician's wife would be handled today. Even then, Nigel Dempster in the *Daily Mail* kept plugging away at her and her activities, and she used to talk regularly to her friend Lord Goodman about it. He dissuaded her from doing anything until he felt the time was right, then he pounced, and she won about £20,000 in damages for harassment.

I was always intrigued by Antonia's great spiritual, as well as physical, beauty. I used to ask her, as she was a devout and serious Catholic, how she squared that side of things with having such an extraordinary personal life. But she saw no problem about that at all, saying that you could always have your personal life and be true to your faith. And, after all, there was always the safety valve of the confessional box.

I always went with her to the same, very nice restaurant in Abingdon Road, Kensington, the Trat Two. I asked her why she always went there, and she said that she used to go there with Jonathan Aitken. I said, 'Well, he might be here one day, and he'd come and punch me on the nose.' Sure enough, one day, there he was, sitting with another woman. Nothing was said, he left the restaurant and walked straight past us.

Eventually, we left and went to Antonia's car – in those days she had a wonderful little Mini which was painted up in the colours of her book, *Mary Queen of Scots*, light blue with gold facings – and there was a piece of paper folded beneath the windscreen wiper. She opened it. The message was written in capital letters on House of Commons notepaper: 'Darling Antonia: lowering your sights a bit, aren't you?' You cheeky bugger, I thought! A few days later, I went to the book launch of *The Female Woman*, Ariana Stassinopoulos's riposte to Germaine Greer, without Antonia. The place was jam packed with people and I suddenly came face to face with Jonathan Aitken. 'Oh hello,' I sneered. 'How are you?' 'Very well, thank you.' I turned around and he'd gone. He disappeared instantly from the party. He had simply vanished. And so, from my life, had Antonia. But it was certainly fun while it lasted.

14

Spills and Thrills with Patricia

When I came out of hospital I went to see, much against my wishes, a musical playing in the King's Road called *The Rocky Horror Show*. It had opened in the Theatre Upstairs at the Royal Court in 1973 and had transferred to a converted cinema in the Kings Road, where it had become a long-running cult hit. Chris Downes was mad about it, and had seen it roughly fifty times. Early in 1975 he begged me to go along and see it with him; he thought it might cheer me up, I suppose, although I had no particular interest in tacky actors in suspender belts.

The producer was Michael White, and as I was about to work for him in *Murderer*, I felt I better go along. I went to a five o'clock performance on a Friday night with Chris and an actress who had been in *The Day of the Jackal*, Olga George-Picot, who always said that Linda Lovelace's claim to be the queen of oral sex had undermined her own reputation in that field and had ruined her career. Little did I realise that this innocent outing would eventually lead to my lasting friendship and partnership with the actress Patricia Quinn.

I was completely knocked out, and I remember going backstage to congratulate Tim Curry and Little Nell, two of the leads, as well as the extraordinary, bewitching Patricia. Tim was amazing as Frank 'N' Furter, the transvestite rocker in black suspenders, while Nell (real name, Nell Campbell), who later opened a famous nightclub – Nell's Club – in New York, had become an overnight cult sensation in the show.

Patricia Quinn, my fourth wife, 'milady Stephens', says she remembers that first backstage meeting of ours so vividly. As I was back-slapping Tim Curry, she and Nell were pushing in to gain their share of attention from 'the great actor' (I think she means me!) visiting the cast. She played the film-struck usherette who sang the big hit 'Science Fiction' at the start of the show, and was then transmogrified into the kinky Magenta, who takes over the Transylvanian castle with other dissatisfied domestics.

I was pretty undomesticated myself at this time. I was living with Chris and Illtyd who were always complaining about my propensity for setting the bedclothes on fire with my cigarettes. I smoke wherever I am, and they kept moaning about holes that appeared in blankets and curtains, quite unreasonably, I always thought. It was a tiny apartment, and dear old Chris put the most enormous ashtrays all over the place; I managed to miss nearly all of them. Maggie had in effect kicked me out, and I had nowhere else to go. So I stayed with Chris and Illtyd, on and off, for several years.

Jeremy Brett always kept a room in his flat for me, but staying there always involved terrible bridge evenings with Charlie Kay and Penelope Keith. *And* Patience Collier, a dear old character actress and *grande dame* (she's dead now, alas) who looked like Mr Punch and sounded like Martita Hunt under sedation. That scene was all a bit too precious and old-maidish for me.

Patience was always surrounded by pretty young men. After the first night of Larry's abysmal production at the National of *Love's Labour's Lost* she barged into the dressing rooms of all the moaning Minnies who were in it – Derek Jacobi, Charlie Kay, Ronald Pickup and so on – and yelled, at nobody in particular, 'Well, what about that! What were *you* doing [singling out Charlie], young man, do you suppose?' They were all terrified of her. And in thrall, at the same time.

Soon afterwards, auditions were held on a freezing cold December morning by the producer Michael White, the director Clifford Williams, the author Anthony Shaffer and myself for *Murderer* at the Fortune Theatre, and by the last morning we had not seen anyone suitable for the role of my girlfriend in the play. Or anyone, to be frank, that I fancied all that much. We had three girls to go, and I was prepared for a postponed opening. The first girl was no good. The second didn't turn up. The third one arrived in a great long shoulder-to-ankle racoon skin fur coat and a mass of dark red curly hair. So it was impossible to see what the creature looked like. We sat down and started to read the text. No sooner had she begun when the director, Clifford Williams, interrupted her with the time-honoured phrase, 'Thank you very much.'

I was in despair when Michael White suddenly said, 'Hang on a minute, that's Patricia Quinn who played the usherette in *The Rocky*

Horror Show.' I immediately said, 'Give it to her; she was brilliant.' It was all a big risk. You couldn't hear her speak, because, as she admitted later, she was dreadfully hung over. She had been out partying the night before with the film director Stephen Frears and the photographer John Vere Brown. Tony Shaffer said, 'Oh, I see; all you've got to do is shoot somebody full of novocaine and they get the part!'

Anyway, we offered her the part and she accepted immediately, on condition that she had her name up in lights. She always kept us to that promise because her great *Rocky Horror* chum Little Nell had a flat opposite the Garrick Theatre, where we played. We used to sit in there eating Little Nell's Mum's home-baked sultana cake from Australia while looking at our names up across the road in red neon lights.

By the time *Murderer* got to Brighton on tour, the race was on for the only available girl in the cast. (The fine actress Caroline Blakiston, who was also in the cast, was *hors de concours*.) Pat was married to the actor/director Don Hawkins, by whom she had a son, Quinn, then about five years old. This fact did not deter the runners on the starting line, who were myself, the author Tony Shaffer, and the director Clifford Williams. Of course, as soon as Pat knew that I was in the running, that knocked the others clean out of contention!

She was, and is, gorgeous, and I'm afraid to say that she was not entirely well behaved in her private life. Pat is the daughter of a legendary Belfast bookie, James Connelly Quinn, with a brother and a sister to whom she is still very close. She's a beautiful, bubble-haired redhead, with a slender figure, blue-green eyes and an infectious, unforgettable throaty laugh. She was, and is, totally adorable, and I was determined to let her know my feelings. She had several lovers on the go, one of whom was the rock star Meatloaf, who told her that he had been voted the best high-school kisser in Texas. Pat always confirms that he was the best kisser – in Texas!

In her native Belfast, Pat joined the British Drama League, won lots of school prizes for acting – and, as it happens, gymnastics! – and started to work with the Arts Theatre in the city. She then came to London to train at the Drama Centre and from there she joined the Glasgow Citizens' in its first full flush in the early 1970s under Giles Havergal and Philip Prowse, before appearing in the original Royal Court production of Heathcote Williams's seminal drugs-and-sex play, *AC/DC. The Rocky Horror Show* followed soon after.

I made her promise me that we would get to know each other more intimately in Brighton, but as this sounded to her more like a threat than a promise, she decided that our tryst should be made in London before we went down to the coast. So we consummated our passion in Chris and Illtyd's flat one Saturday afternoon when I was due to meet Antonia for tea at the Ritz. I insisted she took half a sleeping pill so that she would still be there when I came back! Then we all went out to dinner together – Pat, Chris and Illtyd – and we've all been together ever since.

The next day, Sunday, we went to Brighton. I have always been immensely fond of Brighton, and Pat was just the sort of person one hoped to get to know very well there. She suited the place perfectly. The production was billeted in the Royal Crescent Hotel, which has a marvellous theatrical history of its own. Larry's house was just around the corner. Binkie Beaumont kept a flat in the hotel. Brighton was always the last stop before London on the pre-West End tour, and the actors and directors and producers always congregated in the hotel after the show to discuss notes and changes.

The Royal Crescent used to be run by a Mrs Taunt. She and her husband had separate offices, and they both drank all day. She drank port, he drank whisky, and they were always pissed. And I must say they were always very, very kind to me! Sir Ralph was fond of them, too. Mrs Taunt used to greet him always with a brimming glass and a bouquet of flowers for Mu, his wife. Once, Mrs Taunt took them along to their room, and as she opened the door, there was a terrible scream from Mrs Taunt and she banged it shut. And Ralph used to say, in his most mysterious of voices, 'And no one will ever know what Mrs Taunt saw in the wrong room!'

I already had some spicy memories of the place in general and that hotel in particular. The year after we opened the National, and soon after I had met Maggie in *The Recruiting Officer*, a Canadian company from Ontario came to Chichester with, I think, *The Taming of the Shrew*. Larry wanted us all to go down and make them feel welcome in the theatre, which was the National's outpost. So Rosemary Harris, Billie Whitelaw, Colin Blakely and myself – regarded as senior actors in the National, with ambassadorial responsibilities – all went down there. The three of us were in the first half of a double bill, Beckett's *Play*, which only lasted about forty minutes, so we were out of the theatre by half past eight.

When Maggie heard about this proposed little jaunt, she said, 'Oh, that's nice, I'll come too.' We all went down together. After we read the letter of welcome, there was a party, which was obviously going to go on all night. Maggie had a matinée at the Old Vic the next day, so we skedaddled and went across to Brighton for the night. The Adelphi was full, so we went to the Royal Crescent. In those days, there was a porter there with a funny eye. I signed us in – this was in the early stages of our hectic romance – as 'Mr and Mrs Robert Stephens' which at the time we were not.

The funny-eyed porter took us to the room, and we were just settling in when the telephone rang and this importunate underling said, in typically porter-ish tones of lubricious discretion, 'Excuse me, Mr Stephens, don't mind me for asking, I can't really restrain myself; but isn't that Miss Maggie Smith with you up there?' I said, 'No, it most certainly is not.' And he started having an argument with me: 'Oh, I'm sure it is, I know 'er; we've had all the greats staying here at one time or another, you know.' Most annoying of all, it was clear that he was not including me among their number.

A couple of years later, I was in Brighton without Maggie, in *The Dance of Death*, and Larry said to me that he couldn't put me up because Joan's relatives were staying, but that he had booked me next door at the Royal Crescent. It was their wedding annniversary. I went in and out for meals with Joan and Larry but slept in the hotel. On the Thursday night they all went out for a celebratory family supper and I went to the hotel and had my cold supper on a tray, whch was brought up to me by the porter with the funny eye.

'You down here acting this week, sir?' he asked. 'Yes,' I replied. 'I'm with Sir Laurence Olivier in *The Dance of Death*.' 'Oh yes, sir,' he said. 'We know all the great theatrical figures here, sir. John Clements, Terence Rattigan, Dora Bryan, Mr Binkie Beaumont, Kenneth Williams, Maggie Smith. Oh, yes, I could tell you a funny story about that Maggie Smith.' 'Oh, what's that?' I enquired, hardly daring to breathe. 'A couple of years ago, she came here with some fellow or other and I called him up and said I was sure that he was up there with Maggie Smith. And he denied it, the crafty bugger! I know 'er. But this crafty bugger wouldn't say anything! Don't really blame him, though. I expect she just wanted a bit . . . !'

On that last Saturday night of *Murderer*, everyone was running around the Royal Crescent as if they were in a Feydeau farce. Jonathan Kent, now the director of the Almeida, had come down and was due to return to London with us after the show. However, we all went out to dinner and had a bit too much to drink, so we decided to stay over. But the Royal Crescent only had one double room left, and as my affair with Pat was still supposed to be secret at that stage, Jonathan magnanimously booked it and offered to accommodate Pat.

Pat was happy to room with Jonathan, whom she'd known for a long time. They had shared rooms together previously and nothing had happened. But on this occasion he suddenly, and sweetly, said, 'I think I'm in love with you.' To which Pat replied, 'You can't be, I'm having an affair with Robert!' Meanwhile, I had been ringing up Pat from Chris and Warren's room, where I was parked on the floor, saying that I didn't want her to spend the night with Jonathan Kent.

So we roamed the corridors together until the porter with the squint found us the last single room in the hotel – it was no more than a glorified broom cupboard, and there we spent the last night of our heady Brighton sojourn together. Chris Downes and Warren Clarke slept soundly in their twin beds while Jonathan Kent relaxed in solitary splendour, no doubt thinking of what might have been, in the big double-bedded room. That was the night we realised we might have some sort of serious relationship: all very jolly and entertaining, which is a good deal more than you could say of *Murderer*. At one point, when Pat was running up and down the corridors staving off Jonathan Kent, the man with the squint said, 'Where *would* you like to spend the night, madam?' It was highly ridiculous and, in retrospect, immensely funny.

The play itself was a mess, though the first twenty minutes of pure dumb show were brilliant. The audience thinks at first that George, the character I played, has killed a woman. He is painting a nude model, then wanders around behind her and strangles her with a silk scarf. He carries 'the corpse' up to the bathroom, takes off all his clothes (down to his underpants), puts on a white plastic apron, gets out all his knives and saws, and chops her up. In fact, it's a dummy.

A knock at the door: it's the police force, embodied in the singular presence of Warren Clarke. The woman across the road – there were big windows giving on to his light-filled room – has seen George commit this 'heinous crime'. Under interrogation, he breaks down and confesses that he is addicted to re-enacting famous murders; the model he murdered, played by Pat, is in effect still alive. What he doesn't tell the police, of course, is that he is building up a sort of 'Cry Wolf' alibi, because he plans to murder his wife, played by Caroline Blakiston.

In the second act, George comes in and his wife, who has a stutter, calls out from the bathroom, which is full of steam, 'Is that you, G-g-g-george?' and he goes upstairs and murders her by drowning her in the bath. It turns out to be his girlfriend who had been doing an imitation of his wife. When the wife comes back and realises what has happened, that George planned to murder her, she sticks a knife into him and departs. His phone calls to the police station, as he expires, covered in blood, are met with disbelief and derision. Although I have heard from people who really think the play is extremely good, I felt that it all became a bit silly and pointless after a while. There were no effective tricks in it after the first twenty minutes.

I was assured that Tony Shaffer would do a lot of rewriting on tour, as his brother Peter endlessly did on his plays, when sufficiently bullied into doing so by John Dexter, and indeed as Tony himself had done on *Sleuth*, at the insistence of Tony Quayle. But on this occasion he never did. We did two weeks in Brighton, where the producer and the director stupidly invited Ken Tynan to come and see it. He was a friend of Clifford Williams and Michael White, and they'd all done *Oh! Calcutta!* together. Ken made a lot of suggestions involving music and blackouts, but nothing helped, and the whole thing started to creak.

Everything always seems to go wrong in Brighton, but there's always fun to be had. Jack Tinker lives there nowadays, and I remember first meeting him at Chichester one year when I went to see a dreadful musical with Topol in it. Virginia Fairweather, Larry's old press officer, had a tiny little cottage there. Chris Downes and I ended up there on the night in question with her and Jack, whom I'd never met before.

He was full of admiration not for any of my performances, but for a light windbreaker jacket I was wearing which I had bought in Los Angeles. He went on and on about it so much that I gave it to him. He's still got it. But he can never wear it because he's so tiny. It's too big for him. He was such a funny little man. He still is. He always seems to be laughing.

There was also, that night, in the tiny cottage, a very large American woman, a friend of Virginia's, weighing in at about twenty stone. When she went to the loo, she got stuck there. So stuck, in fact, that she passed out. We'd all had a bit to drink by then and we sort of forgot about her. And when we eventually found her, Jack was the only person small enough to get around the back of the loo to pull her knickers up. And I was the only person strong enough to carry her upstairs to a bedroom, with Jack taking the excess weight behind.

It was a dreadful shame about Virginia. She'd done something to upset

Larry, I'm not sure what, and got stabbed in the back by Ken as a result. Larry went in to her office at the Old Vic one day and simply said, 'Okay, pack your bags, clear your desk and get out.' It was awful, especially when you remember that in those days, as an actor in the company, you had to have permission from her to talk to the Press.

Larry was terrified of all journalists and would have nothing to do with them. Later on, Virginia wrote a dreadful book, *Cry God for Larry*, a terrible denouncement of him. But she and her husband David, also a publicist, had been with him all the way from his early days in the West End. She was a great character.

And I always associate Marlene with Brighton, too. She was playing the Theatre Royal in 1964 soon after she had been to see Maggie and I at the Old Vic and had dinner with us. I called Larry's house and asked the housekeeper where Marlene was staying. The Metropole Hotel. So I called and said that as I had never seen her on the stage, could I come along that evening, with two of the stage-management boys who were crazy about her and she said, 'Of course.' The seats were at the stage door with her manager. I sent two dozen red roses into the theatre.

After the matinée at Chichester, I drove over to Brighton, went to the stage door and was summoned to the dressing room. There was a red carpet all the way from her dressing room to the stage. No one ever made a penny out of presenting her; Binkie once said to me that he had never met such a businesswoman in showbusiness. We drank champage and she was about to go on. She was booked for dinner afterwards with someone from the *Sunday Express*, for an interview, and she invited us all along. To English's. She handed me back my roses and said, 'At the end of the show, run down the aisle and present them to me.'

At dinner, she turned her back on this man from the *Sunday Express*, the poor bloke who was paying the bill, while we were drinking Dom Perignon like lemonade. I said, 'You must speak to this poor man.' And she said, 'No, no, he has no stature.' I made her talk to him, eventually, and she came out with fantastic stories, as good as David Niven's, mostly about the war and entertaining the troops. He started scribbling away, and he thanked me profusely afterwards, and in the column on Sunday gave me as glowing a write-up as he gave her, all about the charming, delightful Robert Stephens!

Thus my romancing of Pat Quinn had a Brighton background of pleasant associative memories. She was terribly beguiling, pretty, vivacious. It was love at first sight, you could say. I took her out to dinner a lot after the play – I have always enjoyed eating out after a performance – and Don Hawkins, her husband, didn't like that much. Not unreasonably, he asked me to stop taking her out, and I said, well, it wasn't my fault, she was asking to come out with me. But that was just deviousness on my part.

I never saw the son from my first marriage, after that terrible incident of my exclusion by Nora Ann, until I was on tour with *Murderer* in Edinburgh. After Brighton, we had two weeks in Edinburgh and Newcastle, before we came to London in April 1975. I arrived at the stage door of the King's Theatre on the Sunday night with my friend Christopher Downes, my dresser and amanuensis, to check the mail, and I found his note: 'Dear Robert, I am your son Michael Christopher Stephens and I live here in Edinburgh and I would very much like to see you, but if you don't want to see me I will quite understand.'

He felt simultaneously shattered and withdrawn, as well as relieved, to have made a move towards me. I was immensely grateful that he had bothered, but it has to be said that I never really wanted to be responsible for, nor was I interested in, my offspring until much later in life. Chance had dealt me a bad hand, and I had been excluded from Michael Christopher's upbringing.

Still, I rang him up and he came to the hotel the following day, and although he had my caste of features, he had all the mannerisms of my brother; he would say something and wink at you, which my brother does. He was now about twenty-four. I asked him what he did for a living. He said in his thick Derry brogue, 'I'm a writer.' I asked him what he wrote. He said, 'Stories.' This pleased me, and I saw him every day for a week, and then *Murderer* moved on to Newcastle and London. He went to America and I've never seen him since.

He's a poet, basically, and he lives in Minneapolis or somewhere ghastly like that, although I believe he now has a rock and roll band which he manages. We don't keep in touch. We were always bad at doing that in my family, and it frightens me sometimes to think that my capacity for failure in this direction was inherited from my parents and their parents. I have done a bit better with my other children, Lucy, Toby and Christopher, but it took a long time. I'm proud of them all, and love them all very much; as indeed I do Michael Christopher.

When *Murderer* was over I went to New York to play Sherlock Holmes on the stage and Pat came out to spend a week or so with me. That sealed our fate, and Don Hawkins's. The *Sherlock Holmes* was the 1899 potboiler by William Gillette, a compilation of three Conan Doyle stories. John Wood appeared in it for the RSC at the Aldwych. In America, the role was taken over by John Neville. I had just finished in *Murderer* when I was presented with an enormous bill for supertax which dated from several years earlier. I went down to the supertax offices with my accountant who said to me, 'If I keep mentioning the word 'Bankrupt' don't get frightened, it's a ruse.'

I'd paid £17,000 and they said I still owed £14,000, and my accountant told them that I didn't have it. They asked me what property I owned, and I said none. I had given over everything in the divorce – including my share in Tigbourne Court – to Maggie and the boys, so that I didn't have to pay any alimony or school fees. And anyway, Maggie was always earning much more than I was.

So the die was cast; I had no choice but to take up this offer at the end of 1975 and go to America to play Sherlock Holmes yet again. I was there for about seven months, playing at the Broadhurst, and I made a lot of money, so the tax debt was paid off quite quickly. They offered me a year's tour, as well, but I didn't want to do that.

Pat was reasonably glad to see the back of me at this point and went to work in a Howard Barker play at the Royal Court, *Stripwell*, with Michael Hordern and Constance Cummings. I think I had been a very glamorous affair as far as she was concerned, but there appeared to be no long-term prospects for our relationship. Although I was sending dozens of red roses into the theatre every other day, Pat was back with her husband and son, and getting on with her life.

I took over from John Neville as Sherlock Holmes and it was such a success that they extended my contract and that is when Pat came over for a week. She simply decided, almost impetuously, to visit the States for the first time, at my invitation, and in accepting that proposal, she was most certainly burning her boats and saying goodbye to Don Hawkins. At the same time, I was embroiled in a little local difficulty with one of the most outrageous women I have ever known.

Much more worrying than the odd incidence of strangers or members of the audience falling in love with you, is the case of the obsessive devotee, and undoubtedly the most remarkable instance of this in my career was the case of the actress I met in New York. During the run of *Sherlock Holmes*, this extraordinary woman quite simply decided to take over my life.

I became her obsession, which was terrifying, because it had nothing to do with love. And certainly, as far as I was concerned, nothing to do with sex. I met her for the first time in Sardi's one evening with the Mayor of New York. She was extremely striking, not beautiful in a conventional sense, but keenly intelligent.

She invited me to dinner later in the same week, and from that point slowly began to take over, or try to take over, my life. Whenever I gave an excuse to refuse an invitation, she would insist that I bring along whoever else it was I was going to spend the evening or the lunchtime with. She could drink anyone, including me, under the table. Her drink was Bombay gin on the rocks, with nothing else in it. Ninety-five per cent proof poison.

One day I mentioned casually that I was going to go to Bloomingdale's to buy some shirts. The next day, there were six shirts from Bloomingdale's waiting for me at the stage door. Anything I said was acted upon. If I said 'I love pea soup', there would be pea soup on the table the next time I went. She would talk for hours at a time on the telephone. This business went on for a year, but I never laid a finger on her. I didn't dare, or I would have been in jail, metaphorically speaking, for life.

She used to send me terrifying letters written in a big black Pentel scrawl on lawyers' yellow paper. Chris Downes and I were having a drink in the Algonquin with her and Sydney Edwards, a lovely man who used to write the showbiz column in the *Evening Standard*. Chris happened to let slip that Patricia was coming over the following week, and she flashed round at me in a trice: 'Did I hear you say that Pat was coming over next week? Don't you *dare* bring that woman to my house.'

Pat arrived on the Sunday, and on Monday night we were in Joe Allen's. My pursuer came in, wearing a big long black cloak and a sort of Spanish hat. She looked like the Witch of Endor. She came over and said, 'I've just come to say goodnight.' I introduced her to Patricia and she totally ignored her, turned on her very large heel and swept out of the restaurant. I said to Patricia there and then that I would never go to her house again.

When Pat had gone back, it was Thanksgiving and my obsessive friend was giving a huge dinner between shows for all her friends. I refused to go, and she went berserk.

I thought this was silly, so I wrote to her and suggested we meet for a quiet and sensible lunch in Sardi's, which we did. She arrived shaking from head to foot. I said, 'Please don't think I'm being nosey or impertinent, but I think you should go and see a doctor. I don't think you are nuts, but I do think you are over-energised. You may even have a thyroid complaint, or something wrong in your bloodstream. I'm quite energetic myself and, believe me, it appears to me that you are just a little bit over the top in the way you react to things.' Well, of course, by this time she had had several of her Bombay gins and was nodding quietly in agreement with everything I said.

She followed me to London when I returned to do *Othello* and appeared everywhere, and persisted in writing streams of lurid letters – like novels they were. Thank God she went back. Later on, she became ill and then joined Alcoholics Anonymous, and now puts all her energies into *that* in New York. I saw her the last time I went there, and we got along just fine. She has calmed down a great deal, and is really now the sweetest person in the whole wide world.

I talked to my friend Estelle Weldon, an Argentinian psychiatrist, about it. She said, 'It's very difficult with people who are obsessive; because they are terribly clever to make sure that you are the only person who knows about the obsession.' And that is what had happened.

When Pat got on that plane to New York she walked out of her marriage. By the time I came back, she was playing Lady Macbeth at the Bristol Old Vic, she and Don Hawkins had split up and he was having an affair with the actress Caroline Langrishe. Don realised his marriage was over and he moved out of Pat's flat on Primrose Hill. And I moved in. We had the flat reshaped and rebuilt. And I thought the time was right to get back into some classical work.

The film world intervened in this plan, when I was drafted in as a last-minute substitute for Donald Sutherland in a Gérard Depardieu film, one of his biggest flops, as it turned out, *La Nuit, Tous les Chats sont Gris* ('At Night, All Cats Are Grey'). Depardieu played Philibert, a two-bit, cat-stroking pimp on the Côte d'Azur, who is the invented hero of bedtime stories told to a young girl by her British uncle – played by me. At the end, in England, I go into a pub and there is Philibert for real, sitting in a corner.

The barman was being played by an absolutely hopeless actor who couldn't get the lines right, couldn't draw a pint of bitter. The director, Gérard Zing, had the bright idea that Christopher Downes could play the barman instead. But Chris said, 'No, thank you. I have worked with Mr Billy Wilder, I don't work with second best!'

Our chauffeur was a man called Michel Ménard. When I got in the car I complained that the seat belt had room for two and I couldn't tighten it;

the last person who had sat in the car, Michel said, was Orson Welles. He knew Paris very well and all the best restaurants, and his father had been a chauffeur to Josephine Baker.

When Pat turned up in Paris we had a terrible argument through no one's fault in particular. Pat had arrived on her own and switched hotels from the Pont Royal to the Quai Voltaire. She had then come straight round to see the day's rushes, where everyone, especially the French, was laying very heavily into the whisky. We all moved on to a big table in the Brasserie Lipp, where Pat certainly had her say about the quality (not very good, she felt) of the rushes.

She was deep in conversation with the director's wife over the talents of the American auteur John Cassavetes, whom they discovered they both revered. I intervened, saying what a frightful, dreadful, completely boring actor I thought he was. 'And another thing,' I shouted, turning on Pat, still smarting from her remarks about the rushes, 'you've ruined my day!'

Well, that was probably going too far. She stood up, drew herself together, and slapped me very powerfully across the face. Within two seconds she was being bundled through the door and on to the pavement by two waiters in impeccable black suits and long white aprons. The place froze. The director's wife said, 'I would give all the money in the world to have the courage to do to my husband what Patricia did to you.' A production assistant, the dialogue coach Charlotte Trench, rushed out to look after Pat. They went off and had some brandies together, then she found her way back to the hotel. It was a terrible start to her visit to Paris, poor love.

When I went back to the hotel, there was Pat, cheerful as you like, as if nothing had happened. She'd upset me, I'd upset her, she had whacked me and stormed out, and now it was all over. Pat never bears a grudge and never allows any arguments to linger on beyond their natural length. It's the Irish, I suppose; but it's a very attractive temperament, like living in a squally climate of summer storms where the sun keeps breaking through and the sky, on the whole, is blue more often than it is grey.

So we decided to spend our next evening together, with Chris, in a quiet, refined restaurant in the Quai Voltaire, where nobody would bother us, and we wouldn't have to worry about not understanding French. The whole ambience was relaxed, quiet and sophisticated, with some very charming Americans minding their own business at the next table. Half way through the main course, Chris got a piece of steak stuck in his throat, and started choking and spluttering as if he was going to die. I immediately started pounding him brutally on the back and the piece of meat shot out of his mouth and landed right in the middle of the Americans' table.

And then of course the Americans did notice us, and they found out who we were and asked us to take lots of photographs of them, and then they of us, and then with all of us together, and the evening became very jolly indeed. Chris was saved from death, Pat and I were reunited, and the Americans went home happy with autographs and photographs.

This was a very happy time for me in Paris. Not only were Pat and I settling into a permanent relationship – despite all the hiccups – but my daughter Lucy spent a great deal of time with me. She was studying her Napoleonic law at the Sorbonne, but managed to be around quite a lot, acting as my guide and interpreter. By now she was a very pretty young woman, and people used to think she might be my latest girlfriend. In a way, she was. We got to know each other all over again, and she also got to know, and like, Pat, which made me enormously happy. My career was still in a peculiar state of unresolved tension, but my personal life was pulling together with a little more cohesion, and I was emerging from the dark woods of the early 1970s.

I saw a lot of Lucy over the next few years. When she finished her studies in France, she was employed as a lawyer with a big American company based in the Barbican. I also used to go down to the old Manor House in Chilcomb, near Winchester, where Tarn was, and is, still living, and we would go for long walks together. And when I did *Pygmalion* in Los Angeles in 1979 she came over and stayed with me for about two weeks, and she used to take me through my lines. Lucy is very like me, I always think, and we are very close now. I always listen to what she has to say, and what she has to say is usually well worth listening to.

The boys, too, I have grown much closer to. I always remember that when Toby was little, the nanny had called me up: she had found a dirty great flick-knife under his pillow. I told him that it was an illegal weapon and that I would call the police if he didn't tell me where he had found it. He stuttered out that Christopher, his brother, had given it to him. I told him to pull the other one, and he said that Mr Frost, a builder we had working in the house, had given it to him. I was very cross with him by this point, and he was howling. 'Where did you get it?' I persisted, and now he said that he had found it in the garden.

After they went off to Canada with Maggie and Bev, they came back once a year, through the late 1970s, to visit me. Toby was now nine or ten. I took them both out to lunch and I asked Toby again, 'Where *did* you find that flick-knife?' He just laughed at me, and I was furious. Ten years later, when he was nineteen, we went out to supper together. The subject of the flick-knife came up again. Toby said: 'I was so frightened when you said that you would call the police that I lied to you. I found the knife in Bert Frost's builders' bag, among all the chisels, saws and hammers.'

15

Return to the National, Farewell to Ralph

I had to relaunch my classical career without much help from anyone in the main subsidised companies, so I decided to give my Othello at last in the Regent's Park Open Air Theatre in the summer of 1976, with Edward Fox as Iago. I had performed Albee's *Zoo Story* there in the previous summer, I was living just around the corner in Pat's flat on Primrose Hill, and David Conville, the Open Air's artistic director, was only too happy to have me on board. It seemed a good idea at the time.

However, the experience proved differently, though at least I was not having to spend too much money on bus fares. My original plan was to have Mike Gambon as Iago, but he got a job elsewhere. Edward Fox was a great friend of mine. I'd seen him and admired him enormously in *The Day of the Jackal*, in which he played a smiling charmer, and I thought he'd make an ideal Iago. So I went to see him and took him a copy of the Shakespeare Variorum, the complete edition of the plays with all available annotations, as a present, and told him that he should first study the role, and then play it. With me. He agreed. He read it. He studied it. We rehearsed. We opened. He was disastrous. And so, as a matter of fact, was I.

My director for *Othello* in the Park was another factor in the disaster. He was a perfectly nice young boy called Mervyn Willis, who had been a stage manager at the National Theatre and who now works in a university drama faculty in America. I accepted him as my co-director; I knew what I wanted and what I didn't want.

The casting – and I was as much to blame as Mervyn – was all to pot. Roderigo, a most important part, is always miscast and played for laughs. He should be a cross between Romeo and Henry V, a young man who is lovesick for this girl. He turns the tables on Iago; after 'Put money in thy purse,' and all that crap, he says, 'Look, sort this out for me with Desdemona, or I'll go and tell her what you've done.' And Iago forms a better opinion of him than he had before. Roderigo becomes dangerous and has to be got rid of. He's not some kind of grinning idiot poof, which is what you usually get.

The play was impossible to do in the open air. The make-up was a disaster because it was the hottest summer we'd ever had. One of the reviewers, not without some justification, said that Robert Stephens looked like a melting chocolate ice-cream. The stuff came off all the time. I ended up a good deal less black than when I started. Then I went with it to South Africa and I still didn't get it right, although at least the make-up stayed on. I've suggested doing it again with Adrian Noble at the RSC in what I call the Ken Branagh spot; the Barbican, then Stratford, then a tour to America.

I don't think being white should preclude you from playing Othello, not at all. He's a tawny coloured Moor, not a black man. When my second father-in-law (Tarn Bassett's father) saw Olivier, he said that it was a marvellous pyrotechnical display of acting but it wasn't a Moor. He had been in Arabia with T.E. Lawrence and he said that Moors weren't anything like the way in which Larry played him; they were a strange, wandering tribe of people. Very noble, exotic and loyal. If you reneged on them, they would bury you up to your neck in sand. But they are not Negroes, which is what Larry presented.

I met a Moor and asked him, when Othello comes off and says 'Oh, my fair warrior,' and kisses Desdemona three times in front of his army and the Cypriots, where would he kiss her? And he said, 'On the forehead. It's symbolic, because he is kissing away all the lines that will appear when she gets old. And when he kills her, he would kiss her on the neck.' And he also said that Othello, as indicated, would never take Iago by the throat; a Moorish person would never lose dignity in that way.

My friend said that when his father was angry with his children, he never struck them. He would just stare at them, and his eyes were terrifying. The looks promised much worse things than a slap across the ears or a smacked bottom. Unfortunately, my Desdemona had a squeaky voice and was exactly the opposite of what I wanted. As indeed was the Roderigo, who was played by a terribly winsome creature. My own performance was generally excoriated as ridiculous and riddled with failure, and to be perfectly honest I can see no way of denying that it was anything but.

I was happily ensconced with Pat by now and I did not see all that much of the boys. I was not really involved in their lives in the way Don Hawkins remained involved with his and Pat's son. I would go across to Queen's Elm Square whenever they came back from Canada to pick them up for a couple of hours, but it was always very tense. We'd go out to restaurants, Toby was already well versed in restaurant life. He took a great interest in types of pasta and I even remember him ordering stuffed octopus when he really didn't know what it was.

I first met Pat's son, Quinn, when he was about five, on an outing we made to the Cappanina. The boy had never eaten in a really smart restaurant before, but he took to it like a duck to water. He ordered a Dover sole, squeezed lemon all over it, picked up a fish knife and fork and got stuck in. He was natural restaurant material, which pleased me greatly. He's an adorable boy. And I enjoyed his company, although I was never a second father to Quinn in the way that Beverley has been to my sons with Maggie. I appreciate everything Bev has done for them, but I had no choice in the matter. I was frozen out of their lives for several years.

I cannot bear to be on my own, which is why I needed Pat so much. If I'm not doing anything in particular I don't know what to do with myself when I wake up in the morning. I'm perfectly happy if I'm studying something, but I don't really sit down and just read something to pass the time. It was clear that if my stage career was going to develop at all that I had to get back into the major companies.

When Maggie and I left the National in 1970, we had received a wonderful letter from Larry thanking us for saving his bacon with *The Beaux' Stratagem* and *Hedda Gabler*, which both played to capacity business throughout their runs. But he never asked either of us when we were coming back. Obviously, when he did *Long Day's Journey Into Night* in 1973, he could have asked me to play the elder son, but he asked Denis Quilley instead, which is fair enough, but I wouldn't have said that it was the most ideal casting.

Larry was succeeded at the National by Peter Hall in 1973, the company moved to the new building on the South Bank in 1975. Luckily for me, Peter Hall invited me back to the National at the end of 1978, and I entered with considerable trepidation the concrete morass on the South Bank which was so much less friendly and manageable than the Old Vic. I had four very good roles: Maskwell in Congreve's *The Double Dealer*, Gaev in *The Cherry Orchard*, the Mayor in Ibsen's *Brand*, and one half of a double act with Albert Finney in a very funny play by Charles Wood, *Has Washington Legs?*

Maskwell is a role of venomous, sinewy duplicity: I loved every minute of it! And I was well suited to the description of the character delivered by his betrayed lover: 'Ten thousand meanings lurk in each corner of that various face!' Ralph Richardson was in the company and you always knew you were up against something with him. In *The Double Dealer*, there were some moves he was unhappy about. One night I walked on to the stage as Maskwell and he said, 'Ooh, Maxwell, you are the man I wish to meet . . .'; he always called me Maxwell, never Maskwell.

Howard Sackler, who produced all the classics on Caedmon Records, made a recording with Ralph some years prior to this of *Cyrano de Bergerac*, which had been one his greatest stage triumphs, and Ralph could not remember any of the French names. He couldn't even read them off the script, and what he was saying didn't sound like anything at all, so Howard pieced the vowel sounds together from bits of other words he was saying.

Ralph would grasp my hand as Maskwell – he was a very powerful man, taller than I am – and he'd move me downstage on his line so that he came into some sort of focus, and when you spoke, he'd move you upstage so you came into focus. It was totally unexpected when he did this, but it was never in order to upstage you. On the contrary, it was all to do with making you, and himself, be seen and heard to the best possible advantage at the right moment. It was also all to do with instinct and his feeling for the house and the audience, the mood on the night. He was a genius at living in the atmosphere of each particular performance.

One night he said that the scene in which we came down the stairs was wrongly positioned, it was not focused properly. It felt all right to me, but he asked me to come in before the next performance at five o'clock in the afternoon, just the two of us, and he re-staged the whole scene in terms of the steps we took, when, how many, and it was much, much better. He never directed plays himself, he wasn't interested enough, but he would have been frightfully good at it.

He knew what's what and, like all the great actors, had this total awareness of everything going on around him. And you couldn't see what he was doing at all. Albert Finney was quite right in saying that Ralph wasn't an actor at all; he was a magician. You couldn't see where anything came from, or why he said a word in a particular way. Who ever spoke like Ralph Richardson? Nobody. His stresses were completely his own and inexplicable.

All the great actors have this special ability to be heard, almost overheard. When Michael Redgrave played Vanya at Chichester, that great impossible barn of a theatre, he spoke perfectly naturally without raising his voice and you heard every single syllable as clear as a bell. Olivier as Astrov, too, was totally audible, but of course his enunciation, unlike Michael Redgrave's, was so pronounced.

I asked Redgrave how he did it. He said it was a simple trick that Edith Evans taught him: when each new thought strikes you, it should be expressed at a different velocity and pitch so that the text is treated like music, and becomes endlessly interesting to the ear. You have to orchestrate a speech to make it sound natural. It's not really a trick at all. It's how people address themselves on any subject. And I've always remembered that. If you always speak as if for real, new thoughts bring new energy.

Maskwell was a great part for me. It's amazing, sometimes, the effect you can have in a performance without realising it. The character is the lover of a horrendous, fiendish crocodile of a woman, and he's also trying to get her off with her nephew, while he himself is in love with the nephew's girlfriend. He's wheeling and dealing and in the end becomes so confused he doesn't know what to do. Somebody sitting behind Pat said, 'Oh, if only I knew a man like that!'

It is interesting the number of people you meet after the event who say things like, 'Oh, I was an usherette when you were playing at Chichester and I fell madly in love with you during *The Royal Hunt of the Sun*.' The girl who said that told me she had been sixteen at the time, but that when I came back the following year in *Armstrong's Last Goodnight*, she was even more in love with me. I was flabbergasted and could only say that I wish I'd known, but there was nothing I could have done about it. 'Well,' she said, 'Albert tried. But he didn't get anywhere, because it was you I was in love with!'

There was a girl from Philadelphia who turned up backstage on *Private Lives* one night. Chris Downes asked me if I wanted to see her, and we let her in, and we went and introduced her to Maggie along the corridor in her dressing room. This sort of thing happens all the time, you have a polite chat, and then you say goodbye. Which is what happened in this case, except that she was rather adamant, I thought, in saying, as we went in to see Maggie, 'It was *you* I came to see.'

Subsequently, she turned up wherever I appeared, in New York, Los Angeles, wherever I went. I can't remember her name. She was a very attractive girl and inevitably we jumped into bed in America. There was nothing I could do about it in England, but she still followed me back to London and was hanging around in the bushes of Regent's Park while I did *Othello*.

That first season back at the National was good for me, but I don't think the productions were outstanding by any means. Peter's production of the Chekhov was very disappointing. And *Brand* was such a boring play, and it was dreadfully directed by Christopher Morahan but I came out of it all right, because the Mayor is the voice of the audience and he expresses their common-sense reaction to Brand's crazy ideas all the time. He gets all the laughs and, in the end, all the notices: perfect!

Michael Bryant, who was droning on as Brand, couldn't understand that. I told him during rehearsals that he should cut the part; it's far too long and people soon became fed up with him. 'The part is so boring,' I told him. 'You're even boring me!' He was off the stage for only fifteen minutes out of four hours, right at the end. King Lear he is not. And *Brand* isn't even a play. It's a long, epic poem. After the interval, half the audience had gone home. On the other hand, I did get letters from people who had been to see it fourteen times! Heaven knows why. I couldn't have sat through it once.

The Wood play was about making a film about George Washington, so it recycled the idea behind that play *Veterans*, which was about the making of another film, the dread Tony Richardson's *The Charge of the Light Brigade*. The difference was that *this* film had not been made; every movie company in Hollywood was planning to make a film about George Washington; it ended with a call of 'Action' for the first shot on location in Ireland. It was hysterically funny, and you couldn't get a seat for the entire run in the little Cottesloe; I never understood why they didn't put it on in the large Olivier auditorium, and make something much more of all the technical paraphernalia.

Albert played a film director who was a grotesque mix of John Ford and John Huston. His first line was, 'Get John Wayne to play Washington. John Wayne has always wanted to play Washington.' I was the writer, a role written for John Gielgud. I played it with a sort of fluting deference, but with, I am immodest enough to imagine, a more heavy-lidded, saturnine and suspicious nature than John might have managed. He would have been superb; I was different, and quite good. I had a fixation about remuneration, and my character's refrain was, 'Can I have my money now?'

The whole of this National Theatre year was a very good one for me; I had four triumphs. I had a very good time. I've always found that a company environment is the best one, because you know everyone and you know how they work. But nobody rushed to pick up my contract, and there was a bit of a fuss when it became clear that I was leaving. I was later told that a new translation of a Schnitzler play, *Tales from the Vienna Wood*, had been commissioned from Christoper Hampton with me in mind for the leading role. In the event, the part was played by John Wood. And directed by Peter Wood. In the Vienna Wood. *Les trois bois*, in fact!

Peter Hall used to deliver great arias in praise of Albert Finney, who also left when I did, on how he couldn't have done anything without Albert, and on how Albert turned up for rehearsal in a tracksuit like everyone else, and so on. When they came to do *Macbeth*, however, they were completely trumped by the RSC production with Ian McKellen and Judi Dench, which I saw. It was brilliant. Peter Hall begged Albert not to go ahead, because he dreaded all the inevitably unfavourable comparisons thudding in. But Albert refused to be cowed by Ian McKellen. He performed it, very badly, with Dorothy Tutin as Lady M. It looked to me like a very tired production, designed by a very tired designer and badly acted by everybody.

Nor did I ever understand why Albert played Hamlet. It was ghastly. He can't help looking like a rugby player, but he made no effort not to sound like one. Hamlet is nothing if not reflective, which Albert simply isn't; he's an obvious, superb Coriolanus. Macbeth, similarly, is full of self doubt, which is beyond Albert's capacity as an actor. He doesn't know self-doubt. He's like a big oak tree in the ground.

Albert made a balls of Lophakin, too, in *The Cherry Orchard*. He has a potentially tragic scene with Varya, played by Susan Fleetwood, in which he is impervious to her passion for him; it was all set up, it's a gift. The scene, entirely based on pauses, should last about twelve minutes. She can't say anything and he won't say anything. He wants to ask her to marry him but he can't, it's not in his nature; it's a terrible, heart-breaking moment of total inner crisis.

But Albert wouldn't play it that way. He just mumbled quickly through it. I talked to Albert about it, and he said, 'No, no, I don't think 'e wants to marry 'er at all, y'know.' He couldn't share in the sensitivity and emotional shortcomings of the man. There are these great untapped reserves in Lophakin. He reminds me a bit of my father, who used to listen to the radio and weep at things like *Sorel and Son*, or some such sentimental play.

During this time, the film of *The Rocky Horror Show* had been made and had become a huge worldwide cult. Pat was very much associated with it, and rightly so. Her performance as Magenta and the usherette had been a key factor in establishing Richard O'Brien's witty, wacky musical all over the world. Just before rejoining the National, I had been in New York to promote the launch of the film *The Shout* and Pat was there, too, both to see me and to support one of the many worldwide *Rocky Horror* conventions which she has always loyally attended.

Actually, she enjoys them very much, too! Photographs and memorabilia are always laid out for sale and display and, on this occasion, Quinn, Pat's son, came rushing in, puzzled by the fact that they were also flogging pictures of myself at the conference. *Pourquoi?* We finally realised that these photographs were from *The Shout* in which I had a scene or two with Tim Curry, star of *The Rocky Horror Show*! We were dressed not in black silk underwear and suspender belts, but perfectly conservative cricketing whites. That was the nearest I ever came to cult status in the rock world.

John Dexter asked me at this point, in 1979, to go back to Los Angeles and play Henry Higgins in *Pygmalion*. This was certainly a contributory factor to my leaving the National, or at least a mollifying one; there was a chance we would go to Broadway, though we never did. A Canadian actress, Roberta Maxwell, was my Eliza Doolittle. She was excellent, but too old. Most Elizas, including the admirable Roberta Maxwell, make her speak in a comical Cockney voice that has no bearing on anything, let alone the peculiar condition of being bullied every day by Henry Higgins. In Los Angeles, John Dexter had remounted the production he had done with Alec McCowen and Diana Rigg in London. He was very peculiar, John. He asked me how I was going to play the last moment, when Higgins, left alone on the stage, hears the door bang and they're gone, the mother and Eliza.

The stage direction states that he hears the door bang, laughs and jingles the small change in his trouser pocket, showing that he remains totally incorrigible. John thought that I should slowly sink on to the sofa and put my hands in my lap, covering my genitals, and shrink, defeated and castrated by the two women. I thought that idea contradicted the whole point of the play.

We argued about it; the man hasn't lost anything, and he hasn't gained anything, either. Dexter said, 'Trust me, it looks marvellous,' so I did it on the first night, and after he went back to London I changed it back to the laughing defiance. What John seemed to forget is that Higgins hasn't asked Eliza to come to him for elocution lessons; he's been challenged by Pickering, on a bet between two fellow linguistic experts, to turn her into a Duchess. It doesn't really matter all that much to him whether he does or not. It's only a bet. He's not a villain, Higgins. Eliza wants to be a lady. But he's only interested in his phonetics.

I have rarely had misfortunes with wigs or hats on stage, or with telephones falling to bits in my hands, but I did have zipper trouble in *Pygmalion*. Instead of the usual industrial zip, my morning suit had a very light one. In the scene where I took Eliza to meet my mother, Mrs Higgins, I looked down, and the zip had gone. My fly was wide open. But no one had noticed and there was no laughing from the audience. Stupidly, as I left the room, I said 'Goodbye, mother', picked up my top hat and placed it over my fly. The audience roared with laughter and I received a tremendous round of applause.

Ralph Richardson said to me one night, 'I have always wanted to play Henry Higgins.' 'Why didn't you?' 'Nobody ever asked me!' He would have been a brilliant Higgins. Shaw's description of him as a very big man, 'rather like an overgrown baby', but totally without malice, was dead right for Ralph.

Of course Rex Harrison in *My Fair Lady* played it positively brimming with malice, although he was very funny, with that cutting, old-maidish quality of his. Leslie Howard was very good in the 1938 film of the play. He was a tiny man, and he played it with owlish spectacles. And in the same film, Wilfrid Lawson was brilliant as the dustman Alfred Doolittle, returning after he'd been made respectable and speaking through false teeth, with this ridiculous, sibilant, over-emphatic delivery.

Richardson once said to me, 'Did you ever see Wilfrid Lawson? He was a genius.' He never said that of John Barrymore, or of Laurence Olivier. I never knew Lawson, though I used to see him drinking in the pub during the Royal Court years. He'd drink large whiskies with beer chasers *before* the show. An actor who had been in *The Prisoner* with Lawson in 1954 at the Globe told me that when you were on stage with him, you had to adjust to his timing, according to whether he was drunk or sober, because whatever he did had absolute concentration. Lawson was playing the jailer and was reading a newspaper for a great long stretch of the play. And for however long it took him to do that, the audience was riveted.

The same thing with Paul Scofield. I watched Scofield like a hawk in John Osborne's *Hotel in Amsterdam* at the Royal Court in 1968. The play was thin and was about all of Osborne's hangers-on waiting for a tyrannical film director who never arrives, because he commits suicide; that was Osborne's final pay-off to Tony Richardson! Anyway, you could see that Scofield thought the play was no good, and you could sense his whole ear, his whole being, on the audience, to see if he'd still got them. And he would speed up or slow down, speak softly or loudly, accordingly. Scofield, like Lawson, has the ability to be totally attuned to the audience. And of course Richardson had, too. That is what I call great intuitive acting.

I've got the greatest respect for Paul. He's an actor I love watching but with whom I've never worked on the stage. I recorded Edgar on gramophone records in his *King Lear*, which was superb. He had played the part all over the world, and filmed it in the Peter Brook production. We had a very clever academic producer who gave him detailed and really quite insistent line readings, which Paul might easily have dismissed as impertinent at that stage of his career. But, typically, he took every one and responded positively to all the suggestions. He is incredibly open to suggestion and humble in the execution of his work. He always has been. He has a total simplicity about him, and a real dignity.

He asked me at the end of the 1970s if I would play Iago to his Othello, and in normal circumstances I would have done so like a shot. But he insisted on doing it at the National, which I was leaving, so he could do fewer performances in the repertoire. It was dismal. I thought he did the first speech, 'Oh, most potent, grave and noble senators', particularly well, but I told him afterwards that he had to tell his Iago, Michael Bryant, to get on with it. I never understood why Michael played it with a bald head and white hair; the National has a wig department. Iago's a young man. Twenty-six, in fact, not fifty-six.

Around this time, I was invited to dinner with Twiggy, whom I knew from the old 'Swinging Sixties'. She and her then boyfriend and business manager, Justin de Villeneuve, were familiar social beacons of the age, along with André Previn and Mia Farrow. She was planning to play Eliza in *Pygmalion* on television. She was keen for me to be her Henry

Higgins. What I would do as Higgins, I told her, was give her recordings of me speaking so that all she would have to do is imitate me. She would speak exactly like him. It's only when the grammar goes wrong that she screws it up. And it's only when she gets off the agreed subjects of the weather and so on, that things also go wrong. Twiggy liked the sound of all this and told the BBC to make sure that they cast Robert Stephens. But they got their Roberts muddled up and cast Robert Powell instead.

When I came back to London from Los Angeles I went through a strange period of not being able to find any decent work. I allowed myself to become involved in some pretty dire projects, and when I became miserable about them, I started drinking too much and finally walking out. I did a play by Nigel Williams about a policeman in a lavatory, *WCPC*, down in the Half Moon in the East End. I walked out of that, and then went back into it, though I didn't want to. They were endlessly rewriting.

It was all big mistake. It wasn't very good, you got paid about twenty pounds a week and you had to take taxis all the way home, which was a very long way away. And who, frankly, wants to see a play about a policeman hanging around in toilets? Everyone wanted it to be a success, but it didn't work. Every day we worked on a new ending until finally I just felt I was being used to try to get something sorted out.

Then there was *Mary Mary* by Pam Gems at the Donmar Warehouse. That was an even more complete mess. Robert Walker, a great friend of Pat's, was going to direct it, and he's obviously much better at television than he is at theatre. He'd have to be. I said I would do the play if Pam Gems would do rewrites. She came over to see me and I told her what my worries were. The characters were not written fully enough, especially my role, the transvestite Aunt Mary, who runs a petrol station by the road. Pam Gems said she was going to Spain for six weeks to do the rewrites, so Bob Walker and I sat down and talked to her about the play. She came back with exactly the same script!

She said she thought she would find it easier to write as we rehearsed. I thought to myself, 'I've heard that line before.' We started rehearsing, nothing got better and I apologised and withdrew. I said to my agent, 'I'm not going to make a cunt of myself here, or anywhere else, because I'll get the blame and all the flak for this. For being in it to start with, and for all the inept writing.' Alfred Marks took over the role. It was a disaster. The producing management who owned the theatre, the Alberys, threatened to sue me, but they didn't.

Then I was going to do a play in Liverpool, which Jane Lapotaire finally did in both French and English for some reason best known to herself. It was called *The Apartment*, and was directed by Robert Chetwyn. Nobody told me it was going to be in the studio theatre. Just two people in a lavish French apartment. The design was all wrong, the doors were in the wrong place, and I walked off that as well. I wasn't going to make a cunt of myself in Liverpool. And in fact the Liverpool Playhouse did sue me for a couple of thousand pounds, but that came off my income tax.

One is endlessly hoping to be in a new play; I've been lucky with so few. I didn't feel that I was letting all those people down, quite the reverse. I felt that *I* was being let down because, after all, they were employing me to try and boost what they were doing. They were using my experience, my fame and pulling power, if you like, to attract the producers' money and the audiences. So why on earth should I feel I was letting them down? With Pam Brighton, who directed *WCPC* I should have been firmer; with Robert Walker, it was hopeless. I should never have agreed to do any of them. I was out of my mind, really.

The only way you can pull a shitty play out of the fire and do something with it is if you have a director as brutally good and visionary as John Dexter. Dexter would work his arse off to make *The Royal Hunt of the Sun*, or *Black Comedy*, into a good and rewarding experience; and he would make everyone else work their arses off. He knew how to put things together. He'd never tell you to just amble on and make something up, or improvise. It was the same old story when I went back to the National and joined the Bill Bryden company.

I was too old to be messing around like that. And it worked, the Cottesloe was always full, so why should they worry about anything? They came a cropper, though, on the bigger stages. The first show I did with the Bill Bryden mob was *Cinderella* for Christmas 1983, a truly disastrous pantomine in which I played an ugly sister with Derek Newark; they wrote it themselves instead of getting someone in who knew about panto and working with children. I was ridiculous. I looked like an old tart, and I was desperately unfunny. I should have known by then that I was not an innately funny actor. But I was less innately unfunny than Derek Newark.

I also took over Oberon from Paul Scofield in *A Midsummer Night's Dream*, which was not too bad. But the big hit was Tony Harrison's new version of *The Mysteries*. I enjoyed playing Herod and Pontius Pilate very much. But I thought that the company's attitude was so slack towards *being* actors; they weren't doing anything except walking around. I felt totally out of place.

I said to Jack Shepherd, who was playing Lucifer, that although he was dressed as a bus conductor, and although the devil does indeed appear in many disguises, he seemed to have forgotten that he was, basically, an angel who had been chucked out of heaven; and also in the mysteries, the guild plays, he was playing as an amateur actor, and in amateur acting, they tend to overstress things; at least, I felt, he should attempt an accent that was more refined.

I suggested that, as a Yorkshireman, he should try and speak like the Queen. It would have been more comical, and he would have appeared to be a little bit more like the devil and a little less like a coal-heaver, which is maybe what his character might have been in life. All Jack Shepherd ever really played, of course, was Jack Shepherd. He never stepped out of himself to try to play somebody else.

I did quite like Tony Harrison's text, but some of it was very difficult. The first speech of Herod I couldn't understand at all and I asked him about it. He was no help whatsoever. He and Bill Bryden just said, 'Oh, make up anything you like,' and that slapdash attitude drove me nuts. I used to grit my teeth and yell silently at them all, 'Oh for Christ's sake, do something, ACT! Don't just wander around because you're a Bill Bryden actor.' That was their style. They were like a rugby team just turning up to amble round the theatre for a couple of hours before going back to the pub.

I still find it terribly irritating when perfectly good actors like Jack Shepherd obstinately refuse to play with any other accent than that dull Yorkshire or Lancashire. Of course, the minute Jack does that brilliant David Mamet play, *Glengarry Glen Ross*, he can do an American accent right off. So why can't he speak properly in a rich and varied English accent?

I bite my tongue off saying it, almost, but I do think that that crowd of actors were so arrogant – though I did enjoy working with them, and with Bill. He told me how he'd bumped into Trevor Nunn who said 'You've got the best company in England, but I believe they're all alcoholics,' and of course Bill thought that was frightfully funny. They were all so lazy. I got a notice saying 'Robert Stephens has not joined Bill Bryden's company, he bestrides it.' When the company split up, none of them went on to appear in the West End or anything like that; they went back into television, or hung around doing bits and bobs. It is not that

I think this kind of acting is no good to the classical tradition; it is of no use to anybody.

Bill Bryden also wanted me to be in *Golden Boy*, the Clifford Odets play. When I later met Elia Kazan, who had played the part of the gangster Fuseli, who wants to turn his violin-playing protégé into a boxer, he said he thought there was an understated undertow of homosexuality. He said that at the time of playing the role in New York, he had met a gangster, nicknamed 'Gerrah', because he used to say 'Gerrah of here' (meaning 'get out'). He invited old 'Gerrah' along to a dress rehearsal, soliciting any tips in the playing of this mobster. At the end, 'Gerrah' called him over and said, 'You was very good in your part. One thing: don't hollah! They know who you are.' I passed this on to Jack Shepherd but he still shouted all the way through the performance.

The Bill Bryden crowd were at their best in the Mamet play, *Glengarry Glen Ross*. The Chicago accent was very particular, and Mamet was there with Bill Bryden directing, so they all had to learn it like the Bible and learn how to speak it properly.

Then there was a terrible fuck-up over *Inner Voices*, the Eduardo de Filippo play, because Lindsay Anderson was going to direct it for Ralph and he wanted to bring all his regular Royal Court-type actors in. The National said he couldn't. Ralph was miscast and couldn't learn it, and I replaced somebody in it whom he wouldn't work with. The eventual director, Mike Ockrent, replacing Lindsay, was benign but hopeless. I played the man who lived downstairs and they all blamed a murder on everyone else. And of course the old boy's just dreamt it; nobody's been killed at all.

So I went round to see old Ralph and he said, 'Ooh, I'm so glad you are going to play that part. You look like somebody who killed somebody.' Ralph once said to the comedian Dave Allen, 'Are you a friend of Bob Stephens?' 'Yes, I am,' said Dave. 'He's a very strange fellow . . .'. 'Yes, Ralph,' said Dave, 'and so are you!' Later in the run, Ralph became ill and went into hospital, but the show was booked for a big tour, and I was asked to take over his role. I learned it in two days. The only other person I know who is as quick as me in that respect is Derek Jacobi. In my case, the skill is a legacy from weekly rep, whereas Derek is just naturally quick.

The production, in spite of all this, was a great critical success for Ralph, and for me. Ralph was recognised as the most beautiful dreamer and genuine half-awake lost soul of our theatre, and I was pleasingly described as a convincingly Italianate head of the household where the whole thing happened. I presided over a sombre junk house of chairs and hangings. I had a great scene where I broke down and confessed the torment of my daily existence, and Michael Billington described me in the *Guardian* as 'a balding, domesticated Othello in crotch-sagging pyjamas and a tearing temper'.

Ralph's illness – the part was to prove his last in the theatre – coincided with a four-date tour, and the first receiving house, the Theatre Royal at Norwich, was not at all keen on having an understudy in the role they had been advertising as being performed by Sir Ralph. But Dick Condon, the manager, a very nice Irishman, now dead, unfortunately, was delighted when I volunteered to take over. I played it rather more Neapolitan than Ralph did, with a touch more of the 'Godfather', spaghetti-style acting about it. After Norwich, we played in Liverpool, Nottingham, and I think Edinburgh, and then I continued in Ralph's role when we returned to the South Bank. The National was a bit worried that I would object to not being reviewed in the part, but I didn't mind at all. It was a good part for me. And I was honoured to represent Ralph in it.

I was doing a lot of television in this period: John Masefield's *The Box of Delights*, Puccini for Tony Palmer which I enjoyed doing enormously, and a terrible series in Manchester about a recording studio, based on Virgin, for several months. I agreed to be in *The Box of Delights* on condition they agreed to use the music I associate with it from my childhood, a most glorious symphony of carols. The story is supposed to be an allegory about the battle against evil, in particular Adolf Hitler. The rights were owned for many years by MGM, who planned to make a cartoon version. But they dropped them, and the rights returned to the estate.

The BBC, who now acquired the rights, had invented a process of animation with real people called the paintbox, which they sold, stupidly, to an American company. They needed this technique for *The Box of Delights*, so they had to hire it back! There is a famous sequence where a donkey and a cart, with an old man, come out of the picture and into the sitting room, and they give the box of delights, which transports you to anywhere in the world, to the little boy.

I played Abner Brown, a gangster and a magician, who wants the box, and keeps chasing after the boy: 'That boy, that boy, what I won't do to that boy!' and so on. It was a six-part series and because of the animation being mixed with real acting, it took a very long time to make, about nine months. So long in fact, they were frightened that the little boy's voice would break before they had finished. The fact that he also contracted diptheria and was off for a while did not allay these fears. He had to have three sets of costumes made, as it was, because he kept growing taller and taller.

It was a delightful project, and I received a fair amount of acclaim. Pat played alongside me as my partner in crime, the delightfully named Sylvia Daisy Pouncer. This was a very happy time for Pat and me, but it is fair to say that my work seemed to be unfocused and I found it difficult to see further ahead than the latest role in a film, or on television. I was in part compensated by growing closer again to my children, with the exception of Michael, the eldest. Lucy was now my constant delight after the bonding experience in Paris. Maggie and Bev had returned to Sussex from Canada and the boys, Chris and Toby, were now finishing at school and both considering careers in the theatre.

Chris did some stage-management work and looked to be going into that side of things, but he changed his mind and decided to become an actor. He also had to change his name, because Equity already had a Christopher Stephens on their books. So he calls himself Chris Larkin. By the time he went back to LAMDA to train as an actor, young Toby had already started, so the younger brother went through one year ahead of the older. They both moved back to London and used to stay in the house in Queen's Elm Square, so we often met and now we see a good deal more of each other than we used to.

16

*The Biggest Come-Back
Since Lazarus?*

It is a disappointment that the Shakespearean parts I might have been expected to play in the 1980s – Macbeth, Leontes, Antony – evaded my grasp, although there is a great problem with Leontes which I was not sorry to miss tackling. That is his sudden onset of jealousy which is as unmotivated as the decision of Lear to divide up his kingdom.

I hadn't really thought of myself playing Falstaff, although Trevor Nunn had: he invited me to join the RSC in the opening season at the Barbican in 1982, but I was unable to accept. I had other commitments and I did not really feel like rejoining a repertory company. And the Barbican did not sound a terribly friendly place to work in. Joss Ackland played Falstaff in my stead.

My work was varied and interesting in this period, but in 1985 I particularly enjoyed a production of Moss Hart's 1948 backstage comedy *Light Up the Sky* which took me back to the Old Vic after all those years. It was lovely to roar once more to the rafters of the famous old house in a part which certainly demanded that I did so.

I played Carleton Fitzgerald, a somewhat ravaged and emotionally charged-up old theatre director given to such sentimental extravagances as bestowing his leading actress with the necklace Duse once wore on the opening night; and proposing a lachrymose toast to the cleaning woman accidentally enraptured at a dress rehearsal – 'a shapeless, dirty old harridan, this hapless bag of bones who had discovered beauty' – without realising that the bag in question was his mother-in-law in disguise, who was sitting right next to him while he delivered the speech!

I love the writing of those old Broadway comedies, which is why I would very much like to revive Garson Kanin's *Born Yesterday*, an ideal example of the genre and one ideally suited to myself and Patricia. Pat was in the cast of *Light Up the Sky*. Our very good director was her old colleague form the Glasgow Citizens', Keith Hack, and the other actors included such excellent stalwarts as Maxine Audley, Kate O'Mara and Robert Morse. I was unable to progress with the production to the West End because of a commitment to a television series about the Tolpuddle Martyrs, so my role was taken over by Keith Baxter, whose performance as shambling old Carleton several critics, alas, compared unfavourably with a poor thing, but mine own.

During the run of *Light Up the Sky* Pat and I went to dinner with our dear friends and neighbours, Professor Norman Morris and his wife Lucy, who live in Provost Road, Chalk Farm, just around the corner from us in Primrose Hill. Norman is a most distinguished, retired gynaecologist, and his and Lucy's two sons, Nick and David, are both doctors.

Nick was there that night and noticed that I was drinking lots of water. He asked Pat if I got up in the night to go to the loo with any frequency. She said I did. He thought this might be symptomatic of diabetes, and so I checked into the Middlesex Hospital. Afer all those years, I was diagnosed diabetic, which surprised me but perhaps it shouldn't have done: my mother was diabetic, and so is my sister, Jackey.

I immediately started to watch my diet and pretend that I was behaving more responsibly. Before I became too serious about this, I played one of Falstaff's cronies, Pistol, in Ken Branagh's film of *Henry V* (1989) in which Robbie Coltrane was a very interesting fat knight. It was a good film and I was proud to be part of it. But it was a nightmare assignation: two weeks of shooting at night, 6 pm to 6 am, on the back lot at Shepperton Studios which was sprayed every day by the fire department, so you were walking in about two feet of mud. I broke my foot on that picture, though I didn't know until later. Then two weeks of shooting in the same rain, but in the daylight.

We all did it for the same salary, top whack £15,000. But it was fun to do, because if you bung all those actors into caravans – Paul Scofield, Derek Jacobi, Alec McCowen, Judi Dench, Ian Holm – they will talk like parrots all night. Kenneth was brilliant in it, directing non-stop. Suddenly, in the middle of the night, with the cameras rolling, he would jump on to his horse for 'Once more unto the breach, dear friends, once more'. He was admirable, and he couldn't be more enchanting. He knows that he's not the new Laurence Olivier; he's an extremely good actor, though he does not have any charismatic quality on stage or screen. But he's the first person to know that about himself, and he works tremendously hard.

My catalogue of physical misfortunes continued unabated. One year earlier I had fallen over an uneven paving stone on the terrace outside the flat in Primrose Hill. It was pouring with rain, and there was a strike of council workers, so the street lamps weren't working. I did my hip in and it was re-set incorrectly. This gave me a pronounced limp. I sued Camden Council and eventually, three years later, wangled £15,000 out of them.

Later, as Falstaff, I had to turn my limp to advantage. After that earlier fall, my bad leg was a quarter of an inch shorter than the other one, which happens in the mending sometimes. As a result, I developed this ungainly hobble. So when, after my transplant operations in 1994, I fell over and did the *other* hip in, I asked if the surgeon wouldn't mind taking a quarter of an inch off the bone. But that couldn't be done. However, it seems to have all sorted itself out now, and I hardly limp at all; when I can walk, that is!

But I was fine in myself, never finer. I had made the film of *The Bonfire of the Vanities* in 1989 in America. I played a newspaper proprietor and I had a scene in a restaurant with Bruce Willis who was playing a drunk journalist I was taking out to lunch in order to give him a wigging. Willis's character was based in the novel on a journalist called Anthony Haden-Guest, a notorious and good-tempered *bon viveur* who is delightfully renowned for never having to pay for his own lunch.

They told Brucey-baby that he had to speak in an English accent, but he couldn't do it and claimed that his audience wouldn't accept his performance if he did. So they changed the Haden-Guest figure into an American, which defeated the whole point of it. Brucey also changed the script a lot, which was a shame, because it was a terrific one to start with.

The director told him he was playing a terrible shit, that he had to be gross, drunk, slobbering over this girl he pushed to the floor as I walked into the scene. But he wouldn't do any of that. He was a perfectly charming man to talk to, but impossible to act with. He gave nothing back, he never knew his lines and he refused to take any direction. He'd go off to his caravan to change his shirt quite often – he's very muscular man, and sweats a lot – and he'd come back knowing the next few lines of the scene.

I asked the make-up man why Brucey was so unpopular, and he said it was obvious: the money they were paying him, about $10m for five weeks' work. On the *Die Hard* films, he told me that he did three weeks' work out of twelve, and he was paid $15m on the last one. It's all done with stuntmen, apart from the dialogue scenes. He also told me that he was an actor by accident. He simply went along with a friend who had an interview for a part. The producers there saw him and offered it to him instead, even though he wasn't an actor at all. And out of that came this incredible movie career!

Tom Wolfe was paid six million dollars for the rights to his book and never visited the set. When I arrived in New York for the New York sequence, I opened a magazine and there was Tom Wolfe saying what he would have done if he had retained any control over the script: he would have whittled it down in a certain way, hired Mike Nichols to direct it, cast it differently.

I had been off the stage for five years when I joined the RSC at last to play Falstaff in Stratford-upon-Avon in April 1991. My absence had been caused partly by some reasonably well-paid television and film work, but also by my own loss of contact, really, with what was going on. I began to feel that I no longer had any place in the theatre. Whatever I read about it, or heard people saying *à propos*, made me feel like an outsider at my own party.

When the RSC came knocking about Falstaff again at first I said 'No' again. The money is terrible, and I didn't want to go and live in Stratford for months on end, stagnating in a little town with lots of actors. My agent, who was now Michael Foster at Duncan Heath/ICM, talked me into playing Falstaff. After sticking with Maurice Lambert at Film Rights until the late 1970s, I had joined the William Morris agency, partly at Jeremy Brett's suggestion. But they were not a great help to me, and I happily switched to Michael Foster – who said that he had been waiting for me to join him all his life – in 1990 or thereabouts. He said there would never be another such opportunity for me, and that the RSC was unlikely to perform these great plays, *Henry IV, Parts One and Two* for many years. He promised to get me as much film and television work on the side as he could, and he did get the odd thing or two. He made me feel I simply had to accept the offer, if not for the money. He was right, and I am eternally grateful to him.

I talked to Adrian Noble about the play. I liked his willingness to listen to my ideas about the role and I was deeply touched by his confession that, as an undertaker's son in Chichester, he had first considered a career in the theatre because of my performance there as Atahuallpa in *The Royal Hunt of the Sun*.

I was less happy about the fact that the company was unwilling to cast Pat in the company – she would have been an ideal Doll Tearsheet (admittedly this role was taken by Adrian's wife, the excellent Joanna Pearce) or Mistress Quickly, who was not particularly well cast. I needed Pat to be with me in Stratford that summer, and for a lot of the time she was, but at her own expense.

I had never seen the plays, but I read them again and saw that I could do Falstaff without playing some jolly old fat man. Falstaff is the most wonderful part. My received image was of a humpty-dumpty Father Christmas, but he's not like that at all. For a start, he's probably the cleverest man in both plays, terribly devious and, in principle, a great survivor. He's a keenly intelligent, bright and witty fellow who, in the end, gets the boot when there's no further place for him in the life of the prince. The new king is not going to make him Minister of Education or anything like that; their days together are over. And I think that, in the second play, instead of becoming increasingly apprehensive and forlorn, Falstaff becomes increasingly triumphant, knowing that the prince has done exactly the right thing with him. I see more clearly now that in Part Two, he is a completely different person. He only has two scenes with the prince: falling about in the pub, and getting the bullet. Otherwise, you only see him with the Lord Chief Justice and having to put himself about: wheeling and dealing, recruiting soldiers and borrowing money. The second part is really Falstaff without the prince.

The role itself didn't cause me any problems, apart from the need to wear padding: Falstaff *has* to be a fat man, whichever way you slice it. I wore padding during rehearsals. If you get the part right in the first place, the rest will follow. I made a point of observing fat people, or actors like Oliver Hardy, and the first thing you notice is how incredibly nimble they are on their feet, and very careful of where and how they tread. Their hands are very light, too.

But for all that pleasure and enjoyment in the role, I still felt that in going to Stratford one was being ripped off by the RSC. You are subsidising them for the honour of being in their productions. I estimate that playing Falstaff cost me £15,000 of my own money. That amount simply disappeared from my bank account. It is the cost of the Stratford accommodation – I rented a perfectly comfortable, chi-chi little flat right down on the river just beyond the theatre – and the cost of maintaining the London address.

When I got to Stratford it was even worse than I feared it would be. You're spending money all the time. It's not a cheap place because it's a tourist trap. There's nowhere to go, nothing to do. The same people day in day out. So you just go there for the honour of playing Shakespeare. It's faintly ridiculous.

In the old days, you could always see Shakespeare in the reps but these days, apart from the occasional effort in Birmingham, Liverpool, Glasgow or Manchester, that's about it. You rarely see any Shakespeare in the West End, so the actors are forced into the trap of working for peanuts in Stratford. If the RSC are not prepared to pay the actors more money, they should at least find a way of halving the price of the accommodation. They actually own the property they rent out to the actors.

Their excuse for the high rents is that they have to meet all the costs of refurbishment, decorating and painting, but that's so much bullshit. There were thirteen apartments in the complex I stayed in, and they were all carpeted and curtained and furnished in exactly the same way. All job lot stuff. The redecorating was done by the RSC scenery department, the wiring by the RSC electricity department, curtains made by the RSC wardrobe. The company is making a very good profit out of its own actors!

You simply cannot shift them on the top salary. I think my salary was classified a 'Robert Stephens special' which was about £30 more than Derek Jacobi got for playing Macbeth. And I threw in my Julius Caesar for nothing. That was directed by Steven Pimlott, who was making £7,000 a week for having directed Andrew Lloyd Webber's *Joseph and the Amazing Technicolor Dreamcoat* at the Palladium and all over the place. He was simply dying to tell you how embarrassed he was about how much he was making.

However, the important thing about all this, of course, is that I had a lot of fun doing Falstaff, and we played many performances. Everything the old boy says is to the point, and the speech about honour is dazzling. I recited that speech at Buckingham Palace later on, and I wouldn't mind doing it again.

Prince Charles said to me after we opened that he wished he'd had a companion like Falstaff when he was a young man. This underlines a very important point about the character: that he is an example of a sort, an embodiment of humanity and sensual reality, if not necessarily an ideal political role model, which is why Prince Hal has to reject him, but only after he has experienced Falstaff's way of life and philosophy, which is an important aspect of his growing up and preparing for the responsibilities of office.

There was a great sense of homecoming in my success. The critics seemed to welcome me back to the fold, for which I was truly grateful, and most of them remarked on the fact that I was not playing the old boy with any deliberate ingratiation or studied charm. Paul Taylor in the *Independent* noted that my phrase in Part Two, 'If I had a thousand sons . . .' poignantly betrayed the closest I had come to the consolations of fatherhood, and Michael Billington in the *Guardian* also cottoned on to the shafts of pain in the portrayal, the melancholy hunger for lost aristocratic values, 'like some fallen Lucifer with residual memories of a better life'.

I deliberately expunged all hint of geniality from the old bugger. He is not Father Christmas, and he is not a piece of old driftwood catching the tide; he's a canny, cynical old time-server with an eye to the main chance, a disregard for pompous authority and, above all, an instinct for survival. There is indeed something predatory and vicious about him in Part Two, and the role, I found, yielded more to me as an actor with every passing performance. So much so, that I would like very much to have another go at him. I loved playing him, and I revelled in the success we had with those wonderful archetypal English scenes in Eastcheap and Gloucestershire.

When I was in Stratford, I offered to give classes in the use of the 'operative' word; I said I can't hear one operative word when half of those young actors speak. The operative word is the one which makes the whole sentence work and gives it its meaning, the one that operates the sentence or the couplet. In other words, 'I can't *bear* to sit in this cinema', or 'I can't bear to sit in *this* cinema', are totally different ways of operating the same sentence. You have to find which is the correct way with each and every line in a play.

Half the time at Stratford, whatever Adrian Noble, the director of the Royal Shakespeare Company, might say about going back to basic principles of verse-speaking, this simple and fundamental rule is simply ignored. Unless you have that operative word clearly registered, the audience simply won't know what you are talking about. And with all due respect to Adrian, whom I like and admire very much, they don't at Stratford.

Adrian paid me the compliment of saying that I speak Shakespeare as if I am making it up. It is a question of thinking the lines right through to their meaning, not their metre. Falstaff only speaks in prose, but the same thing applies about finding the operative words and the right places to breathe. In verse-speaking, the metre takes care of itself if you make the thoughts count.

My son Toby enjoyed working with Peter Hall when he played Bertram in *All's Well*, but he said he didn't know how to play the part for three months after he had opened in it because he was endlessly thinking about the metrical units, not the meaning of what he was saying. Peter, he felt, gave great notes which had not much practical application to the details of character and performance problems; he's become obsessed with the verse as verse, not as stuff you speak.

Working with Adrian was no different from working with most directors, in that, as an actor, you take in all your own ideas and then embark on a process of selection in which the director is involved. I hated the sets for *King Lear* and the rake was hazardous for everyone, not least the stage hands, and the real rain was horrendous. Doing both those productions in the Barbican was delightful, the stage very good to work on.

The stage at Stratford is a nightmare because of all that space in the wings which sucks your voice straight out there if you speak in profile, so you always have to stand full on, or at least three-quarters on, to the audience. I remember the first time I played there was when we took *Much Ado* from the National during an RSC dark period, and we did a run through on the stage and the stage hands wanted to know if this was a football match, or what. 'No,' we replied, 'it's just a Franco Zeffirelli production. You like it or loathe it, it's up to you.' The RSC's company manager, the late Paddy Donnell, was frightfully patronising after the show, saying, 'Well, we all know what Franco's like . . .' On the other hand, some regulars in the theatre came up to me and said it was the most enjoyable Shakespeare they had ever seen on that stage.

Shaw called the Stratford theatre a sugar factory, not without reason. From the outside, it looks functional, industrial, boring. Inside, despite all the alterations to the stage, nothing much had changed since I had first worked there. The auditorium is an oblong. Well, sound travels in a curve, which is why the old theatres with a horse-shoe shape and steep stacking of the circles – as in the Old Vic – are so much better. The audience is too far from the actor in most modern theatres. The Olivier at the National, and the Stratford main house, are far too big in that they go too far back. The actor must look like a peanut from the worst seats, which he never did at the Old Vic. It is also very difficult to pitch the sound at Stratford, because the audience comes round to your side a lot. The proscenium arch made sure you knew where you were pitching.

After Falstaff in Stratford, and before we took the season to London, Pat and I went to Hollywood for a holiday, principally for the weather, and to stay with the actress/singer Georgia Brown, who is still best known, I guess, for singing 'As Long As He Needs Me' in the original production of *Oliver!* Pat had become friends with Georgia while they were both making the television series *Shoulder to Shoulder* about the suffragette movement and Mrs Pankhurst and her two daughters. Well, the weather was dreadful. It poured with rain and was freezing cold. So we took off for another part of California, where it never rains. And where everybody goes to die. Including, as it very nearly turned out, me.

We stayed in a lovely hotel, but I was terribly tired all the time. I couldn't manage to pull myself out of an overwhelming lassitude. Pat and I were walking along the street and suddenly my legs simply buckled underneath me. I was rushed to hospital and the doctors told me I was anaemic and that I needed a blood transfusion. This is usually as straightforward as taking an aspirin. They take your blood pressure, in you go, and out you come next morning. I didn't. They gave me the wrong blood.

They had given me unwashed blood, instead of washed blood which has been put through saline water. I woke up thinking that I was dying in the last stages of emphysema. My lungs were full of water. I couldn't breathe. So I was pumped out and put on a breathing machine, and I couldn't speak. They had now transferred me to the antechamber of the knacker's yard. I really thought this was it.

It was a dreadful time and I felt totally alone, except for Pat being there. I couldn't really understand why this was happening to me, or the justice of it all. It was as if I was just a punchball. What had I done to deserve this? Luckily, Georgia Brown took care of Pat and a friend of hers, a darling lady called Evelyn Fischelson, lent Pat a condominium to stay in, and arranged the loan of a zippy little yellow Mustang to enable her to get around town. It was a strange and alarming time.

Sitting there in the hospital, I wrote a message to Pat on a piece of paper: 'Please ask them if I will be able to play Falstaff at the opening in the Barbican Theatre on 4th March.' They said to her that not only was that unlikely, but that I only had a twenty-five per cent chance of survival: 'He will never be able to do anything like that again ever in his life.'

This happened twice over. They say you only live once. I nearly died twice. They said I could leave and that there would be some oxygen on the aeroplane for me. But I refused to travel for ten hours on an oxygen machine in an aeroplane; even I might not have made that! So I stayed in that hospital for about twelve days and the bill was $52,000. Thank God for holiday insurance.

Finally, they released me and I came back and went straight into the Royal Free Hospital in Hampstead, North London. They were horrifed by what had happened to me and gave me a new drug which had recently been developed for sportsmen whose haemoglobin level was dropping; but it was terribly expensive. It was concentrated iron and they injected it into my bloodstream for nine hours, a huge bag of what looked like very rich old port. They then shot six injections over six days of something else, straight into my stomach: you feel like Popeye eating the spinach as it goes in.

The RSC paid half the cost of it and I think my agent, Michael Foster, paid the other half. The result was that I missed the six-week season in Newcastle that the RSC always does between Stratford and London, but I was okay for that March opening at the Barbican.

After Falstaff, Adrian wanted to know what I might do next and when he mentioned *King Lear* my first reaction was that there had been too many *King Lears* around. So we decided on Prospero in *The Tempest*. I went off to Canada to make a film and wrote Adrian a very long letter about Prospero, saying that as his daughter should be about eighteen years old, maximum, Prospero should be no older than his mid-forties, fifty top. I didn't see him as some old magician at all, but very violent and vengeful.

I had just posted this letter when he called me up and said that he thought that we really should do *King Lear*. And possibly Shylock later in the same season, but that didn't work out as both productions were finally scheduled to open too close together. My Kent, David Calder, a very good actor, played Shylock, and when I saw the production I was mightily relieved not to be in it. It was hopeless.

I met the director, David Thacker, in Joe Allen's one night, and he said, 'We're going to do *The Merchant* together; it takes place Now, in the City.' I told him that I wasn't doing it, but that anyway, *The Merchant of Venice* does not take place 'now'. 'Now' there are merchant bankers whom you visit to borrow money; you don't go, 'now', to a bloke in a Jewish ghetto with three balls hanging over the front door, and you don't go on to the Rialto, and you don't spit on Jewish gaberdines. 'Now' you don't even wear Jewish gaberdines.

That's what I found was wrong with Jonathan Miller's production at the Old Vic, with Larry playing Shylock as a Rothschild banker in morning suit and monocle. I didn't believe a word of it. Shylock is not a merchant banker, he is a backstreet, two-bit moneylender who lives completely apart from the people who take advantage of him when it suits them to do so. Larry's Shylock was really a load of Shycock. In my view.

The nearest I ever got to the Jewish experience of the Holocaust was in a big TV series of that name, which was very successful, in which I played the role of a German road-builder, and when it was shown in Germany, there was an enormous outcry from the students. They simply don't know what had happened because the Holocaust had been erased from the history books. So there was a huge uproar and the television station interviewed people, including the real-life person on whom my character was based, who turned out not to be a road-builder at all but an architect.

He was asked why he had not used Ukrainians or Russians in his work, because they were much bigger and stronger. His answer was that he used Jews because they were cleverer and they understood what he was trying to do. This character helped save a lot of Jews though his nephew was an SS Officer. It was a good story. In fact, I asked the Jewish producers why they should want to make yet another film about the Holocaust when there had been so many and everyone knew what had happened. And they said precisely that: 'Because it's a good story.' And it is.

The series was shown all over the world. All the Jewish characters were played by American actors, all the nasty Nazis by English actors. David Warner, who is half-Jewish, was playing Heidrich and had to shoot a scene in Heidrich's actual office in Vienna. He broke down during filming, he was so overcome with emotion. The man I played testified at the Nuremberg trials.

I made another Jewish film in which they used an actual former concentration camp in Yugoslavia. Topol was in it. When we went in to film where the gas ovens had been, he couldn't go any further and broke down muttering, 'It could have been me, it could have been me.' He hadn't been able to sleep for two weeks beforehand, tossing and turning with terrible nightmares.

Between Falstaff and Lear I had gone to Canada to make a film with Ben Kingsley about Bobby Fischer, the chess champion. In *The Search for Bobby Fischer*, Ben and I played two chess grand masters in the wake of Bobby Fischer's disappearance from public view. But half-way through the filming, Bobby Fischer suddenly emerged from hiding and announced that he was ready to play the Russians again! The producers went nuts. They couldn't believe it. They had to rewrite the film, because the assumption underlying it thus far was that he was either dead or wandering around the Bolivian jungle. He was neither. He was just hard to pin down. I was becoming a little like that myself, even after all these years.

17

To the Mountain Top as King Lear

King Lear was a happy return to the RSC in May 1993 but I did not get off to a very good start. Thanks to a combination of too tight boots and the ridiculous one-in-ten rake of the stage in Anthony Ward's design, I developed an infection in my foot and the opening was postponed while I went into Warwick Hospital and was pumped full of antibiotics. The understudy did the first few performances, and then everything was fine until the end of the Barbican run, when the same infection flared up again and I missed the last fifteen performances.

I was never frightened of playing Lear. I've never been frightened of anything, much. I've never had stage fright, unlike Larry. Larry was so nervous on his first night of *Richard III* in 1943 that he asked John Mills and his wife, Mary Hayley Bell, to go and hold his hand in the dressing room. He felt that he had the make-up ready but not the performance. The Millses sat with him while he applied his long plasticine nose, his dank, straggly black wig, his great hump. He then shortend one leg. He backed on to the audience for his first soliloquy, then turned, and the house fell about: they screamed with laughter at the sight of this absurd grotesque. And that gave him the spur to play it for comedy; until that moment, when they laughed, he did not know how he would play it. I have never done that, that is, been so unsure of myself that I did not know how to play a part before I went on the stage.

The great point about whomever you play — Lear, Richard III, or Iago — is that you have to feel sympathy with the fool and the villain, even when they act preposterously. Iago is such a silly creature. Half way through the play he's got the job. Othello says, 'Now art thou my lieutenant.' But he goes on because he is power mad. King Lear is not a villain, particularly, but he is most certainly a fool.

It is an odd thing that people assume you must draw on greater reserves of your private self to play a character like King Lear, but I don't think that you do. I believe in what Stanislavsky calls the creative imagination, but you don't have to dress it up in any such fancy terminology; without creative imagination, you simply cannot be an actor. Anyone can do it. The important question is: can you then project the findings of that creative imagination into a large theatre and be convincing, terrifying, amusing or touching. That's the trick of it.

Acting is the projection of certain images that come into your mind through your physical being, which means not only your voice, but all of your body, from your top to your toe. As Larry said to Peter O'Toole when he was directing Peter's *Hamlet*, 'You must be aware of the plasticity of the body,' by which he meant that your body must express what your voice is saying. Beyond that, you can't analyse too much, or you get into a bugger's muddle.

You can play King Lear much more fully, for instance, than you can Hamlet. This is why I have never really wanted to play Hamlet: there is so much about him, so many elements and contradictions, so many complexities, that he is, to be frank about it, unplayable. You cannot play Hamlet, but you can give an edited opinion of him, which is what the best actors do. King Lear goes on a clearly defined journey.

As an actor, I have never played a part without first deciding exactly how I was going to play it. I then proceed to make a series of adjustments or compromises with the director in which I hopefully come out on top. I had a series of long meetings with Adrian to discuss what we thought about Falstaff and Lear, and happily, on both occasions, we agreed. Or rather, he agreed with me. On most things. Except the last speech of Lear. The stress is usually 'I am *old* now.' I felt that everyone else going on about how old he is suddenly annoyed him, and there is a sudden surge of energy through his frame when he carries on Cordelia.

That explains why he has been able to hang the soldier on his way back with his daughter. His dialogue is sharp and terse. There is nothing sentimental or mawkish about it. I decided, therefore, that I would turn on everyone and say, 'I am old . . . *now*,' with a great snarling bark. Adrian would have nothing to do with this and made me change it back to 'I am *old* now.' Simon Russell Beale, who was playing Edgar, implored me to return to my own idea on the line. And I put it back.

I had never seen myself do it until they showed an excerpt at the Variety Club awards ceremony, and it really is very powerful. Adrian thought this interpretation made Lear too energetic. But I think he has this surge of energy, then suddenly has a heart attack and goes. The last thing you want to see is some slow, meandering old tosser subsiding gracefully to the end. I don't see him like that at all. It was a very well cast production except for the women. Goneril and Regan were played as two-dimensional wicked, which they are not. They are perfectly normal girls with this monstrous demon of a father. Their husbands don't help.

The success was even greater than I had enjoyed with Falstaff. There was the most tremendous hullabaloo in the media before the opening which both wound me up and drove me on. Playing Lear is not as enjoyable as playing Falstaff – he's not as loveable and he has far fewer jokes. But it's the pinnacle, the mountain top. You can see everything from up there.

You are onstage in the middle of things for forty minutes on end, which is longer than a single act of *Private Lives* plus the interval. This makes it very demanding, as you can never get off the stage. As a diabetic, I used to like my dresser to be in the wings with a glass of milk stirred with six dessert spoonfuls of sugar. One night she wasn't there, but somebody brought the potion on, thank Christ, in a silver chalice!

After I had missed the first performance, I received a good luck telegram from Prince Charles in Poland: 'Hope you're going to be there on Saturday because I certainly shall be!' This was enormously encouraging and helped me battle back into the part; I certainly wasn't going to let him see the understudy. He has been thoughtful and caring all along since I joined the RSC, of which he is a very active President. After he had seen *Lear*, a play about a monarch who gives everything away, he said, 'There's one thing I've learned from this play: don't abdicate!'

The reaction to *Lear* was extraordinary. I had won the Olivier Award for Best Actor as Falstaff, but the tumult now was even greater. There were leader columns about my come-back in the *Evening Standard* and almost every paper seemed to carry a double-page spread on my achievement. To be truthful, I did not expect any of this, and was only too glad to get away with a decent performance when I was not in the best of health. I never milked Lear for sympathy, nor suggested that he was anything much more than a fond and foolish old man. I appreciated Jack Tinker's remark in the *Daily Mail* that I conveyed 'the humiliation of a human being whose only real fault has been to grow too old and too trusting'.

Some critics – notably Irving Wardle in the *Independent on Sunday* – rightly felt that I was less interested in the tyranny and rage of the man than in his comic potential and his spiritual journey after the storm. It was an extraordinary experience to play that journey night after night and take the audience with me.

The political side of the play was not particularly well developed, and you never really saw the shifts and accumulations of power elsewhere in the action. Lear makes a mistake of dividing up the kingdom and it is a decision he's stuck with, probably against his better judgment, because he has made that mistake in public. Right at the start, Lear says 'Give me the map, there,' and the designer saw fit not to have a map I could reach out and grasp, but placed the map on the floor beneath my feet. The line should have been 'Get *off* the map, there,' which is simply nonsensical, and a good illustration of how little designers take into account the simple physical and psychological requirements of the actor.

The map was covering the floor and twice in the play it was covered in water from the storm scenes. At two performances, I came on and slipped and fell, saying, 'Attend the lords of France and Burgundy, Gloucester,' sitting on my arse, trying to get up. That is no way to make a regal entrance. The man playing Kent was off more than he was on, with a bad back; this was due to the stupid stage rake of one-in-ten, and even the stagehands used to complain about it. So you don't have to ask me what I think about designers.

If you have been bereft of your health in some way, as I certainly had been, it helps playing Lear because you know what it feels like at the bottom of the barrel. It would help, too, playing Titus Andronicus or Pericles of Tyre or Timon of Athens. You have a better understanding of what life can do to you and what you can do to recover from it and look yourself square in the face. Inevitably the part throws you back on yourself. I reflected on the failures in my own life. Anything that has happened in your life, good, bad or indifferent, is of use in acting if you are honest enough with yourself. At the end of *King Lear*, I reach out into the light and grab Cordelia. I've heard that when people are dying, they see a light. So I thought I'd put it in.

As Trigorin says in *The Seagull*, when he sees the bird that has been shot, 'It may be of use,' and he makes a jotting in his notebook. If you don't do that, then acting becomes 'acting' acting, false and insincere and not rooted in any real thought or emotion. I do not mean that when you play a scene about the death of your father that you think of the day your dog died. That sort of sentimentality by association is complete crap, and leads to the worst kind of woolly acting.

You do not make that kind of loose association; you plug straight into the raw experience. Everything joins together into a basic understanding of what life is all about. You hit that level of happiness, despair, frivolity, drunkenness, reckless behaviour, vengefulness; if you are clever and capable, you can use all of that.

If you can't, you should not be an actor. Larry's best performance, for instance, was the Captain in Strindberg's *The Dance of Death*, and that was because he had played all those scenes of a wretched marriage in his private life with Vivien Leigh. Whereas Solness in *The Master Builder*, who refuses to acknowledge the young generation knocking at the door, was a role which defeated him precisely because he could not empathise with that condition; Larry was paranoid about anyone knocking on his door, professionally or personally.

You never really got to know Larry. He was too dark, too secretive, too mysterious. I spent hours and hours in his company and you could never tell what made him tick. Ralph Richardson, on the other hand, exuded such a bare honesty. You didn't have to know anything about him at all to know that he was a genuine person. At the same time there was a detailed carapace of distraction and false scent-laying. But that's all part of the game he played with the public and his fellows. I have no such resources. I'm afraid there is very little guile or deception in my demeanour, except when I have covered my traces at various stages in my private life!

What you see, emotionally, is what you get. And I let long passages of *King Lear* run on emotions very close to the surface. That is not to say that I am very like King Lear, except perhaps in selfishness. My philosophy is that if you are cruel to people, you never forget it. The final cruelty is always perpetrated upon oneself. I have, in my life, been very cruel to people. Never deliberately. And I have never been professionally jealous of anyone, not Brando, not Larry, not Robert de Niro. Except once: of Jeremy Brett. Jeremy is my oldest pal, and when he played Daniello in *The Merry Widow* on television with Mary Costa, the opera singer, he looked fantastic and he sang beautifully – after a three month crash course – and he drove me crazy with jealousy.

But you look at that young boy, Hugh Grant, of *Four Weddings and a Funeral* and then you see him accepting this or that award, and he's giving exactly the same performance. It's not acting. It's a one-flick trick, old boy. I feel the same about Tony Hopkins, who has been hyphenating his words with naturalistic hems and hahs ever since he played André in *Three Sisters* at the Old Vic. He has all those stutters and scratches and coughs and mini-splutters; it's always the same and it's awful. He's a much better actor than that, but these days he always seems to be doing the same irritating, mannered thing. He's forever coughing and spitting and winking and blinking.

At Stratford, during *King Lear*, it was suggested that I might give a Shakespearean master class for anyone in the company who wanted to attend. I readily agreed, suggesting in turn six such sessions, which would give us a structure and something to aim at. I planned what I would do, but the subject never came up again. The directors had subsequently all got together and decided that it wasn't such a good idea; actors might start undermining their authority in rehearsals by invoking my example or advice in conflict with their own. I hated all that paranoia and bitchiness that goes on among the RSC directors.

Unfortunately, at Stratford-upon-Avon, you don't have anybody who knows anything about acting at all, apart from Adrian Noble himself, who is an immensely patient and considerate director, though not in the 'genius' class. You could not begin to compare any of them with Tony Guthrie, Olivier, Gielgud, Dexter, Ingmar Bergman or Gaskill. I can't explain it, because I don't know where the magic comes from. It is something to do with imagination, tenacity, bullying, examination of how best to help an actor. A good director works ten times as hard as anyone else on the production, and you hardly meet anyone like that these days at the RSC or, to my mind, at the National Theatre.

Many of my feelings were reflected in an immensely touching and characteristic letter I received at Stratford from John Osborne. It was the last time I heard from this true and inspirational spirit of my youth, one of my dearest friends. He had come across from his home in Shropshire with Helen, his fifth wife, and sent the letter, dated 30th August 1993, to the stage door (he died just over one year later, on Christmas Eve 1994):

'*My dear old Cock,*
   It was quite wonderful and so exhilarating to see you again, both on and off the green, the other night. I knew all along – for years – that you would be the greatest of all possible Lears. Watching you again up

there blessedly confirmed it. If only: you were not being bedevilled by the crass, utter ineptitude which surrounds you on all sides, behind and below. I know you will forgive me – I hope – for claiming the rights of friendship and affection in not attempting to dissemble. It would have been inappropriate, to say the least, after the performance and in the presence of others.

The crippling rake and bunch of chorus boys prancing about like ninnies in a touring production of Perchance to Dream *in 1949 . . . what is Noble (ill-named) trying to do to you? The first scene crumpled up and thrown away like that silly paper map on the floor. Come not between the dragon and his wrath!* No chance. *Let me not be mad . . . I'm trying not to be. Time and time again your face and very presence is stamped upon, whether wilfully or with the sheer malignity of stupidity I know not. If I could get hold of A.N. I would do such things . . .*

Even Wolfit was shrewd enough not to surround himself with such dross and silliness, but gave himself at least the chance to make you feel the very roof of the old King's Theatre, Hammersmith, would split open and the heavens hurtle down upon you. Even horrible old Dickie Goolden – amateur that he was – made a more tolerable and less tiresomely intrusive Fool. It's not his *play. As for that fucking music . . .*

Anyway, Wolfit was never half the actor you are. As for those three bag lady daughters: they look, and sound, as if they should be doing the school dinners . . . enough of that, my lord, or I shall mar all . . .

I only longed to be able to assist in some way, to brush aside all those tadpoles blurring and masking your trapped greatness. Dexter's instinct was so right in seeing you truly placed as a full-frontal God . . . May we all meet sometime for an extended lunch/supper, perhaps when you're settled back into London?

I'm off to the dentist this week and next (another five or six thousand). Trying in the meantime to earn something. I have known for quite some time that my own days in the theatre are truly over. It is harsh and bitter to accept, but it's foolish to deceive oneself. Where is thy lustre now? With Peter Hall, Richard Eyre – yes, and A Noble. Thank heavens you are still there, a good deed in an ungifted, overweening and arbitrary world.

Believe me, dear friend, with abiding and renewed admiration, and much love to you both.

John

For all its extremity and flaying rudeness to others, I treasure that letter almost above any I have ever received. It cheered me up through those dismal and demanding autumn months of the Stratford season. We turned the corner of the New Year and although I was not particularly well, and permanently devoid of energy, we kept going. Pat and I were especially cheered to be invited by Prince Charles to Sandringham for Palm Sunday weekend, just before Easter 1994.

My leg was playing up a bit, so I was bit slow getting the tickets for Kings Lynn at Liverpool Street Station; Pat ran ahead on to the train. She certainly wasn't going to miss the weekend even if I was! But I hobbled on to the platform with her shouting encouragement, and just made it. We found ourselves sitting next to John Wells, the very funny satirical writer and actor, but we had no idea that he was going to the same place as we were.

There was a fleet of Range Rovers waiting for us at the station. When you enter the house, you walk straight into a huge room – there's no hallway at all. And laid out on tables, for as far as you can see, is every kind of drink imaginable and limitless amounts of same. Pat and I drank the most delicious champagne. We were all rather nervous. Ted Hughes, the Poet Laureate, said how nervous he had been. He had gone out to look for a pub in the village. But there wasn't even a village, he said, let alone a pub.

However, the Prince is brilliant at putting you at your ease. He is so charming and funny. After drinks, we were taken to our rooms. Pat and I had the most wonderful suite, with the biggest bath in the world. There were three wash basins, one for hands, one for face and one for teeth and naturally, as someone who usually does what I am told, I used all three as separately instructed.

When we reconvened for drinks before dinner, the Prince, who knew which room we were in, said to Pat, 'Don't you just love that bath?' And she said that she hadn't had time to try it; she had merely washed and changed, so she gave herself away as a dirty midden. Just fancy: unbathed at dinner in Sandringham!

When *King Lear* opened in London at the Barbican that spring, the performance was acclaimed all over again, and I think I even improved on various aspects of it, certainly in the vigour and rage departments of the earlier scenes.

I had made my point, and completed my come-back. Nothing gave me greater satisfaction than the fact that my children – Lucy, Toby and Christopher – all took pleasure in my restoration to the forefront of British classical acting. I'm proud to think that I have given them, at least, and at long last, something to remember me by.

I re-entered the Royal Free Hospital in Hampstead in late August 1994, having missed the last performances at the Barbican due to the recurrent foot infection and exhaustion. I was given a blood transfusion of two pints and immediately felt a lot better. But one of the young doctors, K.J. Patel, told Pat that unless I had a liver and kidney transplant, I would be dead within three months. I had been given some drugs at Palm Springs which can be very injurious to the kidney, despite the fact that this medication had been quite unnecessary. I had been having transfusions all the time since the bad blood business in Palm Springs, and the doctor said that all they were doing was patching me up. Because of my infected feet, the Royal Free were simply not going to operate. While I was lying there, Pat went on the warpath and the upshot was that King's College Hospital were prepared to take me in and operate. At which point the Royal Free agreed to do it themselves.

The result is that now I have three kidneys, because they gave me one new one but left the other two in there! It is the biggest operation anyone can have and I have been incredibly lucky to recover from it. I do have a very strong consitution and an enormous will power, and that has probably pulled me through. They do put you through about ten thousand tests beforehand to establish the viability of putting you on the operating table. And they also tell you what will happen if it does go wrong.

Nothing frightened me about it all because you are never in a position to be frightened. It was simply a chance of living as opposed to certain premature death, and once they give you a shot in the arm, you don't know anything about what's going on. My liver was not particularly weak, but the drinking had not helped it all that much over so many years, and the business in Palm Springs had weakened my entire system. The new liver and kidney were flown in to London by helicopter, rushed to the Royal Free on the Sunday night, and the operation was done the next day, Monday 19th September 1994.

Even when I can get to my very painful feet with the aid of a crutch or a stick, it is a real problem to get up and down the stairs. Pat was away at this time on tour in *The Rocky Horror Show*, so we had no option but to find some sort of nursing environment to look after me for a while, which is how I ended up in Denville Hall, the actors' convalescent home at Northwood, about twenty miles north-west of Central London. It is a very restful sort of place, surrounded by golf courses – which are of no use at all to the old actors – comfortable and well appointed.

The staff are superb. But I am not a slippers and bathchair sort of person, and I hate institutional food in any shape or form. I could not wait for visitors to arrive and whisk me off to lunch or dinner. Also, although I am reasonably gregarious, my idea of fun is not sitting around with a lot of old actors reminiscing and going over the past. There was one dear fellow there, a resident of ten years, with whom I had appeared in a very brief stint in rep in Dublin, between my engagements in Morecambe and Preston in the early 1950s, but neither of us could remember what we played in.

I had a very nice room, and adorable nurses who spoilt me appallingly. One of them even took me home to the family and out for an Irish hooley the night she left to work somewhere else. While I stayed there, Pat went off for a much-deserved holiday on Goa – to a resounding chorus of 'She's a right little Goa' – in order to recover from her year-long tour with the revival of *The Rocky Horror Show* and also prepare for the tedious ordeal of looking after me. She has done that so brilliantly for twenty years, I dare not think that I am making any further demands upon her tolerance and charity. I love her more deeply than I can say.

And now that I am at home, I return to the Royal Free Hospital every two weeks for a blood test, and they keep an eye on me, with the occasional top-up of steroids, and a liver biopsy to make sure the organs are prospering as they should. I am allowed the odd glass of wine, but not a barrel of whisky. I am not supposed to smoke a single cigarette, but I'm afraid I can't be doing with that. Not to be allowed my Camels really would give me the hump!

I have never felt like giving up on life in the way that I did during the filming of *Sherlock Holmes*. Something like that teaches you a lesson, and you learn to take all the set-backs and disappointment with more *sang-froid*, more equanimity. Acting is only a job, and one is lucky enough to be indulged and employed from time to time. My dark moods and depressions are a thing of the past. I can't imagine, though, what I would do without acting. I could teach, I suppose, or direct, which I have done.

I still cannot remember my dreams, but at least I don't grind my teeth in my sleep as I'm told I always used to. And with my new 'liver and lights' I sometimes feel I am starting all over again. I don't think I've changed at all over the years. I've had to 'butch up' a bit and learn how to survive, but I still treat everyone exactly the same as I would have done forty years ago in the Manchester Library Theatre. I don't have much side, I am no good at all at false deference or hollow manners.

I really have been very lucky. I read and I watch films but I also think about the parts I could play. There's Willy Loman in *Death of a Salesman* by Arthur Miller or old Tyrone in *Long Day's Journey Into Night*. Maybe I should do *Othello* again. I'd love to play it with Toby as Iago; Iago is twenty-six, so Toby would be ideal. I am very proud of him, and of Christopher. They were very well raised in Canada and London by Maggie and Bev, and after all the difficulties, it gives me enormous pleasure to know that we are now much closer to each other than we have ever been.

My illnesses, I suppose, have been a catalyst in cementing our new relationships with each other. Lucy has always been there for me. Tarn has been so sweet and helpful and more than sympathetic. Maggie started ringing up again when I hit rock bottom, and we are now in constant touch with each other. She even gets along quite well with Pat, for which I am extremely grateful.

Toby's career has got off to a flying start, but I suspect that Chris will be at least as successful in the long run. Chris won all the verse speaking competitions at LAMDA, and many of my friends, whose opinion I value, rate him very highly indeed. He's not 'Handsome Harry' like Toby, who appeared in a big TV series, *The Camomile Lawn*, before putting in a very considerable and highly successful few years' stint with the RSC. That sets him up perfectly now, I would have thought, to have a good look at any movie opportunities. Chris is an amiable beanpole, but Toby tends to put on weight a bit more easily, as I do, though he's been very good at looking after himself. He even works out on Saturday nights!

I do enjoy eating and keeping good company. I am supposed to be cutting out the drink and reducing the cigarette consumption. But I find that very hard to do, because then you find yourself asking if life without such pleasures is worth living at all. I have come close to death a few times which has only gone to show how very important it is to realise that you only live once. I have drunk the sediment and I have heard the chimes at midnight. And survived.

Posterity will gossip in any case, as Jean Giraudoux said. But I have tried to put down the truth about my life and times in the theatre as far as I can reach it. In summing up, I would say the one big hurt I have had to live with is my removal by Olivier from the kingdom. I have never really recovered from his rebuff and our falling out after seven or eight glorious years. Maggie and I had our good times, our bad times, she fell in love with her career and out of love with me. But it's all water under the bridge and life goes on. Just about. I'm fighting to stay fit, fighting fit! Wonderful, grand, pluperfect! And several projects have been occupying my time inbetween keeping the doctors happy in the Royal Free. In the course of work on this very book, I mentioned to the publishers that Prince Charles had asked me to send him some tapes of his favourite Shakespearean speeches, as he rarely had time to read any.

The result is an audio-book, *The Prince's Choice*, in which the Prince himself has participated, playing Prince Hal – very well indeed – to my Falstaff. Other items include Maggie Smith as Volumnia with Toby as her son Coriolanus and myself as Menenius, my own version of the big speeches of Jaques in *As You Like It*, Sir Toby Belch in *Twelfth Night* and Hamlet. And I am delighted that such distinguished colleagues as Alan Bates, Richard Briers, Glenda Jackson, Alex Jennings, Charlie Kay, Alec McCowen, Antony Sher and Peter Ustinov have all chipped in. The director is Glyn Dearman of the BBC, and a hefty percentage of the royalties goes towards the Prince's charitable fund.

After Falstaff and Lear, what happens next is sheer serendipity. It is not important, as long as I manage to keep a few pennies in the bank. And having lovely Pat means so much to me. I have been fortunate and I have been fulfilled. Think of me as a tree that has nearly been axed through, but the sap has found a way of working its way up. The tree, miraculously, still stands. The roots which have held me in place go down deep. And I've still got people telling me about the dreams to come.

EPILOGUE

by Michael Coveney

Robert died in the small hours of Monday 13 November 1995, just ten days after the first publication of this book. It was an exit timed to perfection and rounded with a sleep. His revels now were well and truly ended. Once again, he was in the Royal Free Hospital, Hampstead, where he had been readmitted in early October with a tumour on the bladder. This misfortune, just one more, led to other complications, the onset of severe liver rejection and a period of rapid decline. He was plugged into a dialysis machine three times a week, but the doctors knew there was little hope of recovery.

His friend Jeremy Brett had predeceased him in September, succumbing to heart disease after a long illness. Robert paid tribute to him in *The Guardian*, describing him as the first true gentleman he ever met, and noting his kindness; also, that his hitherto unrevealed ability to sing, in a television version of *The Merry Widow*, had driven him, Robert, into paroxysms of jealousy. It was typical of Robert that he went straight to the point about his oldest friend and was incapable of dawdling in the realms of sentimentality or gibbering emotion.

Throughout his final illness, Robert remained in good spirits. He rarely gave the impression that he would not soon be running around as usual. His belief was such that his visitors would believe it, too. When he was moved to the renal transplant unit in the hospital in the second week of October, milady Pat was told that her titan now had only the remotest chance of survival. Should Robert himself be told, in case he wanted to sort anything out? 'Absolutely not,' she replied, 'Robert has never sorted anything out in his entire life!'

He carried on receiving female journalists, some of whom scurried away to say how ill he looked and how much, poor deluded gals, he had flirted with them: Robert flirted with everyone! Odd, as Robert himself remarked, that women can feel free to discuss their lovers in print – it's always revenge, after all – but the men who do so can be accused, as he was, of a lack of gallantry. The sentiment might appeal to Dame Barbara Cartland, one feels, or to a stickler for starchy details of etiquette, but not to many real people. Robert retained affection and respect for all his lovers, and it shows. He always celebrated his women.

Robert's skin had turned yellow, his demeanour slightly confused. Pat recounted waking him as she arrived one day, and he turned to her and said, 'Darling, you look marvellous!' How did he feel, she asked? 'Wonderful!' Did he want something to eat? 'Most certainly!' Steak and kidney pudding, ever one of his favourite dishes, went down particularly well. No more champers, though. One felt that, without a cheering drop, there really was little point in Robert carrying on.

Robert would lie back on his pillow and wonder why the hell he couldn't get out of the place. When he finally realised there probably was no escape, he became depressed and, for a moment or two, according to Pat, just a little frightened. But he always bucked up when doctors or friends walked in. One day, Pat said, 'I've seen him playing King Lear, and that was magnificent; now he's *doing* it, and it's really strange.'

I paid my last visit to Robert on the afternoon of Monday 6 November. He had been moved yet again to another ward. I took him a bunch of freesias – it was our standing joke that I would always take in a bunch or two of these pretty flowers and solemnly intone a chorus of 'Freesia jolly good fellow!' He was not really with it, and he fought hard to focus his attention.

Amazingly, he did. Where was I off to this evening, he enquired. 'To Greenwich, to see a new production of *The Country Girls* by Clifford Odets.' (This play, ironically, is about a heavy-drinking actor given one last chance by a brilliant young director who saw him at his peak; a paradigm, in fact, of Adrian Noble's hiring of Robert at the RSC as Falstaff.)

'Fucking awful play,' Robert spluttered, 'who's playing the actor?' Corin Redgrave, I replied. 'Jesus Christ, *he'll* never be able to do it!' I assured him that I felt he might. In the event, Robert was correct, although his exclamation was undoubtedly fuelled by an envious implication that he was the right bloke for the part, as indeed he was. Redgrave the younger, in one of his father's famous roles, seemed to lack the animal appetite that Robert was suddenly embodying in his dwindling, pathetic state. Heavily sedated with morphine, he lapsed once more into a state of physical inertia. He had made an effort for me. After just five minutes, it was time to go.

Two days later, on Wednesday 8 November, Robert was paid an impromptu visit by the Prince of Wales, who had insisted that Robert be moved to a private ward on the twelfth floor of the hospital. (He had already telephoned the hospital several times. When it was announced to the staff nurse that the Prince of Wales was on the line, she at first assumed it was the local pub wishing one of their regulars a quick recovery.) Robert was asleep when he entered the room, with no fuss and minimal security. The prince held his hand and Robert immediately awoke. 'Robert, your are wonderful,' said Prince Charles. 'No sir,' exclaimed Robert, '*you* are wonderful.' He thought very highly of the prince's performance as Prince Hal in their recordng of the great tavern scene from *Henry IV, Part One* on *The Prince's Choice* CD.

In that scene, Falstaff at first bluffs his way out of a corner while inaccurately recounting his exploits during the Gadshill robbery. The fat knight and the prince then exchange roles in a mock encounter between the prince and his father, the ailing King Henry IV. In an unprecedented theatrical duet between a real-life heir to the throne and one of his own ragamuffin knights, the scene is shot through with ironies and strung with a tension born of the fact that we know just who the actors really are and that they know we know.

Prince Charles is particularly good at Hal's effortless assumption of rank while exploding in disbelief at Falstaff's accumulating fiction – 'O monstrous! Eleven buckram men grown out of two! ... Why, thou clay-brained guts, thou knotty-pated fool, thou whoreson, obscene, greasy tallow-catch ...' – while Robert, a man whose whole life was riddled with harmless deceptions and elaborations of the truth, sounds just as he did when bluffing his jovial way through bars, green rooms and, latterly, hospital wards – 'By the lord, I knew ye as well as he that made ye.'

With Pat and his stepson, Quinn, also in attendance, I am sure that Robert now felt that his business in the world was complete. He could die happy. His Falstaffian reality would not be rejected by the heir to the throne, as prefigured in the mock encounter in the Shakespearian tavern – 'Banish plump Jack, and banish all the world' and Hal's bone-chilling response, effectively delivered by the real prince, 'I do, I will' – but embraced as a meaningful physical facet of our future king's experience in the world.

This meant a lot to Robert. His friendship with the prince was genuine and uncomplicated. For his part, Prince Charles has said on more than one occasion how much Robert's performances as Falstaff and King Lear meant to him.

On the following Saturday morning, I turned up at the Royal Free and saw that Robert's brother, John, whom he had not seen much of in recent years, was by his bed, so I left them to it (Robert was out for the count, really) and returned home. Pat and Toby rang me from his bedside so, knowing that his family would be with him on Sunday, I delayed my next visit until about 10.30 am on the Monday morning. I rushed a little more urgently than usual from my house, which is just five minutes' walk away. The private room was empty, and staff were cleaning it in readiness for the next incumbent.

In such circumstances, the nurses are not allowed, quite properly, to report the patient's demise to a mere visitor, and Robert had not been on this ward long enough for them to be sure of my identity. A nurse said I should ring Lady Stephens, and an orderly I had spoken to on the Saturday morning gave away the obvious by the look in his eye. I knew Robert had gone. As I walked home, I felt suddenly bereft: not sorry for Robert, particularly, but sorry for myself in losing his companionship over so many years and the focus of my daily thoughts for the past few months. And, of course, sorry for the loyal, gallant milady. There was a message on my answerphone from Pat.

She was surprisingly good-humoured when I telephoned, not remotely inconsolable. A great battle had been concluded, and she was palpably relieved. She filled in the details. For most of Sunday, as Robert slowly slipped away, she was at the bedside not only with Quinn, but also with Toby and Chris, his sons by Maggie Smith, and with Lucy, his daughter by Tarn Bassett. Toby, Chris and Lucy had left in the late afternoon. Pat read out to Robert a review of his book from *The Sunday Times* that very morning, written by John Mortimer in whose play *The Wrong Side of the Park* Robert had appeared in 1961: 'I remember work or play with him as times of great laughter and enjoyment . . . a magnificent actor, a joy to watch and to be with. I only wish he had taken greater care of himself, but that, after all, is his own affair entirely.'

Maybe he heard the angels singing. There was a magnificent sunset over Hampstead, and Robert relapsed once more into deep sleep. Shortly after one o'clock, Pat and Quinn reached for their coats. A night nurse came in and noticed that Robert had just passed away at that very instant, as if he would keep Pat and Quinn not a moment longer. 'It was wonderful, truly wonderful; I would not have missed it for the world,' said Pat. She went home a widow on the arm of her son.

That same Monday, towards seven o'clock in the evening, the West End first-nighters and critics gathered at the Vaudeville Theatre in the Strand for the opening of *The Shakespeare Revue*, an end-of-term Royal Shakespeare Company smoker devised by Malcolm McKee and Christopher Luscombe (who played Francis, the very funny drawer in the Boar's Head Tavern – 'Anon, anon sir' – in Robert's Stratford comeback). The material ranged from the revue heyday of Herbert Farjeon and Sandy Wilson to such current zanies as Victoria Wood and Maureen Lipman, via the Shakespeare sketch from *Beyond the Fringe* – 'Get thee to Gloucester, Essex. Do thee to Wessex, Exeter; fair Albany to Somerset must eke his route.'

One item sent an icy blast of sorrow through the house: in 'Ladies of London', a song by Caryl Brahms and Ned Sherrin from their 1959 musical *No Bed for Bacon*, Dolls Common, Tearsheet and Overdone announced their departure for the funeral of Merry Sir John:

> 'We're ladies of London, and it won't be the same;
> He was sprightly twice nightly, and lord he was game . . .
> He owed for his drink and he owed for his rent,
> He owed for his shirt, but we're sorry he went . . .'

Everyone in the theatre was thinking the same sad thought. It is fair to say that the obituaries in Tuesday morning's papers were the most extensive and exuberant for any actor since those for Olivier, Robert's great hero, in 1989. This was not necessarily to do with the magnificence of his career. As Michael Billington justly pointed out in *The Guardian*, Robert was a formidable actor 'who periodically achieved greatness. He lacked the consistency of an Olivier or a Gielgud'. His story, and his character, had touched a nerve, and the nation knew that a great spirit had been extinguished.

The playwright Ronald Harwood, biographer of Donald Wolfit, said that the tradition Robert represented, that of the full-blooded actor, was, alas, dying out. Adrian Noble, the artistic director of the RSC, also touched on this profound sense of loss: 'A great light has gone . . . He could speak poetry as if he was creating it. I will remember him as a great raconteur, a great embellisher of the truth, a dedicated smoker, a fearsome drinker, a wicked silver wit, a great actor – and a cat with ten lives.'

Something more than just an actor was slipping away; it was something about the expansiveness, enthusiasm and generosity with which we lead our lives. Or fail to. The actor, writer and director Simon Callow wrote to me saying that Robert's life and belated arrival in the pantheon of great actors should now stand as an example in the increasingly crabbly little world of our contemporary theatre. And, he could as easily have added, the increasingly crabby little world full stop. The quality of public life, as well as of the theatre, was diminished at a stroke by Robert's passing. Callow declared that his forthcoming Royal Shakespeare Company production of *Les Enfants du Paradis*, one of the greatest films of the theatrical theatre, and of romantic love, would be dedicated to Robert 'and to his spirit'.

Pat was inundated with calls and letters, and flowers, and all of this extraordinary reaction helped keep her going through the early period of her loss. Prince Charles sent over to the flat an immense arrangement of beautiful white flowers and a ten-page, handwritten letter that moved her deeply.

The funeral took place one week later, on Monday 20 November, at Golders Green Crematorium. The day was freezing cold. Actors, friends and relatives assembled in a sombre mood before crowding into the chapel of rest for the service. Curiously, as they gathered, a moth-eaten tramp wielding a can of Special Brew lurched around the forecourt. No one dared say anything, presumably in case he was a friend of Robert's that none of us knew about, a denizen of the outdoors around Primrose Hill with whom Robert had bonded after drinking-up time. The jovial incongruity of this far-gone topper reeling among the smartly-dressed and sober-suited thespian crowd added an appropriate tang of bad behaviour. Somewhat disappointingly, the fellow was eventually escorted from the premises.

The RSC was represented by the chairman, Sir Geoffrey Cass, the executive director, Michael Attenborough, and the actress Joanne Pearce, Adrian Noble's wife, (Noble himself was locked into a filming schedule on

A Midsummer Night's Dream). This was not a formal ceremony, however, and the roster of famous names had a pleasing raffishness about it: Alan Bates, Charles Dance, Billie Whitelaw, Shirley Ann Field, Gérard Zing, Graham Benson, Glyn Dearman, Tom Bell, Steven Berkoff, Richard O'Brien, Chris Malcolm, Donald Howarth, Bill Bryden, Sebastian Graham-Jones, Andy Phillips, Terence Rigby, Philip Voss, Nickolas Grace, Ronald Pickup and Charles Kay. The younger RSC generation of actors – Simon Russell Beale, Michael Maloney, Owen Teale, Guy Henry – all adored Robert and found it difficult to contain their emotions.

After a simple address by a local priest, Edward Fox recited with a strange and stunning convolution Keats's poem on rereading *King Lear*:

> 'When through the old oak forest I am gone,
> Let me not wander in a barren dream,
> But, when I am consumèd in the fire,
> Give me new Phoenix wings to fly at my desire.'

Fox somehow managed to transform this cry to burn once more through the fierce dispute 'betwixt damnation and impassioned clay' into a tortured and pitying farewell, his limbs, and jaw, locked into an attitude of mesmerised sorrow.

Next into the nave were Robert's actor sons, both reading beautifully. Chris chose an anonymous 1619 elegy on the death of Richard Burbage, Shakespeare's chief tragic actor:

> 'He's gone, and with him what a world is dead
> Which he revived, to be renewed so
> No more. Young Hamlet, old Hieronimo,
> King Lear, the grievèd Moor, and more beside
> That lived in him, have now for ever died.'

And then Toby ripped into Falstaff's speech in dispraise of the concept of honour, managing to sound at once fresh and beguiling, and vocally his father's son, especially at the sudden *sforzando* of disgust on 'Therefore I'll none of it; honour is a mere scutcheon: and so ends my catechism.' The film director Tony Palmer, who had directed Robert as Puccini in a fine television film, and also in his last appearance, as the poet John Dryden, in John Osborne's *England, My England*, had suggested an excerpt from *Tosca* and settled on 'Vissi d'arte'.

The music swelled to the impassioned, heart-rending outburst of grief with which the aria concludes. Unfortunately, the tape played on, through the dialogue about the mock execution of Cavaradossi, and the stabbing of Scarpia, with all the coming and going, banging on doors and knocking over of tables played out for an increasingly fidgety audience. No one could do anything about the fact that we were all now sitting through most of the opera's second act. It was funny afterwards. Pat told me that when the door-banging started, she thought for a moment it was Robert knocking on the inside of the coffin asking to be let out before the pubs closed.

At last, some prayers, and the final hymn. We were invited to file past Robert's coffin and take our leave of him, touching or blessing the large pine box bestrewn with flowers. Some mourners took a white flower from the beautiful display and threw it on the heap. Outside, the afternoon was grey and raw. Most of the congregation, in various cars, headed for the Hampstead flat of Estelle Weldon who was hosting, with Pat, an appropriate wake fuelled with fine wines and tasty canapés.

The party was splendidly raucous, just as Robert would have wished, and only started to peter out when people realised they wanted to be home in time for that very night's broadcast of the momentous television interview with Princess Diana, the one in which she talked of enemies within the royal family and her desire to be a queen of people's hearts.

Robert was both knave and king of our affections. He had struggled valiantly from his sickbed to play Dryden in the Osborne film and the results were revealed on Christmas Day. *England, My England* is an unwieldy but compelling drama, patched together by Osborne's fellow playwright and friend Charles Wood, and the director Tony Palmer. It is the story of the composer Henry Purcell, illuminated by music and much torchlight, against the background of the Restoratiuon of King Charles II, and the religious and social turmoil, poverty and collapse of public morality that ensued when William of Orange (played with splendid decreptitude, incidentally, by poor old Corin Redgrave) and Queen Mary succeeded to the throne after James II.

The whole magnificent farrago – and there is no point in pretending there is anything neat, coherent or unambitious about Tony Palmer's highly enjoyable film – is framed by the struggle of an angry, unknown playwright in the mid-1960s, working as an actor at the

Royal Court in a revival of Bernard Shaw's *In Good King Charles's Golden Days*, to complete his play about Purcell. The actor, who also plays King Charles in the main body of the film, is simultaneously trying to convince a jolly but easily unimpressed producer (played by real-life producer Bill Kenwright) that he should put it on. His girlfriend, who doubles as Nell Gwynn, is equally sceptical.

Their indifference drives the actor into some classic paroxysms of Osborne rage about the quality of contemporary life. Simon Callow's actor lays into the arbiters of 'correctedness', the proliferation of opinion-makers and phone-ins – 'We've become a nation of babbling backseat cab drivers' – and he describes England, his England, as 'shuffling about like an old tramp begging for a pair of shoes at the tradesmen's entrance of Europe'. No room there for romantic heroism of any sort. Nor would you ever catch Robert discussing the pros and cons of the Maastricht Treaty. The only Brussels of any interest to him were those on his plate with the chestnuts and Christmas turkey.

The sardonic note is beautifully bounced back across three centuries by Robert's periwigged, blotchy-skinned, husky-voiced Dryden, who supplies a voice-over to the action of the film proper, linking the historical narrative where necessary, sometimes in prose, sometimes in Dryden's own rhyming verses.

Near the end, he is allowed the privilege of talking straight to camera as he reflects on the mismanagements and hypocrisies of the age, and he scores a bullseye. His expression of amused disgust permeates the film, validates Callow's own fine performance, and makes another resonating link with his unsentimental, resolutely individual Falstaff.

Purcell's coffin is carried for burial by torchlight to the accompanying aria of 'When I am laid in earth', Dido's lament and one of the most perfect pieces of music ever composed. The notice is finally posted on the Shaw play at the Royal Court, old haunt of Robert and John Osborne, and after an exterior shot of the Sloane Square theatre, the place where the two great friends first made their respective names, we take our leave of the 17th century characters.

The very last frame before the credits roll shows Robert's poet flashing a wink at the historical likeness of Purcell, his fellow artist, muse and Osborne clone/clown. It is a marvellous final image, and fitting tribute to an actor who took his own farewell in a rumbustious entertainment full of wine, women and the very best of English song. A memorial service would be held in the spring of 1996, courtesy of the Royal Shakespeare Company. The curtain, at last, would fall, and the night seem never-ending.

INDEX

Power Play
The Life & Times of Peter Hall
STEPHEN FAY

The greatest theatrical impresario of his time, Peter Hall, is also one of its most controversial figures. Why is he so loved – and so loathed? In this first major biography, Stephen Fay traces the rise of a brilliant empire builder. Using a wealth of unpublished letters and documents, he assesses Hall's triumphs and failures; and reveals, through those closest to Hall, the private face behind the public image.

'compulsively readable and well researched'
Sunday Express

'Stephen Fay is to be congratulated on achieving an admirable warts-and-all account of the life of one of the key figures in post war British theatre'
Sunday Telegraph

SCEPTRE

Billie Whitelaw . . . Who He
BILLIE WHITELAW

'Billie Whitelaw's book is the best autobiography by an actor I have read since Macready's Journals . . . Nothing so thrilling, unsettling, painful, touching, revelatory and remorselessly precise has been written before by an actor of the first rank working on great texts under the cruelly loving gaze of their perfectionist author'
John Peter, *The Sunday Times*

'For Beckett fanatics, of whom there are many, this book is required reading'
Anthony Holden, *The Times*

'She is the instinctive actress par excellence and her writing confirms that her centre is not her head, or even her heart, but her gut'
Michael Arditti, *Daily Mail*

Markova the Legend
MAURICE LEONARD

Alicia Markova is a dancing legend. Her story is a dream come true – as this first major biography reveals.

Born Lilian Alicia Marks in London in 1910, she was discovered by the world famous impresario Serge Diaghileff. Despite enduring astonishing hardships she became one of the greatest prima ballerinas of all time, blazing a trail across the world and dancing in places which had never seen a ballet before.

Written with Markova's full co-operation, this is the enthralling story of a woman with a mission, whose whole life has been devoted to what she symbolises – the perfection of her art. It is also the story of British ballet. Before Markova it simply didn't exist.

'Portrait of brilliance'
The Independent on Sunday

'An extraordinary tale'
The Independent on Sunday

'A lively story of astonishing dedication'
Daily Express

SCEPTRE

Nureyev
PETER WATSON

'It's a fantastic life, the stuff of fairytales . . . (Nureyev) could be the hero of a Grimm Brothers story or an Eric Ambler thriller, either or both at once.'
The Sunday Times

Perhaps the greatest dancer the world has ever known, Nureyev was also the most enigmatic.

In this first major biography since the dancer's death from AIDS in 1993, Peter Watson explores fully the public – and very private – life of the man behind the legend. Interviewing many of those closest to Nureyev, and with unique access to his KGB dossier, Watson tells the full story of:

- his difficult childhood
- his defection from Russia
- his close relationship with Margot Fonteyn
- the homosexual promiscuity which eventually led to his death from AIDS
- his overriding passion for dance

The result is the most revealing, compelling and complete portrait of Nureyev yet to be written

SCEPTRE

So Far, So Good
PAUL EDDINGTON

Hailed as a 'comic genius', Paul Eddington has a career that has spanned over fifty years. In that time he has given us not only some of the greatest theatrical performances, but also two of television's most memorable comic roles – Jerry Leadbetter in *The Good Life* and Jim Hacker in *Yes, Minister* and *Yes, Prime Minister*. Told with extraordinary courage – in the face of his twenty-year struggle against skin cancer – this is the heroic, honest and highly entertaining story of his remarkable life.

'Particularly evocative of the theatre of the 40s and 50s this is a funny and enthralling story. And, in his account of his struggle with illness, a modest and courageous one.'
Alan Bennett

SCEPTRE